# The Japanese
# Management Development System

# The Japanese Management Development System

## Generalists and Specialists in Japanese Companies Abroad

*Malcolm Trevor*
*Jochen Schendel*
*Bernhard Wilpert*

PSI   Policy Studies Institute
AGF Anglo-German Foundation

Frances Pinter (Publishers)
London and Wolfeboro, N.H.

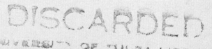

© Policy Studies Institute, 1986

First published in Great Britain in 1986 by
Frances Pinter (Publishers) Limited
25 Floral Street, London WC2E 9DS

Published in the United States of America in 1986 by
Frances Pinter (Publishers) Limited
27 South Main Street
Wolfeboro
NH 03894-2069

**British Library Cataloguing in Publication Data**
Trevor, Malcolm
    The Japanese management development system:
    generalists and specialists in Japanese
    companies abroad.
    1. Management—Europe  2. Management—
Japan
    I. Title  II. Schendel, Jochen
    III. Wilpert, Bernhard
    658´.0094    HD70.E/
    ISBN 0-86187-638-5

**Library of Congress Cataloging in Publication Data**
Trevor, Malcolm, 1932–
    The Japanese management development system.
    Bibliography: p.
    Includes index.
    1. Corporations, Japanese—Europe—Management.
    2. Industrial management—Japan—Cross-cultural studies.
    3. Executives—Europe—Attitudes.  4. Professional
employees—Europe—Attitudes.  I. Schendel, Jochen.
II. Wilpert, Bernhard, 1936–.  III. Title.
HD2844.T74   1986    338.8´8952 86-8432
    ISBN 0-86187-638-5

Typeset by Joshua Associates Limited
Printed by Biddles of Guildford

# Contents

List of Tables     vi

Acknowledgements     vii

Introduction     1

1. Production sector     24

  1.1 Japanese company P1: precision engineering (Britain)     24
  1.2 Japanese company P2: light engineering (Germany)     74
  1.3 Japanese company P3: light engineering (Germany)     80
  1.4 Japanese company P4: electronics (Germany)     85

2. Marketing sector     88

  2.1 Japanese company M1: electrical (Britain)     88
  2.2 Japanese company M2: precision engineering (Germany)     155
  2.3 Japanese company M3: precision products (Germany)     159
  2.4 Japanese company M4: engineering (Germany)     163

3. Commercial and Financial sector     167

  3.1 Japanese company C1: general trading (Britain)     167
  3.2 Japanese company C2: banking (Germany)     220
  3.3 Japanese company C3: banking (Germany)     226
  3.4 Japanese company C4: transport (Germany)     228
  3.5 Japanese company C5: transport (Germany)     231

4. German and Japanese companies compared     235

Conclusion: the task orientation of Japanese Management     249

Appendix: Research Method     264

Bibliography     268

Index     275

# List of Tables

1.1  How managers see themselves in the company (P1)                 66
1.2  How managers see the whole management team (P1)                 67
1.3  British managers' working hours (P1)                           69
2.1  How managers see themselves in the company (M1)               145
2.2  How managers see the whole management team (M1)               147
2.3  British managers' working hours (M1)                          149
3.1  How managers see themselves in the company (C1)               210
3.2  How managers see the whole management team (C1)               211
3.3  British managers' working hours (C1)                          213
4.1  Staff with more than ten years' service                       237
4.2  Perceptions of the climate at work                            240
4.3  Extent of decision-making authority                           242
4.4  Satisfaction with communication                               246
4.5  Type of communication used                                    246
4.6  The success of the firm                                       247
5.1  Management training methods in Japan                          252
5.2  Aims of management training in Japan                          253
5.3  Employees dissatisfied with company training programmes       254

# Acknowledgements

The research on which this book is based was made possible by the financial support of the Anglo-German Foundation for the Study of Industrial Society, to whom we would like to express our gratitude. It was carried out by Malcolm Trevor at Japanese and local companies in Britain and by Jochen Schendel and Bernhard Wilpert at Japanese and local companies in Germany, within the framework of the Japan Industrial Studies Programme of research at the Policy Studies Institute.

We would like to thank the companies and managers, Japanese, British and German, who kindly spared their time to answer our questions and to discuss the issues that were raised. It goes without saying that the research would have been impossible without their cooperation and wherever possible we have tried to reflect the experience of those engaged in day-to-day company management.

The views expressed are, of course, our own responsibility.

Malcolm Trevor, Jochen Schendel and Bernhard Wilpert

# Introduction

## British and German management in the Japanese mirror

'That's not my job', along with such expressions as 'it's not my fault' or 'I wasn't told about it', are common local expressions that Japanese managers in Western Europe strongly dislike. Japanese managers interviewed during previous studies frequently complained of the inflexibility or 'lack of initiative' of local staff, and were puzzled that what is well known as 'demarcation' at operator level seemed to have a counterpart among European managers, known by a number of different terms, such as 'functional specialisation' or 'professionalism'.

Interest in Japanese companies has often focused on 'the Japanese worker' and on Japanese industrial relations systems. In Britain, with its large numbers of multi-union workplaces—but, for obvious reasons, not to the same extent in Germany—interest in phenomena like enterprise-based unions has been considerable. Often a large part of Japan's economic success, beyond relative freedom from strikes, and so on, has been ascribed to such systems.

In the circumstances, this is understandable, but the active role of managers tends to be overlooked—rather as if companies ran themselves according to a 'system', without positive leadership and effort on the part of managers. Some observers in Britain are inclined to forget that the often-cited principles of long-term employment, flexibility at work and 'harmony', of fitting in with the team and its goals, apply just as much in Japan to managers as they do to workers. The managers occupy the senior positions in the company, but they are as much part of it as other employees, and in the big firms there is no external labour market for them as it would be understood in Britain or Germany.

A previous study of Japanese companies in the UK showed a high degree of enthusiasm among British workers for new Japanese management styles. But some operators claimed that British managers, with their 'professional' outlook and career paths moving across different companies in pursuit of promotion, were less enthusiastic. In some Japanese branches in the UK, the lack of clear job descriptions, Japanese expectations that managers would not stick to functional boundaries, related problems of the lack of delegated authority to individual positions and the lack of clearly defined responsibility, were sources of anxiety to local managers.

It soon became clear that expectations covering the nature of managerial work differed between Japanese and British managers; which was particularly difficult for those Japanese managers who had assumed that, while they should expect problems with ordinary employees, local managers would, as senior members of the firm in positions of authority, share their own attitude towards the task and the company. Some Japanese managers were obviously surprised and disappointed that this was not always the case. Mixed management teams, especially in manufacturing, have often worked well, but in some companies there has been a tendency for the local and expatriate parts to go their own way. Disunity of the management team obviously makes it difficult for a company to achieve maximum performance, particularly in a new and unfamiliar overseas market.

Demarcation at shop-floor level in Britain and elsewhere is a well-publicised problem known to many managers in Japan, often through sensational stories in the media. It becomes conspicuous to Japanese managers abroad when they experience what they see as a lack of cooperation or teamwork. One manager in Japan who had worked several years abroad quoted the example of workers who would not help a slower colleague 'unless the extra effort was paid for'. He concluded that there was a 'fundamental difference in value systems' between Japanese and European employees.

Among local managers the problem, from the Japanese manager's standpoint, may not be stated so bluntly, and most British managers are not members of a union that will resist management attempts to cross traditional demarcation boundaries. But this does not necessarily mean that functional specialisation among managers, who must think of their careers against the background of labour market mobility, is less rigid than demarcation. From the Japanese viewpoint, the problem may be more intractable: firstly, because of its unexpectedness, and secondly, because of the highly individualistic way in which managers' careers are conceived and pursued.

Individualism, in the normal British or American sense, is generally considered disruptive or 'selfish' in the context of a

Japanese organisation. In some cases local managers' misgivings about the apparent lack of clear job definition and clearly assigned authority in a Japanese company represent the tip of the iceberg. Their misgivings may seem to be based on no more than abstract principles, but they are connected with real career prospects. They refer to the two different types of career structures for managers in the company and are therefore a serious problem that requires investigation.

The problem is significant because Japanese managers and the particular managerial techniques they are said to use are widely considered to have contributed to Japan's economic advance. Meanwhile, British and German companies in fields like electronics, motor vehicles and machine tools face hard Japanese competition in their own domestic markets, and some of their difficulties are usually put down to problems of management. Does the Japanese example have practical implications for them?

Some evidently think it does. In its basic Quality Control handbook, for instance, the Japanese Union of Scientists and Engineers (JUSE) attacks what it sees as the problem with managers in other countries. 'Anyone can display ability through self-development and mutual-development backed by training and guidance. This concept can hardly be accepted in such countries where education is only given to the élite of the society, where engineers armed with technology guard their privileges, and where a limited number of people with certain social status enjoy opportunities of education, occupation and senior positions'.[1] The phrase about engineers is an attack on specialist possessors of 'private' expertise, who use it to 'guard their privileges', when, in the Japanese view, it should be used for the benefit of the organisation and the achievement of its aims. While in Europe and North America organisations are seen as human products, which can be consciously designed in a certain way, in Japan there has been 'the traditional view of organisations as organic entities'.[2]

The two models of organisation are related to career structures and values. Broadly stated, the European model is commonly identified with specialist career structures and orientations, while in the major Japanese corporations the model is said to be identified with generalist careers and values. It is a major aim of this study to investigate how far this is true in practice.

## 'Generalists and Specialists'

Stated simply, European or American specialists are the owners of jobs and expertise in organisations theoretically designed according to rational principles. Specialists assume the possibility of considerable movement between firms, in pursuit of advancement in the same specialism. Generalists in large Japanese companies are assigned to a task by the organisation, whose structure is usually taken for granted, working as it does with a large number of implicit but clearly recognised rules. Generalists in this case assume, or perhaps in a recession hope, that they will spend the significant part, or virtually all of their careers, in the same company. Typically, they must make their careers in the organisation (until the company's retiring age of 55 or 60, or later if they have reached director level).

In these circumstances, specialisation is claimed to be as rational for European or American managers as flexibility, or the generalist approach, is for Japanese managers. How far the claim can be substantiated in practice will be discussed below. What happens when 'specialists' and 'generalists' work together in the same organisation, as happens in Japanese companies in Europe, will also be discussed. To the extent that both expect to persist with their accustomed types of career structure and their usual concept of their own jobs, the day-to-day functioning of the management team may be put under strain. Mutual incomprehension can arise.

Recognition of the differences is widespread. A Japanese manager at a marketing company in the UK commented that, 'In comparison with the Japanese the difference between well-talented and less-talented people is remarkable. Local staff are individualistic. They attach importance not to the company but to their own status. They don't understand the Japanese style of loyalty and resign from the company when their efforts or achievements are not rewarded directly'.

A recent study comparing the values and attitudes of British and Japanese managers drew the same connection between individualism and 'professionalism', so that Japanese managers saw their British colleagues as 'Regarding the firm they work for as a stepping stone'. The criticism of 'professional' careerism is again apparent. 'The British style of management was often seen to be status-conscious, territory-conscious, authoritarian and conservative ... British managers were over-concerned with a formal chain of command but little concerned with horizontal communication'.³ Previous research has revealed that these are indeed common views among Japanese managers in Britain. How much *actual practice*, as opposed to *perceptions*, varies in the case studies below is relevant to the argument.

Marubeni Corporation, a leading trading company with branches in Europe, has a statement which embodies its six guiding principles: 'Let us acknowledge our individual insignificance and seek strength in our combined efforts. Let us always act with justice and in good faith with freshness and vitality, avoiding arrogance and exemplifying humility'. As with the JUSE quotation above, the moral tone is conspicuous. The organisational principle is 'combined effort' and the 'avoidance of arrogance', which fits the generalist model but not the specialist or 'professional' careerist model. During previous studies, complaints from Japanese managers that British managers hoarded information that the Japanese intended them to share were heard more than once. For British managers, sharing information can be seen as a danger to their own career prospects. In Japan, seniors should help juniors to develop and should not need to watch their backs to the same extent, because of the seniority element.⁴

A recent article on employment systems in Japan concluded that, 'Those who followed a 'lifetime' employment pattern have received higher earnings than job changers'.⁵ Mr A. Morita, chairman of Sony, joked that, 'A Japanese company sometimes looks less like a business than a social welfare organisation'.⁶ This is part of the long-term employment-generalist model, but how such organisations can be so productive is the crucial question, especially for managers in less productive companies and for policy-makers in less productive economies.

Under the heading 'Jobs are ambiguous', a Japanese writer defines the general differences between jobs in Japanese and in British and American organisations. In the Japanese case, 'Jobs are roughly defined and employees are required to do any related jobs ... Job contents change all the time. *Employees are expected to present ideas to improve the jobs*' (emphasis added). In the other case, 'Jobs are clearly defined by contract. It is not necessary to do work other than specified jobs. There are many rules'. The writer also defines the non-Japanese cases as 'bureaucratic models'. The discussion in the article is mainly about shop-floor work, but in both cases there is a pattern that is consistent with that at managerial level.[7] Japanese managers in Europe expect local managers to work with the same concept of flexibility: it is not a principle for workers only, from which managers are 'excused'.

The Japanese long-term employment-generalist-flexibility model has been discussed in many places. The discussion has ranged from educational background and recruitment practices,[8] which will be described in the case studies below, to 'career patterns—Japan and the West',[9] 'No divisional fences',[10] the 'Focus on generalists as opposed to specialists'[11] and 'multi-skilled, generalist managers'.[12] At times the discussion has shown a tendency to deal with principles, perhaps even myths, rather than empirical data.

A British lecturer, to an audience of senior executives and others in London, alluded to job rotation for managers in Japan, contrasting his presentation of the Japanese model with the situation in the UK where, 'It is very difficult at that stage [appointment to the board] to switch to being a generalist ... the Japanese recipe obviously has something going for it'.[13] An article in an American journal refers to the close integration of marketing and production in Japanese companies and wonders whether 'The "professionalism" subscribed to by many individual organisational members in Western corporations might have to be erased ... Perhaps the functional manager will become an outmoded conception as the "professional man" again yields to Whyte's "organisation man"'.[14]

Japanese writers claim that:

Whereas Japan's screening system is based on true *achievement*, [original emphasis] Western systems are based on *qualifications* (education, special skills, previous work experience and not always reliable recommendations). The Japanese system's overall evaluations, including character assessments, are more appropriate for advanced societies ... In order to operate the giant fixed capital of advanced industrial organisations effectively, the division of labour within the organisation must be refined and jobs must be specialised. On-the-job training then becomes indispensable to rotate workers from easy jobs to successively harder ones. Such training, which presumes each worker will stay with the firm for a long time, pays off for management because skills needed for difficult jobs are picked up in the course of easier jobs ... corporations formulate long-range production plans, and as a part of such plans they try to maintain a long-term labour force.[15]

The last point underlines that what may appear to some as the type of concern for employees that Mr Morita of Sony joked about has a readily understandable, calculated business rationale.

Though the reference here is to workers, the strategy of recovering training and other costs by long-term employment is equally applicable to managers—and, it could be argued, especially applicable to managers and their expensive expertise. The emphasis on on-the-job training will be discussed below.

The part of the statement which appears to contradict the generalist concept is that 'the division of labour within the organisation must be refined and *jobs must be specialised*' (emphasis added). Does this mean a modification of the generalist principle, or is it possible, against logical concepts of organisation, for managers to be generalists and specialists at the same time? The issue will be investigated in the case studies.

If the generalist concept is indeed applied in the manner according to the conventional wisdom, serious thought should be devoted to understanding 'Why Japan's Engineers lead' in technical fields that in Europe and America would normally be considered specialised. 'On a per capita basis, since 1977, universities in Japan have graduated annually almost three times as many [electrical and electronic] engineers as in the US, more than four times the total in the UK, almost six times that of France and approximately 70 per cent more than in West Germany'.[16] The problems of engineering in the UK, in terms of training, employment, reward and status, in contrast to Germany, Switzerland and Sweden, have often been discussed; yet both Germany and Britain have become hosts to new Japanese electronic factories, and Japanese motor manufacturers and others have successfully penetrated the German as well as the British market. There seems to be no lack of professionalism on the part of the Japanese engineers. Most Japanese 'generalists' seem to avoid becoming 'amateurs' in the sense of less-than-capable performers. How do Japanese organisations, apparently committed to the generalist model, avoid amateurism?

A Japanese writer who defined the principles of personnel administration in Japan points out that it is 'More than just one of several functions found in any business organisation ... it embodies the corporate philosophy of present-day Japanese management'. He goes on to assert that 'At the level of the individual employee, all superiors, subordinates, co-workers, are expected to manage the personnel and informal aspects of personnel administration, in other words, human relations on the spot'. It is a generalist conception of personnel management, very different from the British 'professional model' with its IPM (Institute of Personnel Management) qualification, for example. Entrants to (large) Japanese companies 'generally feel they were hired for the company and not for any specific job'.

The principle of job rotation is then defined and it is pointed out that 'job descriptions for individual employees' are superfluous because of 'the group task'. The managers of the personnel department are 'not expected to be professionals of personnel administration'.

Is the Japanese personnel department then to be considered line or staff? According to the writer, 'Line-staff organisation . . . is readily accepted in theory but remains denied in practice . . . Mostly sooner than later . . . a staff function ends up in the line organisation. Here . . . interdependence is expected, and accountability is diffused all over the organisation'.[17] There are 'overlapping responsibilities'. The 'strictly functional' authority of Western managers is compared with the 'basically personal' authority of the Japanese manager. 'He is then more efficient in terms of a "generalist" than in terms of a "specialist"; his effectiveness consists essentially in providing his subordinates with the proper work climate'.

In the discussion of the empirical findings below, comparisons with the various definitions of the Japanese long-term employment-generalist-flexibility model will be made, in order to determine subsequently how accurate or otherwise the common versions of the model that are so frequently discussed really are. To the extent that the above descriptions of the Japanese model, as it affects generalist career orientations for instance, are accurate, they clearly show different structures and practices from those that are typical of British and German organisations.

The point was well understood by a Japanese manager with experience of working in Japanese branch operations in Britain and Germany, who will also be quoted in the trading company case below. Writing about the UK, he expressed the view that managers identified themselves primarily with their profession. Taking the almost ideal typical case of the chartered accountant, as a very 'pure' type of specialist, he wrote that, 'He probably feels stronger loyalty to his professional body, such as the Institute of Chartered Accountants, than to the company he works for at that given time. *This kind of self-identification with a profession very seldom exists in Japanese society*' (emphasis added). The point cannot be over-emphasised. The manager went on to explain that 'The training of the manager in Japan is mostly carried out in-house and on-the-job'.[18] As will be seen from the empirical evidence below of British and Japanese accountants, or financial managers, in UK branches, this is an entirely different concept from that of the specialist accountant. In the case of Japanese managers, 'The manager's function is related primarily to his relationship with the people whom he is to manage'. The remark reflects the comment on the 'basically personal' authority of the Japanese manager just quoted above.

The examples of British accountants in particular and of functional divisions and the concept of 'professionalism' in general have attracted the interest of many management writers. One has referred not only to professional training and the attainment of professional qualifications but to the cultivation of a professional mystique, sharply at variance with the task orientation of Japanese organisations.[19] While few people would question the high levels of expertise among British chartered accountants, it does not necessarily follow that divisions between professions in Britain always have a basis that is directly related to their task. 'It is very difficult for a manager to transfer from one occupational caste (say, marketing) to another (say purchasing). The way in which job adverts religiously insist on previous experience is evidence enough. Undoubtedly this is due as much to a feeling of the sanctity of caste barriers as to practical considerations'.[20] This may be overstated, but Japanese managers in Europe complain about precisely what seem to them to be 'caste barriers' among European managers who put functional specialisation and their own professional status before the task of the company.

## Ideology and values

In fact it is not only Japanese managers who are critical about 'professionalism' and the serious implications for task performance that it can have. 'This structure appears to have rather a lot to do with social status and ideology (that is, *being*) and rather too little to do with standards of output (that is, *doing*). While the professions have stood for the self-regulation of proper standards, there has been a tendency for professionals themselves to favour exclusiveness and status at the expense of output or performance', (original emphasis). It is what the author refers to as 'survival type behaviour'.[21] Japanese managers may not always be able to give an explanation of their own organisational principles that are intellectually satisfying to Western managers (or scholars), but their achievements show that they are great *doers*.

Although some expatriate managers appear to believe that local managers' desire for job boundaries, defined authority and professional status is nothing more than irrational obstinacy which threatens cohesive teamwork, it would be as wrong to accept this stereotyped view as it would be to take some local managers' protestations at face value. In the British or American type of labour market, movement between firms is a common way for functional specialists, or professionals, to get promotion. This leads to a situation that is anathema to Japanese managers. 'A man who knows that his promotion depends entirely on the powers that run the accounting department, will emphasise "professional accounting" rather than contribution to the company'. The structure of entry into a specialist function, professional qualification in it and the consequent closure of the in-group against 'outsiders' in the same company conflicts with the Japanese model of all members of the company as 'insiders' and competitors as outsiders.[22]

The Anglo-American professional model has its ideological basis in the well-known (and sometimes exaggerated) concepts of 'individualism' and 'the rights of the individual'. The Japanese model of a company of 'insiders' is rooted ideologically in the values of solidarity and cooperation, about which there has been so much hackneyed discussion. At the highest level of abstraction, the cardinal principle is '*wa*', or 'harmony'. Japan's ruler of the seventh century, Prince Shotoku, admonished the population that 'Harmony is to be valued, and an avoidance of wanton opposition honoured ... When ... there is concord in the discussion of business ... what is there that cannot be accomplished?'[23] The organisational principle of 'harmony', in other words cohesive effort, is therefore of considerable antiquity. It is important to notice that while 'harmony' may appear to be an ultimate or transcendental value, in fact it is aimed at 'what can be accomplished' in a concrete social context: it is directed towards active task performance in the here and now.[24]

'Loyalty' in Japanese companies is not a static but an active concept, aimed at organising and motivating employees to perform. While it would be absurd to contend that Japan's industrial development has proceeded in a straight line from Prince Shotoku and that it will inevitably continue to do so, because of the country's 'unique culture', and so on, it is an empirical fact that 'harmony' calls forth the same sort of emotional and non-rational responses in many Japanese as 'individualism' does in many British or Americans. Ask local staff of Japanese companies in Europe and America.

Japanese writers familiar with Western concepts occasionally characterise a Japanese company, or other organisation in Japan, as a *Gemeinschaft* (community), according to Tönnies' well-known typification of *Gemeinschaft* (community) and *Gesellschaft* (society). The terms express the different qualities of the solidaristic 'community' and the legally and contractually based 'society', with its freely moving independent specialists and professionals.

The distinction is, of course, a broad one and should not be taken to the point of stereotyping everything Japanese as an aspect of 'community' and everything European or American as a reflection of 'society'. In Britain, solidaristic 'community'-type behaviour is commonly found among shop-floor workmates, union members and club members of different types. In Japan, medical doctors, restaurant cooks, carpenters, gardeners and so on, operate as independent professionals. Labour mobility has been gradually increasing, even if it is short of British or American levels. Japan has also produced a rich crop of well-known entrepreneurs.

The point that is relevant to this study is not whether members of Japanese society have an innate belief in 'harmony' but how company managements actively promote the principle as a basis for group achievement. 'In order to foster and maintain cohesion in the group, harmony (*wa*) must be constantly nurtured at all levels'.[25] To what extent the principle obtains in overseas operations will be discussed below.

Exactly how far the actions of managers or employees can be influenced by the propagation of organisational principles is an important question for managements who want to motivate their staff to achieve the company's goals. It is also crucial for organisation builders, especially when, for example, they are designing a new organisation. But the generalist–specialist or generalist–professional dichotomy does not simply depend on value-laden ideas. The already quoted example of accountants is a case in point. The ROI (return on investment) criterion 'Was developed earlier in this century to help in the management of the new multi-activity corporations ... ROI was used as an indicator of the efficiency of diverse operating departments ... and as an overall measure of the financial performance of the entire company'.[26] The purpose of the ROI criterion and its implementation was to promote company profitability—not an accountants' ideology or a 'professional' ethic unconnected with the main part of the business.[27]

By introducing ROI control, 'Corporations achieved a specialisation of managerial talent' or an upgrading of managerial ability. The aim was that 'Managers of functional departments could become specialists and pursue strategies for their department that increased the ROI *of the entire company*. Senior managers, freed from day-to-day operating responsibility, could focus on co-ordinating the company's diverse activities and developing its long-term strategies' (emphasis added). In other words, there would be specialists up to a certain level, with the general management above them. So far from being considered disruptive, or 'demarcated', specialists were seen as the managers with the specific expertise necessary to ensure performance in the form of ROI. It was their job to perform this essential function on behalf of the whole company. The writer of the article argues, however, that what actually happened has created problems for present-day companies. 'In practice, decentralisation via ROI control permitted senior executives to be physically and organisationally separated from their manufacturing operations ... Running corporations by the numbers'—that is, with excessive reliance on ROI measures but without detailed knowledge of divisions' operations and technology—has become uncomfortably apparent'. The dangers of the wrong sort of functional specialisation are precisely what Japanese managers aim to avoid.

This is not the place to discuss the differences between the Japanese, British and German[28] financial systems—or indeed the entire business structure in Japan. But it is a serious mistake to attempt to isolate company organisation and management practices from their financial background. It is equally misleading to attempt to explain management practices with reference to 'culture', or ideology and values, alone when other important factors, such as finance, careers and material interests are in play.

Recently two Japanese writers have taken up the same point of how the financial system influences the type and status of staff within an enterprise.[29] They explain that 'In Japan, partly because financing for capital projects is often done through the banks [i.e. external market], central coordination of internal capital flow is less important than in the US . . . In general, the role of Japanese chief financial officers has been equivalent to that of a chief borrowing strategist, rather than a chief auctioneer of internal capital flow. *Thus, their internal status has not been as high as compared to the US*' (emphasis added). They then argue that, 'Perhaps the most important benefit of a well-developed internal labour market is the opportunity of enlarging each employee's *firm-specific skills and know-how*. Internal development of such capabilities is the norm (and the benefit) in the Japanese internal labour market' (emphasis added). The principle applies to managers as well as to ordinary employees. The authors conclude by remarking that 'Any meaningful international comparison has to analyse the different behaviour patterns from the same common perspective. We hope that we can now understand corporate behaviour in the two countries better and that seemingly "mystical or irrational" behaviour of Japanese firms and other economic agents is no longer so mystical or irrational'. It is a view that is shared here.

## The Anglo-German comparison

'As a country the UK is cursed by specialisms', but in spite of those who see 'culture' as something unchangeable, organisational forms are not as fixed as the statement of this principle might appear to make them. Attempts to cross the barriers of a specialism and make graduate engineers into good manufacturing engineers were initiated in 1974 by the Fellowships in Manufacturing Management scheme of the Engineering Industry Training Board (EITB).[30] 'New pressures are obliging companies and their employees to consider a wide range of new ways to getting tasks done'—among them 'functional flexibility'.[31]

One of Britain's best-known and most successful managers argues that 'Good human relations are not something that can be left to the personnel department. The commitment must come from the top. We do not make a rigid distinction between line management and personnel management. Many senior personnel positions are held by successful line managers, while in turn staff managers are commercially involved . . . the welfare of staff is also the concern of line managers who must be trained in dealing with people'.[32] This cuts across conventional functional boundaries and the 'that's not my job' approach: it could almost be said to reflect 'Japanese' organisational principles. It is an approach at variance with that of the 'professional model' of personnel management in Britain referred to above.

The performance of British industry since 1945, the increasing share of the British market taken by foreign manufactures[33] and the 'economic miracles' of first Germany and then Japan, are all factors that have concentrated attention in Britain on how firms are managed and whether British management as constituted at the present time is competent to perform its task. At a general level it is said, for instance, that 'Precisely because industrial management is not a prestigious career in Britain as it is elsewhere, less vigour, inventiveness and risk-taking is shown by British managers'.[35]

Both the authors of these remarks, Crockett and Elias, and another writer, Mant (see note 21), draw attention to similar and related aspects of the British management problem and reach similar conclusions. 'It always surprises me how little English-speakers are aware that "management", seen as a professional specialism, is a product of Anglo-Saxon culture . . . Equally, I am always surprised how little attention is paid to the Germans . . . In Germany, they have traditionally had no management education at all, as such, and have apparently not needed it'.[36] Mant goes on to describe the visit of a British Institute of Management (BIM) group to Düsseldorf who were amazed, and a little alarmed, to discover that their idea of a 'professional manager' found no echo in Germany. 'The word "professional" in any discussion with German managers generally proved to be an obstacle to the understanding of the role of manager'.

Not that the German managers were amateurs: as Mant says, 'If we judge an industry's professionalism by the integrity of its end products, the Germans are professional by anybody's standards'. Ironically, the British managers, in pointing out that 'Many managers were highly educated in specialist subjects to the level of doctorate', went on to imply that the German managers were almost over-educated. But in Britain, as the National Training Survey and other survey data quoted by Crockett and Elias show, 'The proportion of managers with a university education remains extremely low'—52 per cent have no formal education qualifications at all (a figure almost as low as that of 57 per cent for the general population). Even after they enter a firm, 'Many [British] managers receive no training whatsoever'. In regard to Japan, the extensive graduate recruitment regularly practised by the major companies and the necessity of having attended university as a 'passport' to eligibility for recruitment will be discussed. Reflecting the 'professional' or functional specialisation pattern already referred to above, the same authors quote a 1975 survey, published in 1982, showing that British managers 'Showed less movement between occupations than workers'. This does not of course mean that they did not change their employers within the same occupational framework—the practice so disliked by Japanese managers in Europe. 'If promotion is not forthcoming, the potential manager is likely to move on to another firm'.

Here it may be objected that if British managers remain within the same occupational category, even while changing employers, they must become more proficient at the task 'by experience'. After all, Japanese companies do most of their training in-house and have a mistrust of business schools, which hardly exist in Japan anyway, because of their allegedly 'theoretical' bias. This is not the place to discuss business school training, although it may be argued that managers benefit more from a theoretical broadening after, rather than before, they have had several years experience dealing with real problems 'at the sharp end'.

But the objection on the grounds of 'experience' is misleading. 'We found that *the majority of [British] firms do not train their managers for the job they hold*, other than the usual 'Cooks Tour' of the establishment' (emphasis added). There is 'Little evidence of a relationship between training and earnings'—except perhaps in the obvious cases of chartered accountants and legal experts. As far as British managers in general are concerned, 'The major determinant of a manager's earnings is the particular level reached in the hierarchy of control. We thought it possible that qualifications and training could act as a "passport" to the higher echelons of management. Again, we found little evidence to support this hypothesis'.[37] In spite of the ideology of 'professionalism', people who are neither qualified nor trained can only be described as poorly equipped. When they have to compete in the domestic as well as the international marketplace against better-qualified and better-trained managers from other countries some may appear little better than amateurs. As the authors point out, the implications of the low levels of managerial qualifications and training in Britain are extremely serious for organisations as a whole. 'If managers place no value upon the formal training of managers, then what value do they place upon formal industrial training schemes in general?'

'The greater extent of vocational training in Germany is well known. All the senior staff that we saw in the German factories were qualified engineers (except in one case where he was a qualified technician)'.[38] These remarks, which do indeed underline what should not need underlining, are part of an Anglo-German productivity survey, published by the National Institute in 1985, which has attracted considerable attention. 'If that sounds a bit boring, the results are not. They are appalling'.[39] British productivity is much lower. 'The gap varied from a 10 per cent [German] advantage to as much as 130 per cent. The average differential was 63 per cent'. Obviously there is a link between qualifications and training and productivity, but qualifications and training must be of the right sort, orientated towards performance instead of a theoretically 'professional' or 'specialist' status.

Discussion of the 'high price to pay' of the prevalent British type of 'professionalism', when compared with the situation in Germany, points out that, 'Professionalism, as it has developed in Britain and the United States, is characterised by an isolation of separable tasks and jobs to be claimed as the specialist domain of members of each profession ... the institutional and value systems of professionalism are highly developed in Britain but not in Continental countries ... there has been no debate in Germany about whether management is a profession, ought to be one, or can justify a claim to professional standing'.[40]

The National Institute survey on productivity in Britain and Germany quoted above showed much better task performance in Germany than in the UK. Child et al. argued that 'Criteria of management competence in Germany have been grounded more straightforwardly upon qualifications in the basic core branches of manufacturing, namely in engineering or chemistry on the production side and in business economics or administration on the commercial side'. Manufacturing management is recognised as a special problem in the UK, and is worthy of a separate discussion, but it also provides an example of the absurd lengths to which the Anglo-Saxon notion of 'professionalism' can go. 'It is generally recognised that production *is* a low-status function in Britain. Its members may belong to one of the "professional" engineering associations, including the Institute of Production Engineers, which, however, caters more for those who *advise* on production processes than those who *produce per se*' (emphasis added).

Another international comparison found that:

1. In Germany, the control systems appear to be much more stringent and orientated towards corrective action than in France and Great Britain.
2. In French and German organisations, control is intentionally used as a policy instrument; this is not just a reflection of the quality and behaviour of subordinates.
3. In German companies, chief executives want to make sure they are informed of what is going on; in British companies, chief executives delegate and want only to be warned of unusual matters [cf. the preceding discussion on the ROI criterion].[41]

The quotation is given in full because in the present international comparative study it is important to evaluate the differences between management in Britain and Germany and because any one, or all, of the above points could be significant in investigating how Japanese managers react to their colleagues in the two countries. The further comment, for instance, that 'There was less emphasis on managerial self-development in German firms and more on careers being part of a centralised overall regulation of hierarchies' sounds as if it would fit better with Japanese approaches than the British would, but this has of course to be verified empirically by the fieldwork. Apart from the common observation that 'things work better' in Germany, which can be expected to appeal to Japanese managers, do the latter find much difference between Britain and Germany in terms of job changing and their concepts of 'loyalty' to the company?

Stereotypes are dangerous, and although the 'professional' problem in the UK is often considered to have specifically British aspects, it is, as has been noted, found in the USA as well. An article on German management in one of America's most respected management journals,[42] for instance, referred in a phrase familiar to British ears to, 'The poor management of US manufacturing companies', while warning that, as should be the case in approaching Japanese management, 'There are no short cuts'.

The article went on to analyse the features that make German manufacturing management more effective than British and American. Among these are the relationships between German banks and businesses, which enable German companies, like Japanese, to take a longer-term view in regard to business strategy and personnel. Reminiscent again of the Japanese case is the assertion that 'In most German plants, senior executives can talk intelligently with well-trained workers about the technical aspects of their task [and] the worker–management bond is immensely strengthened'. In the present context the key finding is that 'Germans do not view management as a separate profession. No graduate business schools train them ... by teaching them the theory ... of management disciplines. People who hold responsible positions in German manufacturing companies have usually received undergraduate, and often graduate, training in the technical professions, have had considerable experience as line engineers, and work to keep themselves up to date'.

The authors issue a final warning about stereotypes by mentioning that 'Absenteeism is evident in German industry. It is over 12 per cent and, with the exception of Sweden, is the highest in the world'. One disillusioned Japanese manager, when asked to express his view of 'German punctuality', commented that what had impressed him was how punctually staff left the office at five o'clock. In other words, it is not just a question of the popular stereotypes of the hard working, disciplined German population, and so on. '*The practices that lead to competitive success are usually not culture-specific*' (emphasis added).

There is now an international three-year course organised by the European School of Management Studies, backed by the Paris Chamber of Commerce. One year each is spent in Paris, Oxford and Berlin, with a period in industry or commerce in each of the three countries. British students who have taken part in the scheme have not been slow to draw their conclusions. 'France and Germany have institutions which are designed to produce business managers ... British management suffers from tunnel vision. Marketing people often don't talk to people in sales or production. In Germany, I found that each job is related so that you feel part of a whole. The British identify with their social equals, not with their companies. In Germany, you can't easily distinguish the managers and the managed'.[43]

It is argued here that the 'professional' problem in management in Britain, in contrast to the approach to management in Germany, is both deeply seated and with serious implications for task performance. The present research may be able to give some pointers towards possible solutions in the light of Japanese experience in Europe, although there is no space to examine all the institutional factors involved in detail. While agreeing that social relations between managers, accepted norms of behaviour and, for instance, negotiating styles in decision-making are related to broader social differences specific to particular societies at a given moment, the approach is opposed to the over-use of the term 'culture'. Vague generalisations and the ascription of certain characteristics to a catch-all 'cultural' explanation, seldom defined with any precision or awareness of social change, are unfortunately common in Japan, USA and Europe. They frequently mask the motives of those who use them.

Thus, in Britain 'culture' is often advanced as the reason why 'you can't do that'. 'Culture' becomes an alibi for not changing, for not taking a serious look at the seeds of competitive sucess elsewhere and, in the present context, for persisting with approaches to management and 'professionalism' that are no longer productive. At a general level, 'culture' is commonly seen as an expression of 'national character', in spite of the data on the high rate of absenteeism in Germany. As Max Weber, the German father of social science observed, 'The appeal to national character is generally a mere confession of ignorance'.[44]

## Aims of the research

To sum up, the research aims to investigate as empirically as possible the nexus of the above interrelated problems. For example, how far do the models of generalist and specialist managers respectively accord with actual company behaviour? Do they reflect objective data, such as career profiles, training and job assignments, or do they reflect ideas, ideologies or perceptions? What is the relation between ideas about managerial work and management structures? If differences exist between Japanese, British and German approaches, what are the results in mixed organisations? Do the differences lead to mutual incomprehension and to a lowering of effectiveness? What are the implications for the efforts of Japanese companies in Europe that want to introduce new ways of managing?

For practising managers, of whatever country, in Japanese companies in Europe, these are immediate problems, but they have a wider significance. In countries experiencing the pressure of Japanese competition there is considerable discussion among managers about the 'transferability' of Japanese management. Here there are three questions. The first, which is so obvious that it is sometimes overlooked, is whether in fact Japanese companies in Europe *are* using practices which they normally use at home. The second question is what are the results of the practices, if any, that they have introduced from their operations in Japan. The third question is whether, on the basis of the results, there are useful implications for European managers. The approach here is that it is always valuable to learn and understand what others are doing, without which one becomes inward-looking, complacent and ultimately less able to compete. It then requires careful investigation and analysis beyond the stereotypes to determine what inferences can be drawn and what practical measures introduced that will increase competitiveness.

Here the popular term 'transferability',[45] or 'exportability'[46] may be misleading. It tends to be forgotten how many managerial techniques Japanese managers themselves have adopted or adapted from Europe and the USA, including in the post 1945 period,[47] and that they have spent years of painstaking effort to sharpen the competitiveness which has now become famous for its cutting edge.

It is futile to import 'hardware' alone, without the necessary management 'software' that can make it work. It is naive and dangerous for European firms to attempt to import a half-understood 'package' of what is conceived to be 'Japanese management' and, like other management gimmicks, to try and stick it on an unchanged structure in the hope that it will lead to a rapid doubling of profits. Japan's own business and industrial experience since 1868 and again since 1945 indicate that the long, hard efforts of Japanese managers have been directed towards dealing with the fundamental problems of management, within the framework of their own society and the economic conditions of the time: not with the superficial rearrangement of organisations according to what the popular expression vividly expresses as 'the flavour of the month'. Japanese success, proved not once but many times in the international market-place and by the preferences of international customers and consumers, suggests that it would pay us to look seriously at the ways in which that success has been achieved and on what it is based.


## Notes

1. JUSE, *QC Circle Koryo*, p. 49.
2. T. Ishida, *Japanese Society*, pp. 99–100.
3. R. Miyajima, 'Managerial Values'.
4. Cf. J. McLoughlin, 'Comfort in Suntory's happy song'.
5. R. Evans, 'Lifetime earnings in Japan for the class of 1955'.
6. N. Lyons, *The Sony Vision*, p. 76.
7. T. Kono, 'Japanese management philosophy: can it be exported?'
8. Y. Watanabe, 'The role of academic background in Japanese society'.
9. A. Weiss, 'Simple truths of Japanese manufacturing'.
10. M. Moritani, 'Behind the screens of technology'.
11. A. Okumura, 'Development in Japan: Japanese and US management models compared'.
12. D. Taylor (ed.), 'Learning from Japan'.
13. P. Sadler, 'Educating managers for the twenty-first century'.
14. J. K. Johansson and I. Nonaka, 'Japanese export marketing: structures, strategies, counterstrategies'.
15. Y. Nakagawa and N. Ota, *The Japanese-Style Economic System*.
16. G. Gregory, 'Why Japan's Engineers lead'.
17. H. Inohara, 'The personnel department in Japanese companies'.
18. Y. Funaki, 'Japanese management and management training'.
19. G. Cleverley, *Managers and Magic*, esp. pp. 38–50.
20. Ibid., p. 96.
21. A. Mant, *The Rise and Fall of the British Manager*, pp. 181–2.
22. P. F. Drucker, *The Practice of Management*, p. 270.
23. K. Singer, *Mirror, Sword and Jewel: A study of Japanese Characteristics*, p. 62.
24. Cf. R. N. Bellah, *Tokugawa Religion: The Values of Pre-Industrial Japan*.
25. Inohara, 'The personnel department'.
26. R. S. Kaplan, 'Yesterday's accounting undermines production'.
27. In the terminology of Max Weber, it was an action motivated by *Zweckrationalität* (expediency or purposive rationality directed towards a particular end, especially a concrete and shorter range aim). It was not primarily motivated by *Wertrationalität* (value

rationality, or values and ideals, frequently of a fixed type). See Weber, *The Theory of Social and Economic Organisation*.

28. Cf. Y. S. Hu, *National Attitudes and the Financing of Industry*.
29. K. Imai and H. Itami, 'Organisation and market interpenetration'.
30. M. Walker, 'Engineering tomorrow's managers'.
31. J. Atkinson, 'Manpower strategies for flexible organisations'.
32. Lord Sieff, 'How I see the personnel function'.
33. See, for example, S. J. Pollard, *The Wasting of the British Economy*.
34. 'On Britain's industrial decline', *Financial Times*, 23 January 1984, listed 'major problem areas' in which the balance of trade had deteriorated significantly. The list was headed by cars and commercial vehicles (down by over £1,000 million in the previous eleven months), aero engines, electronic components and other standard industrial products. These are official Department of Trade and Industry figures and are not to be compared with media sensationalism.
35. G. Crockett and P. Elias, 'British managers: a study of their education, training, mobility and earnings'.
36. Mant, pp. 15–16.
37. Crockett and Elias. Cf. also B. Alban-Metcalfe and N. Nicholson, *The Career Development of British Managers*, pp. 29–31.
38. A. Daly, D. M. W. N. Hitchens and K. Wagner, 'Productivity, machinery and skills in a sample of British and German manufacturing plants'.
39. R. Eglin, 'Give us the tools and we'll mess up the job'. For a European-wide comparison, see R. Johnson, 'Adult training in Europe'. The author argues that training should not be 'An optional extra for the favoured few, but a vital necessity for everyone'.
40. J. Child et al., 'A price to pay? Professionalism and work organisation in Britain and West Germany'.
41. J. Child, 'Culture, contingency and capitalism in the cross national study of organisations', pp. 343–5.
42. J. A. Limprecht and R. H. Hayes, 'Germany's world-class manufacturers'. Cf. 'Much has been made of non-militant German workers, implying a deep-rooted psychology which harmonises the interests of workers and employers. This article argues that West German workers are as sceptical of employers' motivations as their British counterparts'. (A. Lane, 'Industrial efficiency and the West German worker').
43. P. Wilby, 'Hard work? It's just not cricket'. The institutional roots *per se* of the British management problem are outside the scope of the present study. They are discussed in Mant. It has led to complacency, ignorance of management in other countries and unwillingness to consider change. See, for example, K. Kumar, 'Why Carlyle should be living at this hour'.

44. R. Bendix, *Max Weber: An Intellectual Portrait*, p. 65.
45. M. H. Trevor, 'The problem of transferability: some theoretical considerations'.
46. M. H. Trevor, 'Quality control in Japan: technology transfer and self help'.
47. H. Ishida, 'Exportability of the Japanese employment system'.

# 1. Production sector

## 1.1 Japanese company PI: precision engineering (Britain)

Production started in the mid-1970s in a new factory on an industrial estate. Like all the other Japanese companies in Britain and Germany in this study, it is a leader in its field in Japan and can call on the technological resources of the parent company. Company strategy is based on the perceived need for a manufacturing base within the EEC to head off protectionism and to increase market share—a strategy which applies to Japanese manufacturers in engineering, electronics and, as the example of Nissan in the UK shows, automobiles, in general. Japanese Company PI is therefore a typical case as far as the above characteristics are concerned.

The British personnel manager stressed the 'commitment to product quality and service' and the 'high development level of manufacturing techniques' of the company and its plans in Japan, which he has visited. He referred to the 'long-term transfer of responsibilities to local staff' and the British deputy plant manager is a director designate of the company. This is not found in many other Japanese companies in the UK at present but in this and other respects the start-up date of the operation needs to be borne in mind. The first Japanese manufacturing operation in the UK did not start up until 1972. Local branches are therefore at an early stage in their development cycle.

### Quality philosophy

From a personal visit to the main plant and discussions with the plant director and production managers in Japan, it was possible to learn at first hand about the company's approach to quality; the importance of which in the field of precision engineering goes without saying. Great efforts have been made to transfer this philosophy to the UK, and managers and employees are keenly aware of the importance of quality.

Instructions formulated by the personnel manager and issued

to employees at all levels of the organisation explain the following background:

Comparing our plant with normal British features, our standard of housekeeping is of a higher level. But if we do not try to improve standards, then in time present conditions will deteriorate. Looking to other British companies offers no help in improving ourselves and simply saying we want to improve our factory will not make it happen. So we need a system that will help us bring about a positive and lasting improvement in housekeeping and to make easier working methods. Such a system exists in Japan and has worked for many Japanese companies. We now have UK personnel with first-hand knowledge of the system and its application. Therefore, we intend to use the system as a vehicle to improve our factory.

Under 'Purpose' it is stated that, 'through the active participation of every plant member', the aim is to: '1. Create a pleasant working environment. 2. Make existing working methods easier to perform'. But these are not simply ends in themselves. The point is that 'The above items will naturally lead to some benefits for productivity and quality, resulting in improved job security and rewards. Of course, it will not be the only way to bring about such benefits'. In other words, the focus is on the task and on results.[1] Naturally the management prefers managers and employees to be as content as possible at the workplace, because they judge that this will improve motivation and performance, but there is no room for interpretations which are unduly orientated towards a 'human relations' approach.

Overseas investment involving sophisticated manufacturing techniques is costly, and Japanese managers have additional worries that stem from the differences in recruitment, selection and training systems between the main company in Japan and its overseas offshoots. Candidates for the managerial stream in first-class companies of this type in Japan go through a meticulous screening process; based on the expectation that they will stay with the company until the official retiring age of 55 or 60—or later if they have risen as high as director.[2] By definition, local managers and staff engaged in Britain and Germany do not go through this process. Given local labour market conditions and local conceptions of work and career, there is also not the same expectation of a high degree of stable long-term employment. This has several major implications (which will be discussed in the Conclusion below) in relation to recruitment policy, selection criteria, recovery of investment in training and the company's overall employment policy.

Management puts considerable thought and effort into communicating with all levels of the organisation. The personnel manager stated that general company information is distributed to all employees and that the organisation chart is given to all managers. Management ensures that all understand the company's business aims and production procedures. In the former case it can be said that 'nothing succeeds like success'. All are aware that the company is almost the only one on the industrial estate which is expanding even during the recession—no mean achievement. Elsewhere on the estate several operations which started up when the estate opened in the 1950s and 1960s have already closed down. The link which Japanese managers emphasise between company performance and individual prospects is only too apparent.

As regards quality, little is left to chance. The system to ensure the smooth running of the plant is based on a mnemonic, of the type one often sees in plants in Japan, of 'the four A's'. In outline these are:

1. Arrangement: Have designated areas, standardised storage and identification throughout the plant.
2. Accessibility: Ensure easy access to items and information most frequently used.
3. Area housekeeping: Keep it clean and tidy!
4. Affirm: Ensure that above conditions are kept.

'Management by detail' in a Japanese factory in the UK was described in a previous study.[3] The four points above are amplified by specific details, and in the present context it is significant that the amplification of the first point on 'arrangement' gives the following explanation: 'The reason for identification and uniformity is so that *all plant personnel* are able to clearly understand the purpose of area or function, *whichever department they are in*' (emphasis added). This presupposes a degree of flexibility, or lack of demarcation and functional boundaries, and a conscious management policy of not dividing up the organisation into watertight departments. But to what extent does it reflect generalist or specialist concepts?

On a research visit to plants in Japan it became apparent how aware Japanese industrial managers generally are of the need to ensure the momentum of any management programme. Here it is pointed out under 'affirm' that although continued effort 'is the responsibility of all personnel . . . those in a supervisory position should set an example, especially at their own working area'. Responsibility to lead from the front is placed squarely on management's shoulders. 'Setting an example' is a cardinal, task-centred, principle of Japanese managers at their best.[4]

But even, or perhaps especially, in an environment characterised by high levels of commitment, management knows that generalised exhortations by themselves are not enough. They must be given precise form and content. The company's 'Quality Assurance Principles', which are similar to those found throughout first-class manufacturing in Japan, point to the general business strategy and also to the precise tools which alone can make it a reality.[5]

The two Quality Assurance Principles are:

1. To make a contribution to the development of society and industry through our enhanced quality products satisfying our customers' needs.
2. We therefore seek to reward our customers' confidence in us at all times by means of maintaining and improving existing quality standards using all of the *specialist knowledge and managerial techniques* at our disposal [emphasis added].

Details follow of how Quality Assurance (QA) systems are to be monitored by means of maintaining the accuracy of measuring instruments, clarifying specifications, reviewing and improving the QA systems of suppliers, and so on.


## Personnel management

The personnel manager plays an important role in the company. He is an IPM (Institute of Personnel Management) qualified professional and was recruited as personnel manager through an advertisement in a local newspaper. This is the company's normal method of recruiting employees at managerial level. He was initially interviewed by a recruitment agency, again following local practice.

The company is unionised and recognises one of the major unions as sole bargaining partner. Because of the changing and complex nature of industrial relations legislations in Britain, and unfamiliar negotiating styles, the Japanese management were keen that the responsibility for direct dealings with the union should be given to an experienced local professional. But this does not mean that management policy towards the union is determined by the personnel manager alone. Although his advice is sought, the policy comes from the senior Japanese management, which he then has the task of implementing. This is the usual pattern in Japanese manufacturing operations in the UK, almost all of which are unionised, and in those distribution and other service companies that have made an agreement with a union. But in the companies in the commercial or financial sector it is rare to find a personnel professional.

It may be conjectured that the personnel manager's energetic and flexible attitude would have appealed to the Japanese managers who conducted the final interview—'attitude' counting for a great deal in selection in Japan. The combination of skills and experience contained in his curriculum vitae would also have been appreciated, because it shows familiarity with production management as well as expertise in personnel. At his previous, American, engineering company, the personnel manager spent a year each as process engineer, production controller and production supervisor, respectively. During the three-year period he took the Diploma in Management Studies at a polytechnic on a part-time basis.

He then spent one year as training officer and three years as personnel and training officer with the same company, studying during the first year for the final year of a three-year accountancy course and taking the first two stages of the IPM course during the remainder. After that he spent nine months as personnel and training officer at an electronics company and completed three short courses. The first was an Industrial Society action-centred leadership course, the second a supervisory management course. Both lasted three days. The third course was a week's course on safety.

During his time with the Japanese company he has completed the third stage of the IPM, of which he is now a Member, and a five-day course on interpersonal skills at Ashridge Management College. Although he is a professional with broad experience, he has worked six months on the shop floor, which is not common in such cases in Britain.[6] He has taken the IPM journal for nine years and occasionally speaks at outside meetings with other personnel managers on the industrial estate.

His own work is not restricted to the personnel function as it might be seen in many British organisations and includes accounts, purchasing and 'general management involvement', all areas where his previous training and experience are useful. He sees all functional managers in the company as having general management responsibility and considers that for top managers the crucial abilities are 'Flexibility of thought—initiative. The critical difference here is the emphasis on leadership, on leading the team'. On the other hand, little except the title and a company car distinguish managers from others in the company in status terms. There is a single-status canteen, uniform clothing to be worn by all personnel at all times and an absence of reserved parking spaces and other overt status indicators.

The personnel manager's reasons for joining the firm were the good conditions offered, such as salary and the prospect of secure employment, and most importantly, the affinity between his own ideals and the company's philosophy, particularly the voice of the personnel department in the overall policy of the company.

Personnel management in the UK has been made into a profession in recent years, with a recognised corpus of knowledge, professional validating body and professional ethics—a situation far removed from that in Japan, where members of the personnel department are not accredited specialists and where there is no parallel with the IPM and its activities. But, at least in theory, personnel management in Japan does not have to struggle for acceptance and many companies have a slogan such as 'Our most important asset is our people', which is by no means an empty one. It might be said that this principle has a strong imperative behind it, in a heavily populated resource-poor country, without assets like North Sea oil.[7]

Yet in Britain, for all its professional status and qualifications, personnel management in practice faces many problems. These often arise from the situation in an organisation, where the personnel department's power and influence are restricted, leading to considerable gaps between the prescriptions of personnel management textbooks and what the personnel manager can actually do. Other colleagues may be glad the personnel department is there to handle problems like industrial relations, while remaining sceptical of personnel management in general and preventing the expansion of the personnel manager's power and importance by defending their own areas.[8]

At a higher theoretical level this can be justified by appealing to the concept of functional specialisation and the advantages claimed to flow from it. In the present case, the personnel manager's words show his awareness that the management system in the company is not one with a characteristic split between personnel and production management. The reasons given for his decision to take up his post with the firm suggest that he saw an opportunity to work in an environment with a personnel philosophy similar to his own, where the emphasis on teamwork of the top management, who would, so to speak, hold the ring, would ensure that barriers based on function did not arise. Implications for the direction in which personnel management in Britain is developing will be discussed in the final Conclusion. Here the personnel manager's experience in production and on the shop floor should be emphasised.

The company set up a pension scheme in the year of the start-up. The personnel manager is widely involved in helping employees when necessary to, for example, find accommodation, obtain company loans and arrange transport to work and concessions over working hours in case of family illness. He is available for private meetings or discussions in the company and, like the top management, is committed to employee welfare.

But this does not imply that the company is not tightly run. He says a friend described the organisational principles as 'modified theory X'[9] explaining that the Japanese managers feel they cannot allow mistakes in a subsidiary overseas that they would allow in Japan, and that they are afraid of 'the British disease' and the consequences that it would have for the success of the operation. Tight control is implicit in the strong task orientation.

The personnel manager sees 40 per cent of managers in the firm as generalists and 60 per cent as specialists. In this inter-pretation, a generalist is a manager who has responsibility beyond the functional limits of the job. The personnel manager sees himself more as a generalist, reflecting what was said above about his duties, but this does not detract from his view of himself as a personnel professional at the same time. Specialists 'are the same really, whether they are British or Japanese'. The particular example given was that of engineers, 'though the Japanese engineers have a broader view'. There are five Japanese technical advisers, or 'departmental engineers', compared to nearly 200 British staff in line departments. Four more Japanese managers are in the staff departments, compared to some 70 local employees. The total strength of the company is approaching 300.

Bearing in mind that the plant opened in the mid-1970s, the average length of service of employees in 1984 was 4.16 years. Recruitment policy has been to go for younger managers, and where possible to promote internally, and this is reflected in the age distribution of middle and top management. Forty per cent are aged 41 to 50; 50 per cent, 31 to 40; and 10 per cent, 21 to 30. There is no formal policy of 'lifetime employment', but the company places emphasis on stable employment. This is aimed at by tight manning to keep costs down, and careful selection, to ensure as far as possible that technical expertise is accompanied by the right attitude. The latter should ensure adaptation to the management style and working practices of the organisation, and therefore increased prospects of long-term commitment. As many Japanese managers make plain, it is only under these conditions that investment in human resources can be attractive.

Use of overtime is practised, both for providing the necessary elasticity which particular orders require, and as a means of continually assessing and spurring the motivation of managers. This broadly follows the pattern in Japan, where, although employment in a first-class company is to an extent guaranteed, managers cannot take their own promotion prospects for granted.

The four above factors—careful selection, tight manning, use of overtime and the encouragement of stable employment—need to be considered together as mutually consistent and reinforcing parts of an overall strategy aimed at producing concrete results. To abstract one feature, such as stable employment, and to seek to explain it in terms of so-called cultural factors would be a serious mistake. Stable employment, if accompanied by a strong motivational system and continuous assessment of achievement, is the company's best guarantee of performance and return on investment in training, in the broad sense of the word.[10] As such, it is rational in business terms and does not stand in need of cultural interpretations.

This is not, of course, to deny the values linked with long-term employment and that what Japanese managers see as the 'disloyal' behaviour of local staff in some companies can produce strong emotional reactions. In the present case, one middle manager has left the company voluntarily, but there have been no dismissals, and employment to date has been quite stable. Excluding secretaries, three managers report directly to the general manager. There are seven grades between him and shop-floor operators. Ten to fifteen employees are subordinate to the first level of management.

The company has job descriptions for all grades between operators and general manager. They are described as 'reasonably tight' by the personnel manager, on whose initiative the job descriptions for local managers and employees were drawn up. The company also has comprehensive written working procedures, routine procedures and work-scheduling programmes. In other words, there is considerable use of detailed written instructions. As noted above, the company fills managerial vacancies internally when it can and only advertises externally if it must. Initial interviews are held by the personnel manager, who makes a recommendation to the general manager and deputy production manager. The matter is then discussed by the group. The decisive criterion for selection is the 'attitude to responsibilities'.[11]

Being unionised, hourly paid employees are paid according to collective agreements, but managers and salaried staff are paid individually, with reviews of their performance.

Managers having already been recruited on the basis of their expertise and attitude, training is mainly on-the-job and little use is made of external courses. Training in Japan, for which managers are chosen according to the needs of a particular job, varies between three and eight weeks. Its main purpose is familiarisation with the parent company and its operations and with the company's way of doing things.

Promotion is according to a mixture of seniority and achievement. In one instance the local QC manager was promoted after six years' experience in the company in this function. Given the size of the local operations, the personnel manager did not rate local promotion chances very highly and saw no possibility at the present time for local managers to be promoted outside the branch. For Japanese managers, he saw little except perhaps honorific promotion in the branch, but believed that their prospects outside the branch were quite good. He considered that their overseas experience would assist their promotion, although in some companies the situation seems to be ambivalent, due to Japanese managers' fear of losing contact with the head-office network.

The personnel manager saw the general manager as having a

considerable degree of autonomy. The sales company would state its needs, and the general manager would assess the plant's capacity. A decision would then be worked out between the top management at the plant and the parent company in Japan. The latter was the origin of the most important decisions with, in decreasing order, the plant top management, middle management and administrative departments following. There is no job rotation for managers. One manager who failed to meet expectations was given further training.

Many meetings are held. The personnel manager attends a monthly general management meeting, meetings with work teams three to four times a week. He holds daily morning meetings with his own staff. He finds the meetings quite useful (4 on a scale of 1 to 5) and is personally fairly satisfied (3). Contact with other departments and between his subordinate and the next level are good (4) and the willingness of subordinates to cooperate, very good (5). He feels well informed about the current situation (4) but insufficiently informed about the company as a whole and the local operation's plans for the future (2), apparently because of a reluctance to put forward ideas that had not actually been agreed.

The climate at work was said to be sometimes too task-centred at the expense of the personal side, because of the hectic period of expansion and the very tight manning levels which led to considerable amounts of overtime being worked. It was said to be unknown to relax at work.

The personnel manager's communication was 80 per cent face to face, 10 per cent in conferences and five per cent each estimated for the telephone and written messages or notes. Communication difficulties across the language barrier were solved by talking, explaining as much as possible and by diagrams. There is a consultative committee, a safety committee and a sports and social club but no formal suggestions scheme. There have been no serious differences with the consultative committee. With the exception of safety, for which the deputy plant manager is responsible, the personnel manager is in charge of all employee relations matters.

As already stated, he plays a major role in the company and scored high on the scale of 1 to 5 in answer to the questions on decision-making. He can appoint his own subordinates entirely on his own responsibility (5). With other matters—for example, organisational changes, determination of recruitment procedures, working hours, and so on—he participates equally with other managers in the decision (4). In regard to making a larger capital investment, he is informed before the decision is taken (2). This is not unusual in Japanese companies in the UK that have been established in the 1970s and that continue to receive investment capital from the parent company in Japan.

The personnel manager's scores on the job satisfaction questions were at the top end of the scale (4 or 5), with the exception of dissatisfaction over the long hours worked (2). Two key questions received the most positive score on the scale (5). They showed, firstly, that the perception of the firm was of one that was much better than others and, secondly, that job security was rated very highly indeed. The implied comparison is, of course, with other British firms known to the personnel manager, since he had had no experience of other Japanese companies.

The success of the firm was also highly rated. In comparison with other firms, profitability, efficiency, adaptation to the market and technological knowledge were rated higher (4). Motivation, growth rate and quality of product and service were rated as much better than others (5). This reflected what was already stated about the dynamism of the organisation and the strong emphasis in company policy on manufacturing quality products and providing customers with such good service that they would place further orders.

### The Japanese managers: overseas assignments

The normal tour of Japanese managers in the UK is between four and five years. This is characteristic of Japanese branches in the UK as a whole, though it is possible to find significant exceptions where a senior Japanese manager is kept in place for seven, eight or even more years in order to build up and nurture a new operation. The problems that can arise in overseas branches, or indeed in any organisation, from the regular turnover of managers, in terms of familiarisation and communication for example, are not the main focus of the present study.[12] What is significant is the ability of the parent company to assign managers to overseas branches in accordance with its strategic priorities and how this may affect managers' career structures.

In boom conditions, a posting overseas in an expanding organisation may help a manager's promotion prospects. When business is less buoyant, and opportunities correspondingly scarcer at home, a manager may feel that his remoteness from the networks in the parent company and its continual decision-making processes is a disadvantage. Many keep in constant touch with colleagues in Japan by telephone, but the possibility of 'being out of sight, out of mind' is a real fear.

The anxiety is more serious in first-class Japanese companies, of the type found in the UK and Germany in this study, that hire managers for 'life', than it would be for British or German managers, who follow more individually orientated career paths in a more fluid labour market. Some Japanese managers may be reluctant to be posted overseas, on career or other grounds, but they must follow the company's decision. If they succeed abroad, they may return to a hero's welcome. If they are less successful, they can harm their promotion prospects. Managers may feel that the cards are stacked against them because companies overseas cannot function in exactly the same way as they do in Japan. This inevitably increases the risks, so that some decide to adopt a low profile and avoid adventurous and possibly dangerous actions.

## Japanese managers' careers

None of the Japanese managers from whom data were collected had worked for another company. This is characteristic of a first-class enterprise. The form of their career development is apparent from the following profiles:

*Assistant (engineering) to general manager*

| Function | Years |
|---|---|
| University, mechanical engineering course | 4 |
| Machine-shop engineer | 3 |
| Production engineer | 2 |
| Machine-shop project engineer | 3 |
| Overseas project engineer | 2 |
| Machine-shop engineer/coordinator | 4 |
| Project engineer | 1 |
| Assistant (engineer) to general manager, UK plant | $4\frac{1}{2}$ |

The manager stated that he had completed the normal six months' introductory training for graduate entrants. This consisted of three months visiting plants, familiarisation with engineering processes (but not accounts or other functions), plus three months as a shop-floor operator. There followed two years' on-the-job training (OJT), with the status of 'trainee engineer'.

As a production engineer he did a year's theoretical self study and undertook self-development, so as to be able to train staff engineers. He also completed a six months' QC course, arranged in three-hour sessions after work. This ended his formal training, but from his comments he was obviously engaged in a continuous process of learning, when he had the chance to see other processes, as a project engineer for example. He was ordered to be a union representative for two years, although he described his own philosophy as conservative.

He sees himself as a generalist and considers his development has been typical for the company. He stated that he wanted to be a generalist, especially in man-management, control, and so on, but that he had to be a specialist in several areas. Even in the machine shop there were several specialists, but to work as a manager a person should be a generalist. He sees 20 per cent of managers in the UK branch as generalists and 80 per cent as specialists. Up to section leader they were specialists. Above that they were generalists.

He is critical of the British training system whereby an engineer who wants to become a Member of the Institution of Mechanical Engineers has to study 'other functions, such as accountancy' over two years. This was considered inappropriate, because they might leave the company, which would be very uneconomical. He himself has been a member of the Japanese Society of Mechanical Engineers for twenty years, since a Japanese engineering graduate is automatically eligible. Professional associations in Japan are not as numerous as they are in Britain and, with the significant exception of the Japan Medical Association[13] they tend to be less influential. It follows from the differences between the Japanese and British labour markets that their *raison d'être* and activities are not identical. The assistant to the general manager currently subscribes to a Japanese machinery magazine and has subscribed to several others in the engineering field in past years.

He says that he follows company rules and procedures very strictly (5 on the scale of 1 to 5) but that his job area is very flexible. Managers should lead people. Their actions should be instructive. Top managers needed a long-term view. They should train and educate subordinates.

As far as communication is concerned, telephone, written notes and face-to-face communication each account for one-third. It is 'case by case', but the manager tried to record things in written form as much as possible, so as to have a record or evidence. The problem with local staff was that they didn't like 'abnormal communication'—they wanted it strictly top down without skipping levels.

The manager sees the success of the firm as better than that of its competitors in the same industry (4). He is 'confident of our technology'. International expansion is a question of competing against Japanese rivals, as well as of becoming 'a worldwide company' and of increasing market share in competition with foreign companies.

*Assistant (administration) to general manager*

| Function | Years |
| --- | --- |
| University, foreign language course | 4 |
| Personnel department | 4 |
| Finance department | 5 |
| Assistant (administration) to general manager, UK plant | $2\frac{1}{2}$ |

The manager stated that training in his first two departments, where he was a 'member' without a precise title, consisted mainly of on-the-job training (OJT) and self study—nothing formal. Like his colleague above, he was told to spend two years as a union representative, as part of his career development. He subscribes to *President*, a Japanese magazine for senior managers, but is not a member of any professional association.

His work is largely with accounts, but he sees the job as very flexible. As is normal in Japanese companies, he does not have a professional qualification in accountancy, which might be expected under the British system. Nor does he see accountancy as a distinct or separate profession. Accounts should show the company 'the real situation' and what it should be. Accounts should produce useful information to help the company's performance. The remarks are instructive in the light of the discussion of the implementation of the ROI criterion in the Introduction above.

He sees himself as a generalist with wide but shallow knowledge. He feels he may sometimes need specialist knowledge which is lacking. In his view, two-thirds of the plant's managers, including the British first-line management, are generalists, while one-third are specialists. The latter include the Japanese engineers and the engineering assistant to the general manager.

Sixty per cent of his communication is face to face, with 20 per cent using the telephone and 10 per cent each estimated for written notes and conferences. Contact with other departments is very close (5) and he is very satisfied with the amount of information about the company's situation and plans both in the branch and the company as a whole (4). He finds the monthly general management meeting fairly useful and the willingness of subordinates to cooperate fairly good (3).

In his view, which is largely similar to that of the British personnel manager for instance, it is the parent company which has been responsible for the most important decisions. This is followed by the top management, middle management, the consultative committee and, finally, the administrative departments. The position of the consultative committee may be surprising.

He views the firm as rather more successful than its competitors (4), although he forebore to comment on profitability, because 'I don't know other firms' profitability'. He sees the technical level of the branch as quite good but dependent on the transfer of technology from Japan.

To survive in a competitive world, and because the home market is limited, the company must become a multinational, and some of the company's customers are also expanding overseas. But the manager emphasised that he was not top management, so he did not know the details.

### Quality Assurance Engineer

| Function | Years |
| --- | --- |
| University, engineering course | 4 |
| Quality Assurance division | 9 |
| Quality Assurance division, UK plant | 4 |

The manager has had two months' management training and six months' statistical Quality Control (SQC) training in Japan and has served as a union official. He is a member of the Quality Control Institute and has subscribed for four years to a well-known Japanese management magazine. But this is a general management magazine, not one of the magazines specifically for QC. He sees his role in the company as that of 'manager' and his main job function in the UK as developing English managers and engineers in order to establish a better QA system.

Although he perceives his job to be strictly marked off, with boundaries that he must observe, he still sees himself as a generalist. He is quite happy with the description (4). He sees 80 per cent of the British and Japanese managers at the UK branch as generalists and 20 per cent as specialists. Subordinates are 'fairly well qualified' (3).

### Mechanical Engineer

| Function | Years |
| --- | --- |
| University, engineering course | 4 |
| Production engineer | 2 |
| Machine shop engineer, UK plant | 2 |
| Production engineer, UK plant | 2 |
| Machine shop engineer, UK plant | 2 |

The manager has had 'no particular' training; in other words, OJT without formally organised courses. He has not been a union official, nor does he belong to a professional association. Since he has been in the UK, he has subscribed first to *Newsweek* and now to *The Economist*.

He considers his role as that of 'manager' and does not perceive his job to be tightly bounded. He sees himself as a generalist but is not very happy with this description (2). In his view, his colleagues at the UK plant are divided equally into specialists and generalists. He rates his subordinates as highly qualified (4).

### Staff Engineer

| Function | Years |
| --- | --- |
| Technical college | 4 |
| Operator | 3 |
| Staff engineer | 12 |
| Staff engineer, UK plant | $4\frac{1}{2}$ |

The only training mentioned is the standard one-month general introduction training given to all entrants, but as an operator for three years, the manager will have received constant OJT. He is not a member of a professional association but has subscribed for eight years to the Japanese *Machinery* magazine. He is pleased with his job. He does not see it as strictly delineated but still sees himself as a specialist. He is fairly happy (3) with this description.

He considers his Japanese subordinates to be better qualified (5) than his British subordinates (3). In contrast to the other Japanese managers, he specifically mentions having wanted to join an engineering company as a major factor in joining this particular company.

## British Managers' Careers

The career and functions of the personnel manager have already been described above.

All the senior managers interviewed had worked for more than one previous employer, as might be expected, and comparison of their career profiles with those of their Japanese colleagues of similar age and position is instructive. The use of the asterisk (*) in this and following career profiles indicates a change of employer.

### Deputy plant manager

| Function | Years |
| --- | --- |
| Apprentice toolmaker, engineering | 7 |
| Research engineer, engineering | 2 |
| Project engineer, travel company* | 1 |
| Production engineer, diesel engines* | 3 |
| Production foreman, motor components* | 2 |
| Technical/quality manager, motor components | 3 |
| Assistant production manager, Japanese company* | 2 |
| Production manager | 3 |
| Deputy plant manager | 2 |

The manager has a Higher National Degree (HND) in Mechanical and Production Engineering and obtained his DMS from a local polytechnic. He is a long-standing Member of the Institution of Mechanical Engineers (twenty-two years) and Member of the BIM (British Institute of Management) (three years) and has subscribed for similar periods to *The Civil and Mechanical Engineer* and the BIM *Management News*. In contrast to his Japanese opposite numbers in the management stream, he has not been a union official, but there is, of course, nothing unusual in this. Working fifty-five hours a week, or more, he seldom attends meetings of his professional associations.

He was recruited via an advertisement in a local newspaper. In his first job he spent some time in the drawing office and planning department, and at an aircraft company that was one of the firm's customers. As a research engineer, he did research work on thermodynamics but had nothing formal in the way of training. The diesel engine manufacturer also provided OJT.

No training was mentioned in connection with the motor components company. Training at the present Japanese company consisted first of informal guidance from the Japanese production manager, followed by six weeks' familiarisation training in Japan. As production manager, he spent a further month in Japan, receiving more specifically technical training that included the use of microprocessors and automated systems. He also obtained the Diploma in Safety Management in the UK.

His background is more varied than that of the Japanese outlined above and, in the British sense, more 'professional' in terms of formal qualifications, including apprenticeship, and membership of the relevant professional body. He considers that his development in his present company has not been entirely typical, but he knew that there was a defined development plan for him *if he performed*. Other (British) managers were recruited for specific jobs.

He sees his role as 'manager', definitely not 'entrepreneur', and his job as 'very flexible'—more than in the other companies. But written and unwritten rules have to be strictly observed (5). In his view, managers in the firm are defined as responsible for a function and the employees in it, and for its outputs. Top managers should be good listeners, able to develop subordinates through delegation and coaching—a comment that mirrors one of the two main reasons given for joining the firm. As well as his own career development, he had been frustrated at his previous firm, which had been a traditional British company—especially in regard to human relations.

He said he could not imagine taking another offer, although the question was not to vegetate. He is very happy (5) with the description of himself as increasingly a generalist. In reply to questioning, he stated that he saw no particular difference in the usage of the term between British and Japanese members of the company.

In his view, 40 per cent of the managers are generalists. They include the plant manager and the section leaders. The latter are responsible for the general management of their function, even though the functions themselves are specialised. The 60 per cent of managers described as specialists include in particular the Japanese engineers, the assistant production manager and the QC manager. The unequivocal view expressed was that the main utilisation of personnel was specialised. The Japanese engineers have no general management responsibility and are purely in the mould of technical advisers, concerned with the provision of technical support based on their engineering expertise and experience. This is clearly aimed at the achievement of the necessary quality and productivity and the transfer of industrial engineering expertise to local managers in order to ensure the continued maintenance of standards. It could not be a more technical or specialised function. There is no job rotation for managers in the branch, and the deputy plant manager came because someone else left.

He evaluates the promotion prospects for British managers in the branch as fairly good (3). Internal promotion is stressed, but he points out that in a small organisation the number of posts likely to fall vacant cannot help being limited. Promotion outside the branch is seen as unlikely for the foreseeable future (1). The size of the branch and the relatively short duration of overseas assignments means that for Japanese managers also the prospects of promotion in the branch are low (1), except perhaps 'in a status sense'. Their task in the UK was to train, not to carry out a function. On the other hand, the manager still believes that they will enjoy better prospects in the home organisation if they have worked overseas (3).

For British managers there is a short basic course of from three to five days. Otherwise training was done individually. Managers should be personally highly motivated. The accent is on self-development. This is clearly part of the motivational system, aimed at making the plant as productive and efficient, and therefore as cost-effective, as possible.[14]

For the deputy plant manager, communication is primarily face to face (55 per cent), followed by conferences (20 per cent), telephone (15 per cent) and written messages or notes (5 per cent). He is very satisfied (5) with the climate at work but experiences problems with the meaning of words. Just translating words was all right, though it took time, but the difficulty was the connotation. Here the first problem is to realise that people do not necessarily understand the same thing from the same words. Once this has been recognised, the solution is to talk things over thoroughly until understanding is reached. This need to talk things over at length until both parties finally understand (or perhaps believe they understand) what the other has in mind was mentioned by a great many British managers in similar situations in the companies studied. It will not, therefore, be repeated in every single instance below.

In the deputy plant manager's view, the major decisions affecting the branch come from the parent company and the top Japanese management together. Next in order of significance is the middle management, followed by the staff and administrative departments. This is the same perception as the personnel manager's, and the other British managers interviews agreed with this view of the decision-making relations between the head-quarters and the branch.

The manager's own satisfaction with the job is extremely high—5 on all points except future salary prospects (4). 'Development' was stressed as 'self-development'. Company performance, including quality of product and service, technology and adaption to the market were seen as much better than other companies (5). The only exceptions were profitability (4) (see note 14) and motivation (4), which was described as 'good but still not good enough'. This is probably a reflection of personal standards (heightened by experience in the company?) since to an outsider the level of commitment or morale already seems to be very high.

## QC Manager

| Function | Years |
|---|---|
| Apprentice, electrical control gear (company closed) | 4 |
| Apprentice, transistors (company closed)* | 1 |
| Engineer, TV tubes* | 2 |
| Foreman, TV tubes | 2 |

| Function | Years |
| --- | --- |
| Assistant section leader, TV tubes | 2 |
| Section leader, TV tubes | 3 |
| Factory superintendent, TV tubes (company closed) | 1 |
| Trainee manager, Japanese company* | 1 |
| Section leader, inspection and maintenance | 1 |
| Assistant QC manager | 5 |
| QC manager | 2 |

The manager found the company's name through contacts and wrote in. As well as completing his apprenticeship in the first two electrical companies, he has an HND (Higher National Degree) in electrical engineering. As a TV tubes engineer he did two external courses of a week each at local universities: one on method study and the other on glass technology. As assistant section leader, he attended a course on man-management. On his reasons for joining the firm, he commented that Japanese industry had been successful and that he wanted to be part of that success. Prospects were good in a *new* company.

After joining the Japanese company, whose precision engineering field is not the same as that in which he had spent his earlier working life, he was sent to Japan for QC and inspection training. This lasted four months; a long period by comparison with that of those British managers in Japanese companies in the UK who have received training in Japan. As section leader in inspection and maintenance and then as assistant QC manager, he received OJT from Japanese engineers. In the latter part he also attended instruction on decision-making given by a British consultant over two weekends.

As QC manager, he has continued to receive informal OJT from Japanese engineers. Some Japanese managers were said to have expressed anxiety because he did not have a more specific QC background, and it may be inferred that the period of five years spent as assistant QC manager under the guidance of the company's technical advisers had the purpose of providing the necessary technical knowledge and experience. The manager stated that he intended to apply for membership in the relevant professional association, the Institute of Quality Assurance, and he has been a subscriber to *New Scientist* for twelve years. He has occasionally spoken outside the company.

He sees himself as a manager and controller with a very broad area of responsibility. His immediately subordinate manager is very similar but at a different level. Involvement with staff's personal problems is rare and consists of the occasional private meeting—but most people keep problems to themselves.

Rules and procedures have to be strictly followed (5), especially in QC—where people had to have rules, and guidelines, but also had to use their own judgement. He sees managers in the firm as being differentiated by knowledge and experience; in other words by task-orientated rather than by status-orientated factors. Managers had to control manning levels, expenditure, production, quality, and so on. Top managers must know the product, the techniques, the engineering, so they could answer subordinates' questions, rather than saying 'That's your job—that's your problem'—but it depended on the level of decisions.

He sees himself as a specialist and is very happy (5) with this description. He divides the managers in the firm into 70 per cent specialists and 30 per cent generalists. In his interpretation, generalists are those who control people. He pointed out that the company's chargehands, for example, have specialist technical knowledge but generalist management skill and that they could be moved to learn a new job. By comparison with his present job, previous jobs in British companies were much more demarcated. The possible interpretations and connotation of the term 'specialist' and 'generalist' will be discussed further in the Conclusion at the end of the book.

The QC manager sees the promotion prospects within the branch for British managers as fairly good (3) because the company is expanding, but low (1) in the company as a whole. The opposite is the case with Japanese managers. He sees their chances within the branch as low (1) but as quite good in the wider company context (3). They work hard in the branch, developing themselves, and several have been promoted after returning to Japan. It is possible that they were on the track before being sent to the UK.

There is no job rotation for managers in the branch as a policy but if someone leaves, the gap must be filled, and this may necessitate other changes.

The manager is very satisfied (5) with the climate at work. His decision-making is at its highest level in the appointment of his own QC subordinate (4) and lower in all the other hypothetical cases discussed. He attends the monthly quality meeting and several other management meetings. The company has intended for some time to set up Quality Circles, even though quality consciousness is already high, and weekly team meetings are held in order to get shop-floor people to work in teams.

The QC manager rates his own contact with other departments as very close (5), and the flow of information from his direct subordinate to the latter's direct subordinate and the willingness of subordinates to cooperate as high (4). He rates the meetings he attends as useful (4) and is personally fairly satisfied (3). He is more satisfied (4) with the information he receives about the branch than that referring to the company as a whole (3). His own communication is 80 per cent face to face, with 15 per cent written, often to back up what was said, and 5 per cent on the telephone. There are some misunderstandings with expatriates due to the language, but this is not serious: it is overcome in the same way of talking things over until they become clear that was mentioned by several local managers. It is as clear from the QC manager's responses as from those of other managers above that the most important decisions affecting the local operations, such as whether to make a large capital investment, are centralised on the parent company.

The manager's scores on job satisfaction are high. They include 'job security' and the 'possibility of realising your potential and interests' (5), which represents what would be important to a 'specialist'. As with the personnel manager, satisfaction is lower over working hours (3), and there was the same score for 'future career prospects'. 'Training and further development' scored 4, and the firm was seen as much better than others (5). The success of the firm was evaluated as very high (5) in all respects except efficiency (4) and profitability (2). The latter low score is explained by the relative newness of the firm and its commitment to investment, which would be expected to pay off according to the long-term strategy. There was said to be 'regular information' about profitability, which was 'put out to the shop floor'. 'Adaptation to the market' was said to be particularly good because the organisation was market-led.

*Assistant production manager*

| Function | Years |
| --- | --- |
| Industrial engineer, food | 1 |
| Production superintendent, food | 4 |
| Production planning manager, food | 1 |
| Production manager, confectionery* | 2 |
| Assistant production manager, Japanese company* | 3 |

The manager replied to an advertisement in a national newspaper for an assistant production manager. The company where he had hoped to get promotion was taken over and he wanted to get back into engineering. He saw good career prospects in the Japanese company and liked a small management team. He has a BSc in Mechnical Engineering, which he took externally, and has been a Member of the Institute of Production Engineers for eighteen months.

In his first job he received 'internal company training', followed by two financial management courses of three days each at the company training centre and several man-management courses of one week each during his time as production superintendent in the food company. In the confectionery company he attended two short technical courses, of four and seven days respectively, at the company's own training centre. The Japanese company has sent him to Japan for seven weeks, which was fifty–fifty technical training and man-management; but training in the branch is mainly OJT, occasionally with an external course for specialists. He has experience of serving on works councils at all his previous plants.

The manager's job is 'very flexible', although written and unwritten rules, company procedures, and so on, have to be very strictly followed (5). Managers were treated the same as everyone else, but they had to set an example, be seen to be better and follow the rules. They had to show leadership. Top managers were very different from other factories. They had to be seen to be leaders, although people operated as groups rather than individuals.

The manager sees himself more as a generalist and is fairly happy (3) with this description. He divides the management team into 40 per cent generalists and 60 per cent specialists. The latter include engineers, especially because the area was too big for one person to master the field. He rates his (British) subordinates as very highly qualified (5), although only one is a graduate engineer and the other two are unqualified. Technical control from the parent company is tight.

There is no job rotation for managers in the branch. He sees promotion prospects in the branch as limited (2) and unlikely (1) in the parent company. Japanese managers came to the UK as consultants and can hardly be promoted in the branch (1). But they return to promotion, and their prospects in the wider company are very bright (5).

Contact with other departments is very close (5), and the flow of information between subordinates and their willingness to cooperate are highly rated (5). The managers attend MBO (Management by Objectives) and production meetings once a month and weekly meetings with section leaders. The meetings are fairly useful (3) and 'improving'. The manager's personal satisfaction with them is high (4), but he does not feel sufficiently informed about the company's operation, either in the branch or the company as a whole (2).

He is moderately satisfied with the climate work (3). For him, communication is mostly face to face (70 per cent), with 20 per cent on the telephone and 10 per cent in the form of written messages and so on. Like the QC manager, he tends to write things down for confirmation. Language problems crop up less frequently than before. Most Japanese could speak reasonable English, although they sometimes said they understood it when they didn't. Any problems left over can be cleared up in private conversation after the meeting, and it sometimes helps to write things down.

Similar to other managers above, the manager views major decision-making as centred on the parent company, which provides the investment. His own decision-making is limited in most cases to having his opinion taken into account. He is fairly concerned (3) with the welfare of his subordinates, which at employee level is taken care of through the section leaders.

Satisfaction with the job is high, except for working hours (3), and the atmosphere is not felt to be more than fairly friendly (3). There is a feeling that now the company has grown to a certain size it should look again at the organisation. Tiresome restrictions connected with time off were mentioned. Company performance was very highly rated, with only 'motivation' (3) scoring less. The feeling was that the company was very profitable and paying off the investment, although the manager felt he had not been with it long enough to make a properly informed comment.

Referring to his training in Japan, he said that considerable flexibility was expected, which he personally liked. The Japanese philosophy was very task-orientated and flexibility was a good thing. Managers knew what their responsibilities were, but there was some give and take. In the branch, QC, production and production planning were all very close.

The pressure on managers was said to be considerable, in part because their numbers had not increased although the number of operators had. As with other local managers, working hours were the sore point, the view being that managers would work as required but would go home if possible. This was sometimes said to lead to differences of opinion with Japanese engineers. Moves to further increase productivity were also emphasised.

*Section leader, planning*

| Function | Years |
|---|---|
| Science student, research institute | $1\frac{1}{2}$ |
| Assistant production planning controller (clerical), Japanese company* | 2 |
| Production planner | $1\frac{1}{2}$ |
| Progress controller | $3\frac{1}{2}$ |
| Section leader, planning | $\frac{1}{2}$ |

The manager replied to an advertisement in a local newspaper and had three interviews, held by the personnel manager, the assistant production manager and the production manager, respectively. His reasons for joining the firm were good career prospects, relatively high job security and nearness to home.

He has an HND in applied biology, which he used in the research institute, but he has been a Member of the Institute of Production Control for three years. In his first three and a half years in the company he received OJT. As progress controller, he attended night school over a period of two years in order to take the Institute of Production Control course, which he passed with distinction. In his present job he will take man-management courses after the section has expanded. He does not see his development as typical because there are no specific lines of promotion on the planning or office side. In his view, the typical pattern in the company would be production-orientated, with promotion up through the grades according to a structured process.

The rules, were said to apply to everyone—especially about not smoking, not eating, and so on, and had to be very strictly followed (5). As regards functional areas, all the managers in the plant were linked in together in a team. It was a big interrelationship.

Total responsibility was what defined managers. In a Japanese company, top managers should be able to make 100 per cent genuine efforts to be excellent communicators up and down. They should have self-discipline and set an example. But, most important, they should be very adaptable to new situations. They should be able to accept criticism. The manager himself says he works long hours (between fifty and fifty-five hours a week or more) like other managers and is clearly impressed by the example of the senior Japanese manager, who normally works until 9.00 pm.

He sees himself as a specialist, but Japanese companies didn't have a view of the difference. A manager had to be in charge of an area, starting as a specialist and then expanding. In his view, 60 per cent of the management team are generalists, who are expected to have specialist expertise too. The 40 per cent who are specialists are expected to share information.

On training, his view is that day-release was only possible if you could do your normal work. He expects to go to Japan for six weeks' training. He sees promotion prospects in the branch as very high (5) but meagre (1) outside it. Individual assessments are important. People are not promoted beyond their capacity. They do the work first and are then confirmed. Japanese managers are promoted up when they come to the UK and have good prospects when they return home.

There is no job rotation for section leaders or managers. The manager attends the weekly section leaders' meetings and the monthly planning meeting. The department manager holds meetings twice a day. The meetings are very useful (5), though personal satisfaction is lower (2) because of the high aim and the need to avoid complacency.

Contact with other departments is quite close (4), and levels of information about the company in the UK and Japan are good (4).

Communication consists of 20 per cent each by telephone, written messages, face to face, conferences and correspondence with Japan—the first manager to refer specifically to it. Problems in communicating with expatriates came from believing one has understood. They are overcome as far as possible by discussion. Satisfaction with the climate at work is not high (2), because there is no direct comparison with the pay of hourly or weekly staff not on shift work. But pay itself scores 3 and future salary prospects 4.

The manager sees important decisions as being taken by the parent company, following the centralised pattern identified by other managers. He can decide the appointment of his own direct subordinate but not that of another junior employee.

Not having worked for a comparable firm before, he was unable to compare conditions elsewhere but scored high (5 or 4) on all job satisfaction items except working hours (3). He sees technology, growth and quality of service as the company's outstanding successes (5). There are no claims back from customers. The policy of no redundancy meant the company had to maintain the volume of production, which influences its adaptation to the market (4).

### Section leader, assembly

| Function | Years |
|---|---|
| Trainee, light engineering | $\frac{1}{2}$ |
| Engineer, Japanese company* | 1 |
| Section leader, assembly | 4 |

The manager found the job through PER (Professional and Executive Recruitment, the official agency for more senior jobs). Apart from relatively high job security and nearness to home, his reasons for joining the company included the structure and techniques of the management team; in other words, the management style. He also particularly emphasised that the absence of demarcation was a major reason.

In his first job, in light engineering, he was trained up to the Industrial Technologist level under the EITB (Engineering Industry Training Board) scheme and obtained block release to get a BSc. in Mechanical Engineering at a polytechnic. In the present company he has had six weeks' training in Japan. As section leader, he has attended a four-day external course on management techniques run by the Industrial Society, but the main thing has been self-development. He does not belong to any professional association. Like other managers, he is able to see technical or professional magazines connected with his work which are provided by the company, in this case *The Engineer*.

He sees his role in the firm as manager, promoter and example setter. Rules and procedures must be strictly observed but the work area is flexible. A manager in the company is one who has the authority and responsibility of the company at heart. A top manager should be, first, a leader, secondly, a good communicator and, thirdly, available to people.

The manager sees himself as a generalist, although he has specialist knowledge. In his view, 85 per cent of management colleagues are generalists and 15 per cent specialists. He sees the graduate Japanese engineer he works with as more qualified (4) than his British subordinate (3) but points to the different, more important role of engineers in Japan—a reflection of what was already said in the Introduction about the numbers and importance of engineers trained in Japan.

Like most British managers already referred to, he evaluates promotion prospects in the branch as better (3) than in the company as a whole (1); while for Japanese managers the situation is the opposite—better in the wider company context (4) than in the smaller UK branch (1). There is no job rotation as such. The exception was when one manager left; but there is flexibility. This mirrors the remarks of the deputy plant manager and the QC manager, for instance, who made the same point about what happens if a manager leaves; although this has not been a common occurrence and has hardly required a special system.

The manager is prepared to help staff with personal problems in any way necessary: 'I take the long view and the important thing is to build relations'. This could be described either as part of a recognisably diffuse 'Japanese' approach to the responsibility of a manager, or simply as good management.

He is on the committee of the sports and social club, which meets monthly. He attends a considerable number of meetings: shift handover (daily), engineering (weekly), preventive maintenance (weekly), chargehands (weekly), section leaders (weekly), safety (fortnightly), budget (monthly), engineer handover (monthly), quality (monthly), budget review (half yearly). The example shows the company's concern for communication and detail and the high level of development of its communications structure. Having said that, the manager personally feels no more than adequately informed (3) about the company's plans for the branch and less than that (2) about the company as a whole.

He is moderately satisfied (3) with the climate at work. The subjective nature of these perceptions should, of course, be borne in mind. Like other managers, most of his communication is face to face (75 per cent). This is followed by written notes (15 per cent) and telephone (10 per cent). Language or cultural difficulties with expatriate colleagues are rare and can be dealt with by the characteristic method of talking face to face.

Unlike other British managers already quoted, this manager sees the head of the local British or European operations as having the major say in important decisions, with the parent company in second place. The middle management are then third, with no other bodies such as staff or administistative departments exercising significant influence. His own major decision-making power (5) concerns the appointment of his direct subordinate.

Job satisfaction is high (4–5), including hours of work (4), which are 'self-imposed'. But there are doubts about future career and salary prospects (3) and, most clearly, about opportunities for further training and development (1)—the lowest score on this point. On the other hand, job security is highly rated (5) and the firm is seen as considerably better than others (4). The performance of the firm is evaluated as high (4–5).

*Section leader, production*

| Function | Years |
| --- | --- |
| Technical clerk work study, light engineering | 2 |
| Planning department, light engineering | 5 |
| Work study engineer, light engineering | 4 |
| Work study, clothing* | 6 weeks |
| Chief work study engineer, light engineering* | 1 |
| Trainee section leader, Japanese company* | 1 |
| Section leader, production | 7 |

As a work study engineer, the manager had heard that the Japanese company was recruiting and he wrote in for an application form. As well as relatively high job security and nearness to home, the company appealed to him because it was 'different' and had a particular atmosphere. It also offered better prospects and a better job than the previous one.

The manager has a Technician's Certificate as a Work Study Engineer and did the second year of a general engineering course as part of an ONC (Ordinary National Certificate), though the ONC itself was not completed. He is not a member of a professional association.

As a work-study engineer, in his third job, he obtained day-release over three years for an Organisation and Methods course of the Institute of Practices in Work Study. As chief work study engineer he received training in communication skills lasting half a day a week over six weeks from a head office trainer. In the parent company, he has had seven weeks training in Japan—75 to 80 per cent technical and 20 to 25 per cent company orientation. He has attended a one-week Man-Management for the Middle Managers course run by the Industrial Society. Since joining the company, there has been continual OJT—like coaching from the assistant production manager.

Rules have to be quite strictly observed (4): here again the no smoking, no drinking, and so on, rule was specifically mentioned. There is a very long job description, which means that you must do anything required—which to some people might seem like a contradiction in terms; the usual purpose of job descriptions in Britain being to define duties as precisely as possible. The job is flexible and flexibility is given as the first characteristic of managers in the company; the others are freedom, responsibility and pressure. On the abilities required by top managers, the manager stated he could talk for hours, but he particularly drew attention to the need to gain the respect of subordinates by different means; in other words, by leadership.

He is happy (4) to describe himself as a generalist, because he had moved from one shop to another within the company. In his view, 80 per cent of colleagues are generalists and 20 per cent specialists. He likes his job, having seen the company start from zero, which meant a lot to him. To think of moving would be hypothetical. Another green-field operation, but not an old company, might be alright; but only if the salary were 50 per cent higher. This suggests a move is hardly a serious consideration.

On the other hand, there is some worry about promotion prospects. These are not perceived as very high in the branch at the moment (2) because people felt they did not know where the company structure was going. This compares with the figure of 1 for the company as a whole. The latter figure is the same for Japanese managers' promotion prospects within the branch, but their prospects in the company as a whole are rated as excellent (5) because of the flexibility between plants and departments. In other words, flexibility is seen as closely linked to the job assignment and promotion structure. But in the branch there is no rotation of managers.

Like the section leader, assembly, above, the manager attends a considerable number of meetings, which he rates as quite satisfactory (3). Contact with other departments is close (4) and information about the branch's plans good (4) but insufficient about the company as a whole (1). Like other colleagues, communication is predominantly face to face (80 per cent), with 15 per cent written and 5 per cent telephone. The manager had learnt to accept cultural differences, but some subordinates were not used to them. The Japanese became very dependent on the company. They used pressure to motivate subordinates, sometimes with not enough subtlety, but then they were far from home.

The manager sees the parent company as the main source of major decisions. To appoint his own direct subordinate he would discuss the matter with others in the department and with his superiors. In general, he would participate equally with others in the department in decision-making (4), with the exceptions of making a larger capital investment and of appointing a new manager or employee (1).

Job satisfaction is high (4–5) except for opportunities for further training and development and future career prospects, which are in the middle of the scale (3). The success of the company is positively evaluated (4–5), with only profitability slightly lower (3). Technological levels in the branch are rated as 4, but there were more technical standards in Japan. Emphasis was placed on the Japanese provenance of machinery in use in the branch and on the parent company as the decision-making centre.

*Section leader, machine shop*

| Function | Years |
| --- | --- |
| Engineer, coal mine ventilation | 5 |
| Manager, delicatessen* | 3 |

| Function | Years |
|---|---|
| Engineer, telephones* | 3 |
| Machine operator, Japanese company* | $\frac{1}{2}$ |
| Chargehand, machine shop | $3\frac{1}{2}$ |
| Section leader, inspection | 2 |
| Section leader, machine shop | |

Recruitment was by personal application to the company, after hearing about it from a friend. Career prospects, security, nearness to home and the fact that 'the previous company didn't pay enough' were the deciding factors.

During his career the manager has had considerable training. While working in his first job, for the National Coal Board, he obtained day-release over a period of three years and completed the qualifications of Mining Craft 1, 2 and 3 and Mining Technology 1, equivalent to the Deputy's ticket. His work with airborne dust sampling gave him an awareness of the need for exact work on one's own. In the telephone manufacturing company he attended an eleven-week course on site and worked on adjusting telephone mechanisms.

On entering the Japanese company he had some basic training from a chargehand and expatriate engineers on the job. As a machine-shop chargehand he was further trained by Japanese engineers in inspection techniques and chargehand's duties. He attended weekend courses on man-management given by the Industrial Society and by the personnel manager. As inspection section leader, he spent two months in Japan on a QC Circle course and attended a one-week course at a British university given by a QC expert. There was a year's training at the plant with a Japanese QC engineer four hours a week, and half days and evenings at a local technical college on Quality Management and Quality Techniques. As a machine-shop section leader he has attended a four-day technical course at a local university and received instructions from the senior Japanese engineer on the company's own technical standards. He intends to apply for membership of the Institute of Quality Assurance, having obtained the Certificate in Quality Management and Techniques from the technical college.

The job is entirely flexible, except for one specialised area where entry is restricted to qualified people for safety reasons. Manning is tight. Observance of rules and procedures is a bit stricter than British companies (4) but requires individual judgement on a case-by-case basis.

Managers wear the same clothes as other people and all are on a first-name basis. There is no managers' restaurant or other status differences. The only difference is that the managers have a desk and a chair. Top managers should have a lot of patience. The manager sees himself as a manager and administrator. His subordinate is also an administrator, responsible for low-level disciplinary procedures.

The manager is happy (4) to classify himself as a generalist. He sees 80 per cent of managers as generalists and 20 per cent as specialists; among the latter he puts the Japanese engineers. Both British and Japanese subordinates and colleagues are highly evaluated (5).

He sees promotion prospects more optimistically than his colleagues referred to above (5), though there is little possibility outside the branch (1). For Japanese managers the UK branch is a training ground, in which he cannot judge their promotion prospects, but all engineers had been promoted after their return and prospects for them in the parent company are extremely high (5). He likes the Japanese system, which offers security, and would not be interested in moving. Moves of junior managers in the company have been experimental. The greatest advantage he sees in this is the flexible deployment of managers.

He attends the regular meetings with other section leaders and is quite satisfied with them (3) but does not feel sufficiently informed about the company's operations and plans, whether in the UK or elsewhere (1)—a lower score than most. Contact with other departments is close (5), reflecting earlier comments above. Satisfaction with the climate at work is moderate (3), but language and cultural differences are a major problem. This refers, first, to the need for patience and repetition until language difficulties are overcome and, second, to styles of communication. Expatriate managers meet informally over drinks and discuss work. The feeling was that they may keep information to themselves and not inform people enough in advance. It is annoying when Japanese juniors know things before you do. The manager's own communication is almost exclusively face to face (95 per cent), with five per cent on the telephone. He sees QC programmes as a good way of improving communication and of promoting motivation and teamwork—not just a technical means, although that is included.

The parent company is the decision-making centre. Appointment of the manager's direct subordinate is his own responsibility (5). Otherwise, his decision-making consists of having his opinion taken into account with others (3), except for changes in the level of payment, in which he is not concerned (1).

Job satisfaction is high (4–5), except for salary and future salary prospects (3). Evaluation of the company's success is outstandingly high: profitability, efficiency, growth rate and motivation all scoring the maximum (5). Quality of product and service was described as '100 per cent better than other companies' and quality, adaptation to the market, and technology were all rated above the scale at 5+, although it was pointed out that the scores referred primarily to the company in Japan, which provided 'all technical services'.

The manager is impressed with the high degree of automation—said to be much higher than British competitors. He likes the management style and absence of status barriers. There was no demarcation in the plant. No separate canteens, and so on. The social life, the relationship between Japanese engineers and local staff makes people want to work as a team.

*Trainee section leader, inspection*

| Function | Years |
|---|---|
| Management trainee, tailoring | $1\frac{1}{2}$ |
| Management trainee, tailoring, quality | $1\frac{1}{4}$ |
| Operator, inspection, Japanese company* | 1 |
| Trainee chargehand, inspection | $\frac{3}{4}$ |
| Chargehand, inspection | 6 |
| Trainee section leader | $\frac{1}{4}$ |

Entry to the company was by personal application, after hearing about it from a colleague. Salary and nearness to home were the initial attractions.

The manager has four CSE's (Certificate of Secondary Education) and has had a certain amount of in-house training. This began with OJT on basic work study in his first job, together with QC and the setting of piece rates. In the second stage, as a management trainee in tailoring, he was concerned with quality specifications and was responsible for compiling quality manuals.

In the Japanese company he was given basic training on technical aspects of the production process and OJT for operating tasks. OJT continued throughout his time in inspection, and as chargehand he had a total of ten hours in-house training on disciplinary control. This was followed by a total of twenty hours on the above topics, but in greater depth, and training on the operation of briefing groups given by the Industrial Society.

He sees his role as manager 'mainly as controller', and sometimes as entrepreneur in regard to innovations. The role of his directly subordinate manager is 'control'. Rules have to be quite strictly observed (4), but his functional area is 'not so strictly' marked off from others. There was a lot of management involvement on the shop floor, not strict boundaries: to be a manager in the company does not mean being aloof. Top managers need two main qualities: personal drive and the patience to cope with a different culture and Japanese procedures. But there are no serious communication problems with expatriates and communication problems can also arise in British companies.

The manager sees himself more as a generalist, a description with which he is perfectly happy (5). He had always known that this was the way the company worked. In his view, 70 per cent of the management team are generalists. The Japanese have wide experience. Generalists get involved in various areas and do not just hand over to a specialist. The 30 per cent of specialists include the service group personnel, of whom two are Japanese. Once again, the distinction between generalists and specialists is not seen to split neatly according to nationality.

Prospects for local promotion up to section leader are seen as excellent (5) but less good from there to senior management (2). Promotion prospects outside the UK are not known. For Japanese managers, prospects in the branch are limited (2) but are good in Japan (4), and most managers are promoted on their return home. This comment agrees with several already quoted above. There is no job rotation for managers in the branch.

The manager attends the meetings for chargehands (weekly), section leaders (three hours a week), safety (monthly) and production planning (monthly). He considers the meetings useful (4) but is not quite so personally satisfied (2). Contact with other departments is close (4). Information on the branch is good (4) and on the company as a whole adequate (3). The Japanese would sometimes speak more frankly and reveal more of the company's future plans at the pub than at work. After working hours, the Japanese tend to stay on at the plant, drinking coffee and chatting. The plant manager once caught some of the Japanese engineers having a secret smoke in a hideaway in the plant—and went crazy! The section leader wonders 'how hard they really work in Japan'. To Japanese top management such remarks may appear shameful and embarrassing, but to others it may be reassuring that dedicated company men do have human foibles after all.

The manager's own face-to-face communication is lower (50 per cent) than in other cases above. This is because he puts a strong emphasis on getting it down on paper (30 per cent); it has more credibility. The remaining 20 per cent is accounted for by the telephone. The manager's decision-making is not significantly different from that of the section leaders already referred to. Like the vast majority of British managers, he sees the parent company as the source of major decisions.

Job satisfaction, again, is high (4–5) except for present salary, salary prospects, hours of work and the extent to which the company is engaged in improving working conditions, which are moderate (3). To an outsider, working conditions would already appear well able to stand comparison with those in other plants, and there may not be much room for improvement. Other respondents above rated them more highly.

The success of the firm was very positively evaluated (4–5). It was again pointed out that the high level of technology came from the parent company.

### Chargehand, inspection

| Function | Years |
|---|---|
| Casual employment, building, factory* | 1 |
| Operator, inspection, Japanese company* | 1 |
| Chargehand, inspection | 6 |

While looking for a job, the manager wrote to several companies. He considers that he was fortunate to find a job at all. The Japanese company was the only one near home to offer good career prospects, and he was also interested in the place.

He has an OND (Ordinary National Degree) in engineering, having taken the first year of an engineering course at university but failing it. In his first job he had no training. As an operator with the Japanese company he had OJT on inspection. As chargehand, he has had one afternoon training a week for six weeks on man-management run in-house by the personnel manager.

He has a wide conception of his job as a manager and is very happy (5) to see himself as a generalist. He estimates that 90 per cent of management colleagues are generalists and 10 per cent specialists. He believes that the Japanese have wider knowledge than they use in the British factory. The function of his own directly subordinate manager is, in his view, mainly man-management.

Rules and procedures are to be very strictly observed (5) but the job itself is flexible. With managers in the firm it is very hard to find the difference or the level between them. Top managers should have experience in industry and the ability to cope with the different aspects of the job. At operator level, beginners in the firm are very raw—but they learn by working in the company.

In contrast to other respondents, the manager sees the promotion chances of both local and Japanese managers as uniformly high (4) in the branch and the wider company. He believes that particularly good people are sent to the UK. There is no job rotation for managers in the branch at the moment.

Apart from the daily shift hand-overs, he attends weekly chargehands' and weekly project meetings. These are very useful (5), and he is personally quite satisfied (4). He likes a lot of information and is satisfied (4) with the information about the company's plans for the branch and its wider operations (4). Contact with other departments is very close (5); a result common to other respondents above.

Satisfaction with the climate at work is high (4), and the manager does not now experience language or cultural difficulties with expatriates, although he did at the beginning. His communication is for the most part face to face (80 per cent), with 15 per cent written and 5 per cent telephone. In appointing his direct subordinate, he would participate equally with others in the decision (4): otherwise, his decision-making is limited (1–2). The parent company is seen to be the main source of important decisions.

Job satisfaction is generally high (4–5), though he says he would like a change in the work itself (3), and hours of work, opportunities for training or development and improvements in working conditions also score no more than 3. The lowest score (2) refers to the present limited period for which sick pay is available. The performance of the firm is highly rated (4–5), although on technology no comparison with competitors can be made, and 'the parent company has more information'.

### Chargehand, assembly

| Function | Years |
| --- | --- |
| Electrical mechanic, Royal Navy | 4 |
| Operator, machine shop, Japanese company* | 4 |
| Setter, machine shop | $1\frac{1}{2}$ |
| Chargehand, assembly | $2\frac{1}{2}$ |

The manager heard of the possibility of a job with the Japanese company and wrote in, having been discharged on medical grounds from the Navy. He finds the company characterised by high running efficiency, cleanliness and keeping people happy. He was particularly attracted by the prospect of job security, and then by salary, nearness to home and good career prospects.

Apart from basic seamanship training, he received three months' electrical training in the Navy, which he says resembled an apprenticeship. As an operator, he did a basic six weeks' OJT on the machines. After that you were on your own, though it is always possible to ask advice from engineers or setters. As a setter he did more mechanical OJT, and a weekend Outward Bound course and a basic supervisory training course. As chargehand, he received more OJT on the machines.

He sees his functional area as fairly flexible but adherence to rules and procedures as strict (5)—very comparable to the Navy. His perception of his own role is that of manager, and he has four supervisors, or setter/operators, to assist him 60 per cent with production tasks and 40 per cent with man-management. He is happy (4) to see himself as a generalist, along with 60 per cent of the management. The 40 per cent of specialists include the QC manager, production manager, personnel manager, and so on.

Promotion prospects for local managers are rated as excellent (5). For Japanese managers they are probably good when they return. There is no regular job rotation, though there have been some changes at section leader level; these are seen as good for promotion.

The manager attends the same meetings as the inspection chargehand and finds them useful (4). Contact with other departments and information on the company in the branch and in Japan is good (4). Personal communication is face to face 50 per cent, written 40 per cent and telephone 10 per cent. No communication problems with expatriates were mentioned, and the climate at work was positively evaluated (4).

The parent company was again perceived as the main locus of important decision-making. The manager felt he had adequate decision-making responsibility in his own functional area. Job satisfaction was high (4–5) on all points except two—welfare benefits and so on, and future salary prospects, where it was moderate (3). The success of the firm was very highly evaluated (5) on all points except profitability, which was 4. The final comment during the interview was that discipline was very much the same as in the Navy. Everyone knew the rules, which was very important. Teamwork was very good, again like the Navy.

### Chargehand, production

| Function | Years |
| --- | --- |
| Salesman, machinery | 2 |
| Salesman, motor parts* | 5 |
| Machine operator, Japanese company* | 4 |
| Setter/operator | 2 |
| Chargehand, production | 3 |

Recruitment was through an advertisement in a local newspaper. Working for the Japanese company was attractive, first, because it paid more than the previous job and, secondly, for the other ordinary instrumental reasons of security, prospects and nearness to home.

In his first two selling jobs the manager received some sales training. In the Japanese company he initially had OJT on machine operation from Japanese engineers. As a setter-operator he attended a number of the two-hour sessions on man-management conducted by the personnel manager with the training officer. As chargehand, he took part in the weekend Outward Bound course referred to by the last-mentioned manager. The chargehand group learnt to work together. It was stressed that the fact they were from different departments was a great help.

The manager has a very wide view of his role and sees his immediate subordinate as an aid to him. He can delegate to him. The job itself is very broad: he can do a lot of things—anything. He operates the machines if necessary, if someone is absent. Rules and procedures must be strictly followed (5).

Being a manager doesn't feel different from being an operator, except for the job. There's a lot of responsibility. After 5.30 there are no section leaders, so the chargehands are responsible. Top managers should have two abilities: first, to treat people as individuals; secondly, to build good relationships with subordinates, to be willing to listen and to make themselves and their intentions known.

The manager is very happy (5) to classify himself as a generalist, and he sees 90 per cent of management colleagues as generalists. The 10 per cent seen as specialists included the plant manager and the personnel manager.

Promotion prospects in the branch appear high (5), and the manager believes that eventually the management will consist entirely of local personnel—a view not expressed by anyone else. He also emphasises how the system of internal promotions in the company is appreciated by a lot of people.

He attends the weekly chargehands' meeting, the shift hand-overs at the beginning and the end of every shift and has a monthly briefing for his own shift. Satisfaction with these meetings is very high (5), and he feels well informed about the company's situation and plans in the branch and in the wider company context (4), in relation to the company's expansion, production, and so on. But it's not just one manager that is kept informed—it is everyone.

Satisfaction with the climate at work is high (5). In the early days, during the first two years, the Japanese had had to learn English, but it was alright now. The manager's own communication is mostly face to face (85 per cent), with 10 per cent for written, partly accounted for by the written report system, and 5 per cent for the telephone.

He sees the parent company as having the greatest weight in making important decisions. It is followed, in decreasing order, by the top management of the branch, the middle management, the staff or administrative departments and the consultative com-mittee. Almost without exception, this is the view of local managers and is not unexpected.

Job satisfaction is high (4–5), and the success of the firm receives the highest rating on all points (5). The emphasis is on the dedication of the workforce and the management. There is a good working relationship and little discontent. Everyone pulls together. There are few problems. The shop floor are kept informed through the briefing sessions and people understand.

## Conclusion

The company clearly has a strongly task-orientated management style. This style is related to the precision engineering nature of the task, in which quality is essential if investment is to be recovered and the operation to be made viable by expanding market share. The emphasis on service to the customer, or the ability to deliver the type of product required on time, is part of the same logic. But it must be emphasised that the recognition of such a logic is by no means automatic and that the policies and practices found in the branch depend on purposive corporate decisions. These include tight manning and the use of overtime, for example, as several managers' comments made clear.

The more senior British managers were recruited on the basis of their previous experience and expertise, or as in the case of the QC manager, on the basis of their being able to acquire the extra expertise required. More junior British managers were recruited partly on the basis of experience relevant to their new task, such as that of the last two chargehands for instance, and partly on an evaluation of their 'trainability'.

Managers, particularly at more senior levels, were recruited to fill specific posts, through the normal local channels of newspaper advertising, followed by interviews. There has been little use of external training courses, but the extensive use of OJT, and some in-house man-management training, is obvious from managers' career profiles. Given this interest in training, the tight manning policy, the emphasis on teamwork, experienced through close communication, and the very low turnover of managers, it is clear that the company is not operating a hire-and-fire policy and would prefer to keep the managers it has carefully selected.

Table 1.1  How managers see themselves in the company

---

*As generalists*:

Assistant (engineering) to general manager (J)
Assistant (administration) to general manager (J)
QA engineer (J)
Mechanical engineer (J)
Deputy plant manager (B)
Personnel manager (B)
Assistant production manager (B)
Section leader, assembly (B)
Section leader, machine shop (B)
Trainee section leader, inspection (B)
Chargehand, inspection (B)
Chargehand, assembly (B)
Chargehand, production (B)

*As specialists*:

Staff engineer (J)
QC Manager (B)
Section leader, planning (B)

---

*Note*: J = Japanese, B = British.

Teamwork, flexibility and an 'egalitarian' style do not necessarily appeal to all British managers and, knowing the importance of 'attitude' in the selection process in Japan,[15] it is reasonable to suppose that the members of the management team have been chosen not only for their expertise but also for their positive attitude towards the company's style of management. This can be seen in the comments of the personnel manager, for instance.

Tables 1.1 and 1.2 show managers' perceptions of their own functions and those of their colleagues. A comparison of the two tables shows an interesting contrast. Table 1.1 demonstrates that almost all respondents, including the British managers, regard themselves as generalists. But Table 1.2 is less clear-cut as a perception of the generalist style of the management team. Four of the seventeen managers questioned see the majority of managers as specialists, with one manager responding ambiguously (n.a.). The Japanese scores in particular are less than unanimous and managers seem to have a clearer view of themselves as generalists than they do of some of their colleagues.

Table 1.2 How managers see the whole management team

| Manager | As generalists % | As specialists % |
|---|---|---|
| Assistant (engineering) to general manager (J) | 20 | 80 |
| Assistant (administration) to general manager (J) | 66+ | 33+ |
| QA engineer (J) | 80 | 20 |
| Mechanical engineer (J) | 50 | 50 |
| Staff engineer (J) | na | na |
| Deputy plant manager (B) | 40 | 60 |
| Personnel manager (B) | 40 | 60 |
| QC manager (B) | 70 | 30 |
| Assistant production manager (B) | 40 | 60 |
| Section leader, planning (B) | 60 | 40 |
| Section leader, assembly (B) | 85 | 15 |
| Section leader, production (B) | 80 | 20 |
| Section leader, machine shop (B) | 80 | 20 |
| Trainee section leader, inspection (B) | 70 | 30 |
| Chargehand, inspection (B) | 90 | 10 |
| Chargehand, assembly (B) | 60 | 40 |
| Chargehand, production (B) | 90 | 10 |

*Note*: J = Japanese, B = British.

Replies to interview questions suggest some variations in managers' conceptions of what generalists or specialists may be. Several managers, for instance, saw the personnel manager as a specialist, although he emphasised the wide range of his other responsibilities and saw himself as a generalist. Some saw the QC manager and engineers as a whole as specialists, while others pointed out that although they had specialist knowledge they had broad general responsibility.

The latter included not only man-management beyond a purely technical function but also the premise of flexibility outside what would be a more narrowly defined function under a system of strict job descriptions. This in turn included recognition of the duty to learn new techniques when necessary and to help out with any other type of task when called upon by senior management.

There was however no evidence to suggests that the deployment of managers by the top management was in any way arbitrary, or that managers were 'thrown in at the deep end' into tasks for which their qualifications and experience made them entirely unfitted. Given the company's need to recover investment costs, the variety of reasons that made it essential to succeed in the European market and the strong task orientation already referred to, it would have been surprising if competent senior management had not thought very carefully how to get the best performance out of the management team by using their experience to maximum advantage.

So far, this discussion has centred mainly on managers' perceptions of the management system in the company. Perceptions, whether soundly based or not, are important in terms of motivation and the functioning of a management team as a social unit; they therefore feed directly into task performance. At the same time, perceptions are subjective. They reflect actors' own perceptual apparatus and their own interests. Particularly because of the latter, it can be dangerous to accept actors' perceptions in any situation at face value. In this case, managers have their livelihood and career at heart. Turning, then, from managers' subjective perceptions to the more objective data in the career profiles, what does a comparison of their background, training and job assignments show? Without repeating all the details, two facts emerge.

One, which might be expected, is the difference in mobility between firms; although in a minority of cases the reason for a British manager leaving his employer was not his own but the result of the takeover or collapse of a firm. Mobility between firms, or 'job hopping', to put it more pejoratively from the Japanese point of view, is not seen in the Japanese cases. The second fact, which may or may not be less expected, is that the career profiles of the Japanese managers show higher levels of technical qualifications, such as degrees in engineering, and higher levels of specialisation within a particular discipline than the majority of their British colleagues. In other words, they are objectively more specialised; even if all of them, with one exception, expressed a perception of themselves as generalists. This raises significant questions about the nature of professionalism, which will be dealt with in the Conclusion at the end of the book.

Replies to the questionnaire showed that job satisfaction

Table 1.3  British managers' working hours

| Manager | Hours per week |
|---|---|
| Deputy plant manager | 55+ |
| Personnel manager | 60 |
| Assistant production manager | 55 |
| QC manager | 47 |
| Section leader, production | 53 |
| Section leader, assembly | 47 |
| Section leader, machine shop | 49 |
| Section leader, planning | 55 |
| Trainee section leader, inspection | 55 |
| Chargehand, production | 44 |
| Chargehand, assembly | 48 |
| Chargehand, inspection | 47 |

among British managers was high, with some dissent in two main areas. The first concerns the amount of overtime. Table 1.3 shows the long hours regularly worked by managers.

In companies in Japan, arriving punctually for work and regular attendance are important indices of commitment, which bear directly on promotion prospects. But the end of the working day is not so clearly defined, and to be seen to want to leave at the official time is not the way to create a favourable impression among senior managers with an influence on career prospects.

This is a crucial, not a minor, issue in what might be termed the company/private life dichotomy. In practice, an open-ended commitment to flexible hours is seen by managers in Japan in the same way as the generalist commitment to flexible task performance. In both cases the company has priority: the company, and not the manager's private career or whatever specialist expertise he may have acquired, must be the centre of the manager's attention if he wants to move up the organisation.

In the present case it is clear that, despite the comments about teamwork, British managers had accepted the commitment to work flexibly to a greater extent than they had accepted the commitment to work overtime whenever required. Of course, grumbling is a characteristic of British work culture and should not always be taken too seriously; but for the company's British managers agreement to work with flexibility on the generalist model is evidently not the same as committing oneself to an organisation-centred career in which the company/private life dichotomy is resolved in the company's favour, even in an area and at a time of high unemployment.

Tight manning, the pressures on managers, and their evident commitment suggest that in this case the overtime worked by local managers represented real effort. It would, of course, be an oversimplification to equate the number of hours worked with performance achieved in just any company in a mechanical fashion. Effectiveness and 'efficiency', in terms of cost–benefit analysis, are not always identical, and there is also the emotive question of 'loyalty', whether always economically rational or not. But the overriding aim here is for the company to fulfil its task. This point in relation to managers' working lives and how they see their careers leads naturally to the second main issued referred to above. In discussing differences between specialist and generalist concepts there is always a danger of abstraction, but here the discussion can be brought down to earth by looking at it in the actual company context.

The company has now been running in the UK since the mid-1970s. Thanks to careful selection and the effort it has put into training, the generation of a strongly task-orientated team consciousness and good human relations—not to mention its business success—it has succeeded to a high degree in retaining the managers that it hired at the start up. Since then it has invested in new plant and extended its operations, helping to create a virtuous circle. For managers and employees, especially for those in at the beginning, there are some attractive prospects.

But what will happen in a few years time? Will some managers decide that being 'a big fish in a small pond' is not for them? If the company expands in size to the point where it can offer promotion equivalent to that in large firms that compete with it in terms of career prospects, there may be no problem. Otherwise one would expect managers to feel eventually that, although they did not want to leave the company, they would have to do so in pursuit of their careers. This will be the acid test for Japanese companies in the UK like this one that employ no more than a few hundred people, with correspondingly limited promotion chances for managers no matter how excellently the companies are managed.

All that can be said is that at the moment there is little for the company to worry about. Seven out of the twelve British managers questioned replied that they would not consider another job offer, even if it included a salary as much as 50 per cent higher. One manager referred to the expansion of the plant as a reason for not moving. Another could not imagine taking an offer. A third stated that he never looked at job advertisements. A fourth pointed out that he had originally taken a drop in salary on coming to work for the Japanese company, and a fifth stated that he liked the Japanese system because it offered security.

Of the five remaining British managers, two said they would consider taking a job that offered a 50 per cent increase in salary, but one mused that this was hypothetical—perhaps if it was a green-field site. He liked the job, having seen the company start from zero—and that meant a lot to him. He obviously did not consider moving as a serious possibility. Another manager said he would consider another job carefully if it paid over 30 per cent more but that money itself would not be enough. There would also have to be security; he would need a big lure. Finally, one manager replied that he would think about an offer of 30 per cent more, but it would depend on the job, and another replied that he could not put a figure on it because of the importance of other factors, notably job security. The replies show a high degree of job stability and commitment, in comparison, for instance, with the marketing company below, and suggest that to date the company has largely succeeded in mobilising its managers and generating commitment to the task.

## Notes

1. Cf. R. Harrison, 'Understanding your organisation's character'.
2. See M. H. Trevor, *Japan's Reluctant Multinationals: Japanese Management at Home and Abroad*, Ch. 3, 'Managerial Systems in Japan'. These principles do not apply to smaller, and financially weaker, companies in Japan. Examples exist of medium and small-sized enterprises that have expanded operations into South-East Asia, but they hardly exist in Europe, North America and other developed environments. They do not therefore form part of the present study. The typical Japanese company in Western Europe or USA is the branch of a first-class company in Japan.
3. M. White and M. H. Trevor, *Under Japanese Management: The Experience of British Workers*. See 'details, attention to' in Index.

4. Cf. Walter Goldsmith, former director-general of the Institute of Directors: 'We have had too much management in this country and not enough leadership'. In other words, too many gimmicks, too much chasing after panaceas and too much concern with 'the flavour of the month'. Cf. Sir Peter Parker's New Year Message to the BIM. *Management News*, January 1985.

5. On the difference between Quality Assurance (QA) and Quality Control (QC), including Quality Circles, and so on, as currently operated in Japan, see M. H. Trevor, 'Quality control in Japan: technology transfer and self-help'. The QC carried out by all shop-floor employees in a plant is sustained by management and backed up by the specialist technical expertise of the QA department.

6. Cf. the 'top Toyota executive [who] spent the first six months of his working life as an unskilled worker on the production line [and] a leading public figure who had just launched his son on an executive career in the steel industry—by insisting that the latter spent his first two years in the company's oldest, dirtiest and most unpleasant steel mill . . . Such attitudes, such experiences, are more customary than unusual' (W. Kendall, 'Why Japanese workers work').

7. But are there the makings of an attitude in Britain which is aware of the need to train and develop human resources before North Sea oil production tapers off? Strong orientations towards achievement in Japan have not just been ecologically determined. Nor are they the spontaneous products of some indefinable national essence. Before industrialisation those in subordinate positions were indoctrinated with an *active* concept of loyalty towards superiors as fulfilment. See R. N. Bellah, *Tokugawa Religion: The Values of Pre-Industrial Japan*. Since 1945 Japanese management has consciously fostered employee achievement by attention to motivation, training, team-work, and so on, of which Quality Circles are one manifestation. Similar remarks apply to achievement-orientated education and family upbringing in Japan. See G. De Vos, *Socialisation for Achievement: Essays on the Cultural Psychology of the Japanese*; R. E. Cole's *Japanese Blue Collar: The Changing Tradition*, also draws attention to the importance of upbringing in school and family for subsequent performance in the company.

8. See K. Legge, *Power, Innovation and Problem-Solving in Personnel Management*.

9. See D. McGregor, *The Human Side of Enterprise*.

10. It is not difficult to think of British organisations, particularly in the public sector, where stable employment does not lead to improved performance. This is because there is no proper motivational system, nor effective continual assessment of achievement. The well-known examples demonstrate the fallacy of looking to long-term employment alone as a motivator.

11. A Japanese researcher who visited Japanese companies in the UK referred to the screening process in the recruiting of local employees and to the problems connected with interviewing and evaluating local applicants. According to his account, Japanese managers experienced language difficulties at such interviews. Colloquialisms, regional accents and the correct interpretation of remarks and attitudes are inevitably problematic between two societies with such different behavioural norms or values as the British and Japanese; and in many Japanese companies in the UK, this is one factor that leads to an important role for the British personnel, or general affairs, manager. He can play a major part as a 'go-between'. The Japanese researcher concluded that 'All expatriates confirmed that work attitudes are very important as *they are the key to successful cooperative work*' (emphasis added). See H. Inohara, 'Japanese manufacturing in Western Europe: personnel management'.

12. Decisions to assign Japanese managers to overseas branches, according to what is a process of rotation, depend on the respective priorities and strengths of departments in the parent company. The problem of assigning managers, and their families, overseas is not uniquely Japanese but common to international or multinational firms. Some Japanese managers have argued that the problems with the present system could be overcome if those who are willing to work abroad were assigned on a long-term basis and rewarded accordingly. Apart from the question of whether companies would have enough volunteers, this would create different types of home and overseas managers, which the top management might see as a danger to the unity of the team and its cohesion. In the Japanese case, a special problem is the education of children: crucial because educational achievement determines the rank of company and the grade of entry that applicants in the Japanese labour market can expect when they enter employment after school or university. Children of managers assigned overseas may experience considerable difficulty in being reintegrated into the education system and the home society. These are problems that companies have to consider, even if they do not determine policy on overseas assignments. See D. Willis, 'Child returnees: strangers in their own land', *Mainichi Daily News*, 11 December 1984.

13. For an account of this very successful professional pressure group, see W. E. Steslicke, *Doctors in Politics: The Political Life of the Japan Medical Association*.

14. It is sometimes forgotten that precision engineering, electronics and other plants established in the UK and other countries by Japanese companies represent considerable investments. There are also the costs of human resources, and the deputy plant manager's statements make plain the extent of the supervision and individual

transfer of expertise provided by expatriates. In the short term, Japanese overseas operations of this type must budget for a loss. How soon they can break even or move into profit depends on internal factors for which managers in the branch are directly responsible, such as quality and productivity, and external factors beyond their control, such as changes in the value of the pound or the yen and changes in demand in the wider market. It is not surprising that the combination of factors makes expatriate managers nervous, particularly when their own careers and the prestige of the company are involved.

15. Trevor, 'Quality control in Japan', p. 53.

## 1.2  Japanese company P2: light engineering (Germany)

The company opened a European branch in the early 1960s and some ten years later established its first production operation, in the metalworking industry. The rationale was not only the intended expansion of market share but also the improved possibility of promoting the product. The company now occupies the third position in the German and European markets.

The hierarchical levels are ordered on the classic plan of:

1. Managing director.
2. Functional department manager.
3. Branch and section manager.
4. Warehouse manager.
5. Representative, consultant, technical expert.

Four people, plus two secretaries or assistants, report directly to the managing director, and there are five hierarchical levels between the top and bottom level. On average, the span of control of the lowest level consists of six to seven people.

In order to preserve anonymity, the exact number of employees cannot be given, but the following are the respective percentages:

|          | Male<br>% | Female<br>% | Total<br>% |
|----------|-----------|-------------|------------|
| German   | 55.2      | 30.2        | 85.4       |
| Japanese | 9.5       | 0           | 9.5        |
| Others   | 5.1       | 0           | 5.1        |

Eight per cent of line positions are occupied by Japanese, and they also occupy all staff positions. One German and one Japanese function as 'technical advisors'.

The length of service of employees is:

| Years | % |
|-------|-----|
| 0–5 | 23 |
| 6–10 | 48 |
| 11–15 | 30 |
| 15+ | 15 |

The age distribution of middle and top management is:

| Age | % |
|-------|-----|
| 21–30 | 0 |
| 31–40 | 33 |
| 41–50 | 47 |
| 51–60 | 20 |

Employees' qualifications are:

| Qualification | % |
|-------|-----|
| University | 11 |
| Technical (etc.) university | 9 |
| Further training | 6 |
| Vocational training | 49 |
| Unqualified | 25 |

Absence from work among employees is extremely low. In one year holidays accounted for 2,680 man-days; an average of 16.7 days per employee. Sickness accounted for 764 man-days, or 3 per cent.

In the last three years one middle manager left the firm voluntarily and one senior manager was dismissed. 7.1 per cent of middle managers and 4.1 per cent of other workers or staff are union members. In sum, 4.3 per cent of employees are union members.

As elsewhere, important information and the organisation chart for the entire company are only given to managers, but each employee is given an outline plan for the individual sections. Guidelines for company policy are in preparation. There are detailed written working procedures, job descriptions for workers, staff and line managers and descriptions of routine procedures.

The senior Japanese manager works between sixty and sixty-five hours a week and takes between seven and ten days' annual leave. His German personnel manager works between forty and fifty hours a week and takes thirty days' annual leave.

The organisation's principles and philosophy can be summed up in three words: quality, service and speed. There is no intention of starting a price war. The following principles are also aimed at:

1. Fairness.
2. Helping others, co-operativeness, unanimity in the pursuit of company goals.
3. Harmony; in other words, if necessary not insisting on one's own way.

As far as possible, the management would like to put Japanese personnel management principles into effect. These consist of:

1. 'Lifetime' employment wherever possible; which so far has been realised in practice, with the one exception of a dismissal already referred to above.
2. The seniority principle, which is 'to some extent mixed in with the performance principle'.
3. The performance principle.
4. OJT.

New employees are normally recruited through job advertisements in local or regional newspapers. The managing director is responsible for the final decision in the case of managers, and the personnel manager in the case of staff. Two interviews are normally held. The crucial criterion in manpower planning is economy of operation. Interviews are held both with the department manager concerned and the personnel manager and only then will an evaluation be made. In evaluating a data-processing man, for example, his willingness to cooperate would, next to his technical expertise, be important; and his previous career development would not play such a major role. The reward system is based on a basic salary, which is slightly above the nationally negotiated rate, plus extra individual payments. Salary increases are suggested to the management after discussions with the relevant department manager and the personnel manager. In given instances the management may alter the proposed increase.

Managers' training consists on the average of twelve to fifteen days in the firm and three days on external courses. Almost all Japanese managers and technicians fly to Japan once or twice a year for five-day periods; but according to the personnel manager this amounts to probably no more than two people for an average of four weeks. If a German manager wants to be sent to Japan, he must justify it on the grounds of his competence. The reason for sending German managers to Japan is 'to experience the climate of the parent company'.

The rotation principle 'doesn't work well with German staff as is the established custom in Japan. In Germany people don't really want it'. Over the last three years in the German branch twelve Japanese, with three to five years each in their respective positions, were integrated into the rotation system. The reasons for rotation were:

1. To heighten the sense of responsibility of employees.
2. To train successors.
3. To help managers to understand their place in the enterprise.
4. To become qualified in other areas.

The advantages of rotation were seen as:

1. Heightened awareness of responsibility.
2. Competence in other areas.

When managers' promotion is under consideration, evaluation is based 100 per cent on performance. The promotion chances for German managers were seen as fair (3 on the scale of 1 to 5) in the branch, but low (1) in the company as a whole. For Japanese managers the chances were seen as exactly the opposite (1 in the branch, 3 in the company as a whole). To date no German or other non-Japanese manager has succeeded in being promoted in the company outside the branch. If a manager does not live up to expectations, he receives 'patient instruction'. A well-developed pension scheme should enable former staff to enjoy a comfortable retirement, as the company pays 25 per cent of the last net salary in addition to the statutory pension. The condition is at least thirty years service; otherwise a payment in proportion is made.

It is sometimes claimed that communication is better in

Japanese than in German organisations—a point investigated here. The following regular meetings take place in the company:

| | |
|---|---|
| Section chiefs: | 1 a month |
| Work teams: | 1 a month |
| Branch manager: | 1 a month |
| Sales manager: | 1 a fortnight |
| Quality Circles: | 2–4 a month |

The personnel manager stated that section chiefs met every day. As regards the quality of communication, the top manager interviewed scored an average of 3.8 (on a scale of 1 to 5) and the middle manager interviewed, 4.5.

Questions about cultural or linguistic difficulties received the following answers from the Japanese managing director: 'The difference between the Japanese and German mentality is less in the firm than in the respective countries, but information that German staff obtain in Japan is seldom passed on to others. The attitude is "I am an expert in that field and that is why I attended the course. It would therefore be pointless for me to inform others about it, who would not understand anyway".' Nevertheless the managing director is trying to train his staff in the generalist way of thinking: 'Knowledge should be shared with others, but that doesn't work in Germany. The Germans only make decisions in their own area and are often stubborn and, excuse me for saying so, arrogant.'

Before Japanese are sent to Germany they attend language classes at the Goethe Institute for two months. German is the language in the company. 'We are selling our products in Germany, so we must also speak German.'

The means of communications used are:

| Means | Middle management: (German) (%) | Top management: (Japanese) (%) |
|---|---|---|
| Telephone | 20 | 50 |
| Written messages/notes | 0 | 0 |
| Face to face | 65 | 50 |
| Conferences | 10 | 0 |
| Others | 5 | 0 |

In the factory the suggestions scheme is integrated with the Quality Circles, and at the German head office suggestions are dealt with at the meetings of department managers. Decision-making is divided into general and individual patterns. The general pattern of decision-making shows the hierarchy according to which decisions affecting the branch are made:

| Level | Middle management: (German) (ranking) | Top management: (Japanese) (ranking) |
|---|---|---|
| Parent company | 1 | 1 |
| Top management | 2 | 2 |
| Middle management | 4 | 3 |
| Works council | 3 | 4 |
| Staff or administrative departments | 5 | 5 |

It is not surprising that the parent company is in first place, if one looks more closely at the contact between it and the branch. 'We get all sorts of help from the parent company but it exploits us, and we have to negotiate with it according to the situation'. Although the parent company is only telephoned two or three times a year and reports are only sent when absolutely necessary, individual contact is more frequent. The managing director goes to Japan two or three times a year and specialists come to Germany more frequently. Regarding their own decision-making, the top manager scored 3.5 (on a scale of 1 to 5) and the middle manager 4.3. This is surprising, as it seems to indicate that the middle manager has greater decision-making authority than his superior.

Both the top manager and the middle manager see themselves as generalists and are happy with this description. Both see all the other managers as specialists. On average, the two managers scored 3.4 (on a scale of 1 to 5) in regard to the climate at work and the employer–employee relationship was described as 'very positive'. Differences of opinion were not said to occur more than two to three times a year. Both managers evaluated the success of the firm as fairly good (3.4).

## Conclusion

1. Union membership (4.3 per cent average) is relatively low by local standards.
2. Almost all Japanese managers are technicians and fly to Japan for five days once or twice a year.
3. The pension scheme is extremely well developed.
4. Face-to-face communication and the telephone are far and away the preferred means of communication for both the managers interviewed.
5. Although telephone calls are seldom made to the parent company in Japan, individual contact seems to be close.
6. At first sight it seems unusual that the top manager's decision-making should receive a lower score than that of the middle manager. But this could, on the one hand, be explained by a very liberal style of decision-making and, on the other, by a clearly defined style.
7. Apart from the two managers interviewed, all other managers are seen as specialists.
8. Among all the Japanese enterprises in Germany that were studied this one seems to come closest to German company mentality, custom and practice. It is almost a German firm.

## 1.3 Japanese company P3: light engineering (Germany)

The company belongs to the plastics and metalworking sector. In the early 1960s it established several production operations in Europe and opened its first German branch in the late 1960s. Others soon followed. The company's market share in Japan is 80 per cent and in Germany 40 per cent.

The hierarchical levels are organised as follows:

1. Managing director.
2. Branch manager.
3. Department manager.
4. Foreman.
5. Ordinary employee/worker.

Some ten people report directly to the managing director. Between the top and bottom levels of the hierarchy there are four to five positions. The span of control at the lowest level consists of ten to twenty employees.

In order to preserve anonymity, the exact number of employees cannot be given, but the following are the respective percentages:

|  | Male % | Female % | Total % |
|---|---|---|---|
| German | 32.0 | 53.0 | 85.0 |
| Japanese | 5.8 | 0 | 5.8 |
| Others | 4.3 | 4.9 | 9.2 |

Six per cent of line positions are occupied by Japanese; there are no staff positions.

The length of service of employees is:

| Years | % |
|---|---|
| 0–5 | 40 |
| 6–10 | 40 |
| 11–15 | 20 |

The age distribution of middle and top management is:

| Age | % |
|---|---|
| 21–30 | 0 |
| 31–40 | 90 |
| 41–50 | 10 |
| 51–60 | 0 |

Employees' qualifications are:

| Qualification | % |
|---|---|
| University | 5–6 |
| Technical (etc.) university | 4–5 |
| Further training | 0 |
| Vocational training | 15–20 |
| Unqualified | 70 |

Absence from work is accounted for by annual holidays of twenty-nine days and a 5 to 6 per cent sickness rate.

In the last three years two middle managers left the firm voluntarily. No one has been dismissed. The rate of unionisation is estimated at 10 per cent among first-line supervisors and at 30 per cent among ordinary employees and workers.

In accordance with the system of formal organisation, some 7 per cent of staff, mostly managers, receive all important information. An organisation chart 'only exists in the managing director's head'. There are written documents covering company policy, job descriptions for ordinary employees and workers and for first-line production supervisors.

The managing director interviewed works between fifty and fifty-five hours a week and takes ten days annual holiday. The middle manager works around forty-five hours a week and takes twenty-five days' holiday.

The company's binding strategy is that: 'Our parent company is in Japan. When we expand and export we must behave as the importing countries concerned wish. We should behave like Germans in Germany, so that the customers' wishes can be fulfilled.' The organisation's principles are reflected in these areas:

1. Expansion of sales.
2. Obligations to the customers.
3. Distribution in the territory allocated.

'Without our customers, our people and good shops, we could not fulfil our task'.

Personnel policy is based on two ideas. There is, first, the principle of 'lifetime employment'. Secondly, there is the expectation that staff will work for the firm for a considerable time. Personnel are recruited after two, in a few cases three, interviews with those who have replied to newspaper advertisements. The managing director alone is responsible for selection. The decisive criteria are the work background and personality. Emphasis is put on 'harmony'—but the applicant must also be a competent specialist.

The reward system is based on adaptation to local practice and, for Japanese, to an extent on the parent company's pay system. For a few top managers there are individual salary agreements.

Training appears to be of lesser importance for management. Only technicians are sent for periods of four to six weeks to Japan; but there is the language problem. 'Language is not unimportant, but it isn't everything. A family feeling is developed. New machines are learnt on the spot. The technicians learn how everything works and get to know the Japanese. Then they begin to think beyond their individual horizons.' In the branches in Germany there is no job rotation.

The promotion system is based on a mixed form, in which what the person concerned is able to do and how far this coincides with expectations is considered together. 'With longer service a person understands "harmony" better. He must show that others can follow and respect him'. If a manager does not come up to expectations, he will in around 90 per cent of cases be provided with an assistant. Otherwise he will be transferred to another department (9 per cent of cases) or sent back to Japan (1 per cent). In general, staff are helped to find accommodation, and help through private discussions in the company is available. There is no pension scheme beyond statutory provisions.

Institutionalised forms of communication are not strongly developed. German department managers meet three to four times a month; others as necessary. The quality and usefulness of these meetings are evaluated as quite good by the top manager (3.8) and similarly by the other manager interviewed (3.5). Cultural and/or language problems seldom arise but, where they do, they can be overcome by open communication, which helps people to understand each other better. The differences must be accepted. The middle manager interviewed estimates that the various means of communication are used as follows:

| Means | Middle management: (%) | Top management: (%) |
| --- | --- | --- |
| Telephone | 80 | 80 |
| Written messages/notes | 5 | 5 |
| Face to face | 5 | 15 |
| Conferences | 10 | 5 |
| Others | 0 | 0 |

There is no formal suggestions scheme. Improvements and the best way of doing things are continually discussed and no figure could be put on the number of suggestions that had been put forward.

According to the top and middle managers interviewed,

respectively, the most important decisions affecting the branch were made in the following ranking order:

| Level | According to: Middle management: (ranking) | Top management: (ranking) |
|---|---|---|
| Parent company | 1 | 4 |
| Top management | 2 | 1 |
| Middle management | 3 | 2 |
| Works council | 5 | 5 |
| Staff or administrative departments | 4 | 3 |

As far as individual decision-making was concerned, both the top manager and the middle manager interviewed gave almost identical answers (3.6 and 3.7, respectively).

Both interviewees saw themselves as generalists. The top manager also saw 80 per cent of other managers as generalists and the middle manager saw them all as generalists. The top manager remarked that he was a generalist but didn't know whether he was particularly happy or unhappy about it. The middle manager also expressed the view that he was neither happy nor unhappy in this respect.

The top manager's evaluation of the work climate was good (4) and the middle manager's was quite good (2.9). The latter would move to another firm if the salary was 30 per cent higher. The employer–employee relationship was said to be good, with the branch manager responsible. The success of the firm was very positively evaluated (4.4).

## Conclusion

1. The average age of managers (30–40) is low and there is a high proportion of unqualified workers in the firm.
2. There is no written organisation chart, and there are only job descriptions for the lowest-grade employees and for first-line production supervisors.
3. The rotation principle is not implemented. Managers who do not meet expectations are not dismissed but are supported by an assistant.

4. There are only the statutory pension provisions. Formally organised meetings are rare; the telephone is the main means of communication.
5. In regard to the most important decisions affecting the branch, the middle manager sees the role of the parent company in first place, while the top manager sees it as extremely limited. This is a striking difference of perception.
6. The success of the firm is very highly evaluated (4.4).

## 1.4 Japanese company P4: electronics (Germany)

The company is a comparative newcomer to Germany. It assembles electronics products, and one particular sector of the total product range is covered as far as the European market is concerned by its local production. The rationale of the operation has three main aspects. The first is the avoidance of trade barriers; the second is the improved possibility of cooperation with German components manufacturers, though not on account of price; and the third is the better possibility for distribution in a country where it is producing.

The hierarchical levels are as follows (the English terms are used):

1. Managing director.
2. Manager
3. Administration assistant.
4. Group leader.

It was only partially possible to discover the spans of control, but about five managers report directly to the managing director. There are three or four levels between the managing director and ordinary employees or workers.

It was also necessary to make an estimate of the numbers of employees. About 85 per cent are female. Of the 15 per cent male staff, 5 per cent are Japanese. All have less than five years' service in the firm, due to its recent establishment. Probably 80 to 90 per cent of the managers are aged between 31 and 40, with the remainder between 41 and 50. A rough estimate is that 1 or 2 per cent of staff have a university degree and that 12 per cent are engineers, technicians and mechanics who have received further training. The female workers on the production line are unqualified.

No information was yet available about absence, and there had been no turnover in the first five months. No figures could be given for the number of union members.

Important information is given to those who need to know. Only the managing director and one other manager receive the organisation chart. There are job descriptions only for managers. The managing director stated that he worked 50 hours a week and took three weeks' holiday when the firm had its annual shut down.

The organisation's philosophy and principles are based on two ideas. The first is of working with local component makers and enjoying better cooperation: the second is that distribution is improved by producing locally. Other principles are expressed in such terms as 'harmony', 'sincerity' and 'pioneering spirit'. The principles underlying the personnel policy still have to be experienced in practice, but the basis consists of the seniority principle, 'lifetime employment', OJT and thinking for the long term in order to ensure employee satisfaction.

Recruitment procedures for managers envisage an internal announcement of a vacancy first, and interviews with perhaps ten applicants in the case of an external announcement. Performance and integration into the group are major criteria, but the greatest weight is put on 'personality'. The managing director is responsible for selection.

The reward system is based on the national agreement with the IG-Metall Union, following the average for the electrical industry.

Because of the present limited size of the operation, only the personnel manager attends external courses, lasting two weeks. Japanese staff fly to Japan annually for a month's further training. Again, because of the limited numbers of employees, the rotation principle cannot at the moment be applied. It is still too early to give details of the promotion system, the management discipline system or the pension system.

On the other hand, the outlines of the communication system are already clearly recognisable. There are monthly meetings for department managers and for work groups. The production manager reports daily to the top management. Quality Circles are planned. Satisfaction with the meetings that have been held is very high (4.6). Managers' communication with other managers is mainly face to face, and with other employees mainly written. The suggestions scheme will be formalised when Quality Circles are introduced.

The respective ranking of the various hierarchical levels in decision-making that affects the branch is evaluated as follows:

| Level | Ranking |
|---|---|
| Parent company | 1 |
| Top management | 2 |
| Middle management | 3 |
| Works council | 5 |
| Staff or administrative departments | 4 |

Individual decision-making is evaluated as 3.8 on average.

The managing director sees himself as more of a generalist and is happy with this description. He sees 30 to 40 per cent of his management team as generalists and 60 to 70 per cent as specialists. The work climate is judged to be very good (4.3). It is not yet possible to say anything about institutionalised employer–employee relations but the success of the company is very highly evaluated (4.6).

## Conclusion

1. In spite of reportedly high labour costs in Germany, the company has recently started production there and is employing two methods of keeping costs down as far as possible. The first is to employ overwhelmingly untrained female operators on the production line. The second is to use a high level of automation and robotic systems.
2. The managing director is highly satisfied with the meetings that are held and with the success of the firm.
3. It is still too early to say much about management training or development, because the firm was only recently established and expects ultimately to increase the number of employees sevenfold.
4. At present the management style is almost 100 per cent Japanese. The impression was that employees were very happy with it—an impression that is also reflected in press reports. Each morning the operators are given a performance report by the foreman, who answers their questions and tells them what the day's target is.

# 2. Marketing sector

## 2.1 Japanese company M1: electrical (Britain)

Operations started in the late 1970s on a suburban site where there has been adequate room for the company to expand. The British market for Japanese electrical products is one of the most competitive, and the major electrical manufacturers, including those that manufacture in the UK, have their own marketing bases in Britain. The rationale is clearly to be close to the local market, to expand market share by using the knowledge and experience of local personnel who are most familiar with the market and to be able to fight the competition of Japanese rivals in the same field.

The Japanese electrical and electronics industry operates in an extremely competitive domestic market, and this corporate competition has been extended into Europe; especially into the UK, where no less than nine companies—Aiwa, Hitachi, Matsushita (National Panasonic), Maxell, Mitsubishi Electric, Sanyo, Sharp, Sony and Toshiba—are manufacturing locally in consumer electronics.[1] Another leading manufacturer, NEC, is manufacturing integrated circuits locally, with a marketing company to handle the distribution of electronic business systems. There is a similar situation with Terasaki, which produces electrical switchgear for ships. JVC manufactures in Britain and Germany in a three-way venture with Thorn EMI and AEG Telefunken.

Electrical marketing company M1 has expanded and now employs in the region of 200 people.

### Organisational principles

Respondents who had been with the firm since its start-up stated that there had been the changes normally associated with expanding companies, such as changes in communication and the balance of informal and formal organisation. The Japanese managing director himself formulated a basic philosophy for the company, consisting of five main points:

*Team work*

There can be many interpretations of 'Teamwork'. For example, some people feel that teamwork is achieved by giving an order that is obeyed. However, my feeling is that teamwork is eventually produced after constructive arguments and frank discussions of varying opinions, which will ultimately lead to elimination of complaints and grievances, and thereby create a teamwork atmosphere and attitude.

*Punctuality*

Obviously, from an economic viewpoint, punctuality is important, not only at the start of the day but also with regard to appointments and meetings. However, from my viewpoint, punctuality also means reliability. When a person is punctual they are reliable and trustworthy; for example, if that person can keep a fundamental promise like time-keeping, they become trusted to keep their promises in a business relationship. Human trust is extremely important, especially in business. People who are flexible with their punctuality appear to be undisciplined, and because of this it is difficult to trust that the promises they make will be kept.

*Hard work*

From my experience whilst in this country, it has become apparent to me that the percentage of UK employees wishing to shorten their working hours, but requesting higher earnings, is increasing. Personally, I want my employees to be happy, and one solution is to give them a favourable salary. Of course, I must take into consideration their job satisfaction as well, but my feeling is that if employees work hard, the company will become profitable, can then expand and will be able to increase employees' earnings, encouraging them to be loyal to the company and work harder. A company can only be successful with this rotating system if employees work hard from the beginning to make the company profitable. If a company's starting point with employees is less work for more money, it will never be profitable or able to expand; therefore it will be unable to increase employees' earnings.

*Flexibility*

I have also discovered job specifications since coming to the UK, which I personally dislike; although fundamentally I recognise the need, and that employees wish to protect themselves. However, a company will, in turn, protect itself; for example, if an employee has the potential to move into a higher grade of job, the company would not be able to encourage that person. However, if a company and its employees are both flexible with regard to job functions, an enthusiastic employee can be supported and helped by the company to move in another direction. Also, the company can request support from employees to help in other areas when necessary, thus saving on recruitment and additional salaries.

*Non-bureaucracy*

When a company expands, employees are naturally busier, and it is easy for them to be bureaucratic, especially with regard to correspondence and dealing with customers. Telephone messages taken should always be immediately passed to the employee concerned, and questions asked by customers either by letter or telephone should be dealt with promptly. If time is required to be able to deal with the query, then a customer should be informed of this. Promises made should always be kept, and employees should be well aware that they are representing the company. Requests or complaints from customers must never be ignored; they should be taken seriously. Employees' attitude is reflected on the company, and the company's reputation grows as the company grows. Efficiency saves time and money, which are inevitably wasted if customers are not given their due respect or problems are prolonged unnecessarily.

Discussions with many Japanese managers in companies in Britain show that the 'basic philosophy' reflects many of their concerns and experiences. What is significant is the way in which the principles have been made explicit, and clearly formulated in a way designed to be readily understood by local staff. Under 'flexibility', for instance, the managing director refers to his recognition that local personnel job specifications are important because they bear directly on career prospects, before going on to say why the company nevertheless requires them to work flexibly. But for a considerable number of Japanese managers in Britain local employees' interest in having precise job descriptions is as apparently irrational as the readiness of Japanese managers to do without them (and without clearly delegated authority) is to many British staff. This is inevitable in cases where neither side is sufficiently familiar with the other's employment system. As things stand, it is rational for Japanese managers in this type of large company, where security of employment is virtually guaranteed up to the retirement age of 55,[2] not to worry about tight job descriptions, or for that matter, professional associations and professional validation of specific expertise which would express their value in an external labour market. But in the British case, where the labour market, at least in the private sector, does not operate in this way, managers may feel that they are harming their career prospects by apparently diluting their value as specialists. In comparable British firms selection is not based on the mutual expectation of a lifetime of work, as reflected in a different type of pay structure, and they cannot afford to ignore their external labour market and how they are situated in relation to chances of promotion in another firm.[3] Because there is mutual misunderstanding and ignorance of these points, the formulations of the 'basic philosophy' in such a way as to be accessible to local staff is noteworthy. Such explicit statements are not found in all Japanese companies in the UK, even if some Japanese managers try indirectly to promote the same management style.

Some people argue that managers are paid to make decisions, based on specialist expertise[4] and something like a scientific method,[5] but the first principle of the 'basic philosophy', 'teamwork', fits the generalist approach. 'Top down' orders according to the principle of delegated authority are rejected in favour of discussion, in which the theory is that all viewpoints will be considered. 'Punctuality' also is not seen in a narrow technical sense but in the wider context of the trust that the teamwork management style requires.

'Hard work' may appear self-explanatory but the approach is based on the long-term perspective of the growth of the company. Staff are exhorted to see that their own interests are at stake in company profitability and that identification with the company's teamwork approach will lead to good performance, which will then lead directly to better earnings and increased job security.

Dislike of job descriptions is made very clear, along with the reasons why they appear disadvantageous both for individual career development and for the company. Flexibility means 'saving on recruitment and additional salaries'. In other words, there is the same type of tight manning policy as was already seen in the case of the precision engineering company described above.

'Non-bureaucracy' too is connected with flexibility. It does not, for instance, categorically state that anyone in the vicinity should pick up a phone that is ringing, in case it is a customer, but the instruction is implicit in what is said about passing on messages. The accent on service to the customer is similar to that in the case of the precision engineering company, and staff are clearly being taught to remember that 'the customer is king'. This reflects the intensely competitive nature of the buyers' market in Japan itself (referred to in note 1). The emphasis on 'the company's reputation', that its members should be conscious of in relation to the principle of 'hard work', is also significant. It is another aspect of identification with the company, in terms that can become prestige-laden as well as instrumental.

## Personnel management

The personnel manager plays an important role in the company and is not restricted to the recruitment officer type of level, for instance, that is found in some organisations. He is an IPM-qualified professional and, apart from career prospects and security, was attracted by what he described as the challenge of working for a Japanese firm. He joined the firm after placing a notice in the journal of the Japanese Chamber of Commerce in London.

Like many comparable British firms, the company is not unionised and does not have a works council, but there are monthly staff meetings, for which the personnel manager is responsible. All the managers attend these meetings. The personnel manager is a university graduate and has been a Fellow of the Institute of Personnel Management for sixteen years. He has subscribed to 'Personnel Management' for eighteen years and attends meetings of the Institute once a year on average. On a few occasions he speaks at meetings outside the company. In his previous career he has had some experience in a business field related to that of the Japanese company, which is the fifth company that he has worked for. Otherwise, his development has been that of a personnel professional following a consistent career path across companies.

He left his first job, with a market-research company, after nine months because there was no training. There followed two years as training officer and two years as personnel officer with one

American photographic company. In both positions he received some OJT and attended some external courses. He then gained promotion to senior personnel officer on moving to an American safety-razor company, where he attended some external courses, although the company 'was less keen on training'. He was with the company two and a half years.

The next move was to divisional personnel manager of the record division of another American multinational, where development consisted in 'being stretched'. After three years he moved to another record manufacturing company, spending two years as personnel manager and seven years as group personnel manager. The career profile suggests well-timed moves in order to obtain promotions to the senior level, which it may be inferred strengthens his position in the present company. He sees his progress in the present company as characteristic of the organisation. He has not had any particular training in it.

He described the company as old-established, conservative, proud of its product quality and reputation—genuinely trying to become international. The organisational principles were aimed at Japanese flexibility, a shared task, employee involvement and a high level of communication. His own functional area is not strictly marked off. Rules and procedures are fairly strictly observed. He sees himself as a manager and his immediate subordinate as an administrator. He is very happy (5) with being a generalist and sees 40 per cent of the management team as generalists. The 60 per cent of specialists include the considerable number of engineers. There are a dozen expatriates in the company, of whom four are trainees learning international business. The normal expatriate tour in the UK is five years.

The personnel manager commented that Japanese companies in the UK tend to recruit local staff who had maintained a generalist feeling longer into their careers. At the senior management level the generalist approach was said to be more attractive to British managers, which was what the Japanese wanted. On the other hand, people recruited to the company were assumed to 'arrive fully equipped', and the increasingly high technology aspects of the new products meant that more specialists rather than fewer would be needed. In Japan itself the personnel manager saw the upward flow of information—from those concerned with more technical or specific aspects to those with more general responsibility—as a crucial factor in ensuring that generalism did not degenerate into amateurishness. He also saw company policy pronouncements on generalism as significantly influencing how Japanese managers perceived themselves.

Here again attitude was said to be important. Local managers were expected to accept flexibility and not stand out for their rights or expectations; but moves can cause unintended problems. A British manager who was moved from one product range to another saw this as a personal criticism. Local personnel also tend to think that an increase in responsibility should simultaneously be rewarded by an increase in salary; but the company system is to promise a salary review later, after the manager has shown how he can perform. Anyone complaining in such a case would be damned for life; but this brings the problems back to the discussion above of what is rational behaviour for managers under the two respective types of employment system. Here the gap in understanding is a wide one, as might be expected with systems outside managers' experience on which their own careers do not depend. In the basic philosophy the managing director made his disapproval plain.

There is no job rotation as such in the company, but at the time of the annual appraisal employees can request a different assignment. Internal changes are favourably regarded by the Japanese management, which the personnel manager commented would not be the case in a UK company, where people would be likely to be regarded as rocking the boat. Otherwise, managerial job changes are pragmatic, depending on business needs. Eight managers accepted changes of this sort in the last three years. The ability to deploy managers flexibly and to generate a high level of managerial commitment in the process are seen as important issues by the top management. The Japanese managing director sees all job applicants and stresses the importance of flexibility at the final interview.

It was said to take a year or two for local staff to become accustomed to the system. In new job assignments the two principles are that 'There is no subject which cannot be taught internally' and 'It is your responsibility to learn whatever is necessary'. The former is readily understood in terms of the reliance of Japanese companies on OJT, with more formally organised in-house training where considered appropriate, and little use of external courses. The latter refers to the emphasis in Japan on 'self study'. Thus new Japanese arrivals in the UK branch make out their own lists of who to go and see, whereas, as the personnel manager observed, British employees in a similar situation would wait to be told who to see and what to do.

Following local practice, managerial posts that cannot be filled internally are advertised in national newspapers. Sometimes head-hunters are used. Interviews are conducted first by the personnel manager and the department manager concerned, with the managing director having the final say. As in other Japanese companies, people with specific expertise, experience and a flexible attitude are looked for, which is rounded out by OJT where necessary. New engineers do three to four weeks product training. Occasionally a fortnight's training in Japan may be given to selected engineers. The personnel manager does not identify any consistent pattern in what it means to be a manager in the company. In his view, top managers need good communication skills and forward-planning abilities.

The vertical span consists of five levels between the managing director and ordinary employees. There are on average 3.5 employees under each first line manager. Three-quarters of all employees have been with the firm less than five years. Eight have been with the company over eleven years, with the remainder between six and ten years. One-third of local employees are female. Forty-five per cent of middle and top managers are aged between 41 and 50, 40 per cent are between 31 and 40, 12 per cent are over 60, and 3 per cent are between 21 and 30. Fifteen per cent of employees have university or other degrees; 15 per cent HNC/HND or equivalent; 10 per cent have technical or commercial qualifications of the BEC (Business Education Council) or TEC (Technical Education Council) type; 15 per cent have completed an apprenticeship, City and Guilds (etc.) qualification; and 45 per cent are unqualified.

In recent years there have been two voluntary retirements of managers and two dismissals. In half the cases where a manager's performance was not considered good enough he was allocated the support of an assistant. In 20 per cent of cases he was transferred to another department. In 10 per cent of cases he was given further training, assigned to another function or it was suggested that he should resign.

General information about the firm and, at least in theory, the organisation chart are given to all employees. Following the basic philosophy, there are no job descriptions at any level; but there are policy outlines, detailed working and routine procedures. Pay follows local practice, with the addition of an annual bonus, linked to company as well as individual performance. The sales force gets a good commission. There are typical local fringe benefits. There is a private pension scheme, which employees are eligible to enter after one year's service, free life insurance, long-term disability insurance and a private health scheme (BUPA). Promotion is according to achievement. The personnel manager rates the promotion chances of managers in the branch as high (4) but low outside it (1). For Japanese managers it is the opposite, a judgement that reflects the perceptions at the precision-engineering company.

The personnel manager's responsibility for helping colleagues with personal problems is extremely broad. He himself holds a departmental meeting once a month and attends the monthly management meeting. He considers the meetings meaningful and useful (4) but is not quite so personally satisfied (3). Nor is there a feeling that information about the situation and the company's plans either in the UK branch (2) or in the wider environment (1) is adequate. Contact with other departments is very close (5). The cooperativeness of subordinates is high (4), although communication from the direct subordinate to the next level is no more than fairly good (3). Satisfaction with the climate at work is high (4).

Language and cultural difficulties were said to be permanently in the background, with specific problems cropping up four to five times a week. As in other companies, the method of solving them is discussion for as long as it takes until clarification and agreement are reached. Given the two different types of assumption that expatriates and local managers normally have about organisations, as well as their different social backgrounds, the phrase 'permanently in the background' seems to sum up the latent presence of language and cultural difficulties well. British managers with no experience of organisations in Japan can have little idea of the sort of organisational behaviour Japanese managers are trained to expect, and it takes experience and imagination to appreciate the language problem.

English may be the first foreign language in Japanese schools, as French is in Britain for instance, but it is a considerable leap from there to fluent everyday use in a business situation in an unfamiliar foreign country. It is an everyday experience that literal translation of words misses the point, particularly when, as in the case of English and Japanese, the connotation of words can differ widely.[6] Managers who report that communication problems are negligible may have failed to notice how great the difference between the two positions really is beneath the surface. The personnel manager's own communication is 50 per cent face to face, 20 per cent written and telephone, respectively, and 10 per cent conferences.

In decision-making he can determine recruitment and selection procedures, appoint his own subordinate and other junior personnel (5). Regarding working hours and changes in the level of payment, he participates equally in the decision with others (4). In making a larger capital investment and in implementing time-and-motion studies and organisational changes in other departments his opinion is taken into account (3). He sees the main decisions affecting the branch as depending on the top Japanese management in the UK, followed by the parent company in Japan, and by the hierarchical levels in the branch in descending order.

Job satisfaction is highest with job security and conditions of employment (5). The possibility of realising potential and interests and the friendliness of working atmosphere are also highly rated (4). Satisfaction with the work itself, salary and salary prospects, hours of work and future career prospects is moderate (3). The firm is seen as better than others (4).

The success of the firm is most conspicuous in regard to growth and level of technology (5). Quality of products and service, and efficiency, are high (4). But motivation, adaptation to the market and profitability are no more than moderate (3). The ratings seem to reflect the orientation towards growth, through service to the customer and high technical standards, contained in the managing director's basic philosophy for the company. The moderate rating for motivation may refer to problems associated with reorientating local employees away from the work patterns of their previous British organisations towards the pattern set out in the basic philosophy. Regarding profitability, it might be expected that a company established comparatively recently would still be building up to its peak, or that this process had not been helped by external factors, such as the depressed state of the market.

## Japanese managers careers

*Managing director*

| Function | Years |
| --- | --- |
| University, physics course | 4 |
| Service engineer, consumer products | $1\frac{1}{2}$ |
| Representative, overseas branch | $3\frac{1}{2}$ |
| Quality Control engineer, consumer electronics plant | $1\frac{1}{2}$ |
| Engineering section manager, consumer electronics | $1\frac{1}{2}$ |
| Manager, design engineering, consumer electronics | $1\frac{1}{2}$ |
| Manager, marketing, consumer electronics | $1\frac{1}{2}$ |
| Manager, consumer electronics plant | 5 |
| Managing director, UK | 6 |

The written reply to the questionnaire stated that the managing director had wanted to enter a manufacturing company on graduating from the university and felt that the electrical field was particularly suitable. He had received an approach from the company and had joined because he considered that it had a bright future.

No particular training is mentioned but the career profile suggests a thorough grounding through experience in both the engineering and marketing sides of consumer electronics. From a UK perspective, it could be said that this development shows a high degree of professional competence, using the word 'professional' in a task-related and not a status-related or narrow sense. It is therefore interesting that in the basic philosophy for the branch the emphasis on teamwork and the disapproval of job descriptions in the local sense is marked.

The managing director sees his own job in wide generalist terms but sees only 10 per cent of managers in the branch as generalists and 90 per cent as specialists. He is a member of the (British) Institute of Directors, in his capacity as managing director, but does not belong to any other professional association.

*Financial director*

| Function | Years |
| --- | --- |
| University, economic history course | 4 |
| Factory cost-accountant | 3 |
| Management accountant | 3 |
| Head-office management accountant | 2 |
| Financial director, UK | 6 |

At interview the director stated that he had thought of joining a securities company from university but that the future had seemed better on the financial side of a manufacturing and marketing company, although the securities companies paid better. He saw the company's present success in the UK as due to its persistence in overseas markets, including other subsidiaries that would take time to become profitable—a reference to the long-term marketing strategies of Japanese firms that are often discussed.[7]

His induction training had consisted of the then-standard eight weeks, with 192 other new entrants. This was followed by OJT in his first job as a factory cost-accountant. As a management accountant, he received instructions from his predecessor. Career development is considered to be characteristic of the firm.

Accounting practice in Britain and Japan differs considerably. The financial director's job largely consists of liaison with Japan. In his view, Japanese managers in the UK are for liaison; they have no title. For the UK side of accounting he relies on a British chartered accountant. The case, which is repeated in many Japanese companies in the UK, clearly shows the difference between in-house qualification by OJT, on the one hand, and professional qualification through the examinations of an institution in an external labour market, on the other. As a manager with a liaison function, the director sees his task as providing a good bridge between the UK and Japan. Rules have to be fairly strictly observed but were said to be stricter in Japan. British managers are perceived as concerned with titles and status. Top managers should be good at forecasting and at making general policy.

The director is very happy (5) to describe himself as a generalist, because he likes a flexible job. In the discussion of how many of the management team were generalists or specialists he was one of very few throughout the whole research to raise the question of how the terms were defined. It might have been expected that more managers would have taken an 'it all depends what you mean by generalist' approach but, as the tables in the Conclusion at the end of this section show (see pp. 145–71), there was little hestitation in using them. It should be emphasised that the terms were not put into managers' mouths. A final discussion of the interpretations of the terms and their connotation will be given in the Conclusion at the end of the book.

The director evaluated British managers' promotion prospects in the branch as fairly good (3); better than outside it (2), although he thought they might also have prospects in other branches in Europe. For Japanese managers the prospects were moderate in the branch (3) and excellent (5) in Japan. He thought job rotation might come to the branch later, and in the discussion referred to the policy of flexibility contained in the basic philosophy.

He felt the departmental and management meetings he attended were very useful (5) and that information about both the branch and the company as a whole was good (4). Satisfaction with the climate at work was good (4) and contact with other departments moderately close (3). Sometimes it was necessary to repeat explanations. The manager's communication was mainly face to face (70 per cent), with 25 per cent estimated for written messages and memos and 5 per cent for telephone.

In all the decision-making in which he was involved he would participate equally in making the decision with colleagues (4). He saw the top management in the branch as the source of the most important decisions, followed by the parent company—the same perception as that of the British personnel manager. In descending order, there then followed the middle management and the staff or administrative departments.

Job satisfaction was high (4–5), although opportunities for further training and development were rated as moderate (3). The success of the firm was most highly rated in terms of growth rate and technological level (5). Motivation and the quality of products or services were rated as 4. Efficiency, profitability and adaption to the market each scored 3.

It is again to be expected that in a recently established operation growth would be in advance of profitability, and the prevalence of long-term marketing strategies aimed at increasing market share first among Japanese companies in the UK was already referred to above. The degree of adaptation to the market was said to be a question of the product range. As regards efficiency, it is to be expected that perceptions might vary considerably between British and Japanese managers, as they might indeed between different individuals.

*Department manager, engineering*

| Function | Years |
|---|---|
| University, engineering course | 4 |
| Design and development engineer, radio communication | 7 |
| Head of design and development department | 5 |
| Project manager, radio communication | 5 |
| Overseas manager, electronics | 1 |
| Department manager, engineering, UK | $4\frac{1}{2}$ |

The manager was recommended to join the company by his professor at university—Japanese professors and university appointment offices maintaining far closer long-term links with business, especially industrial firms, than is the case in Britain. As this was a reply to a written questionnaire, it was not clear exactly to what extent the professor might have suggested the manager's name to the firm, but such introductions are common in Japan, where a school teacher's or university professor's report is a useful pre-selection filter.[8]

The manager's job area has boundaries that have to be observed 'to a considerable extent' but in spite of his specialised training and previous job assignments, he sees himself as a generalist, with the management team being split fifty–fifty between generalists and specialists.

He is perhaps unusual in belonging to an engineers' institution in Japan, and the magazines he takes show his interests. He has subscribed for eighteen years to the *Journal of the Association of Japanese Mechanical Engineering*, and for four years each to the *Journal of the Association of Japanese Electronics Engineering* and the *Journal of the American Society of Civil Engineering*.

*Marketing manager*

| Function | Years |
|---|---|
| University, commercial course | 4 |
| Electronics sales | 10 |

| Function | Years |
|---|---|
| Assistant manager, electronics exports | 2 |
| Marketing manager, electronics, overseas branch | 3 |
| Marketing manager, electronics, UK | 1 |

The manager joined the company straight from university because it is a first-class and an expanding company. During his development he spent a period as a union representative. Apart from OJT, training has consisted of one week on export procedures, one month's English and one week's middle management training. He is happy (4) to see himself as a specialist, estimating that 20 per cent of management colleagues in the branch are generalists and 80 per cent specialists. In regard to job boundaries, he wrote that the job was quite different, but in many cases the customers were the same.

The career profile clearly demonstrated the consistent and specialised nature of his job assignments. He underlined this point in the statement that 'I have been working for more than sixteen years in the company and the content of my job has always been the same, even if I am staying abroad as I am now'.

*Marketing liaison manager*

| Function | Years |
|---|---|
| University, electronics course | 4 |
| Design engineer, electronics | 6 |
| Technical support, UK branch sales | 2 |
| Marketing liaison manager, UK branch | 4 |

The manager was recruited through the regular recruiting link that the company maintains with his particular university. During the interview he stated that he had originally wanted to work at a smaller company because it would be more interesting, with more responsibility; but his parents had persuaded him that a big company offered better prospects. He saw the company's overseas expansion in the light of Japan's poverty of resources and consequent need to export and commented that the company couldn't survive only in the domestic market.

The year he had joined there had been a large graduate intake;

the 700 new graduate entrants[9] being divided into three groups for the month's induction training according to the three product areas they were to be assigned to. After that, training was mostly OJT, with visits to different departments over the first six months. The manager had no training in the UK branch. He does not subscribe to any journal personally but sees a number in the company.

His job area is not strictly defined, and there is considerable flexibility between groups involving similar technology. In his view, it is not clearly defined what a manager in the branch is, but he considers that top managers should have the ability to work together. He does not see his own title as important, but doing the job well is. He is content (3) to see himself as a specialist and views his Japanese colleagues as split fifty–fifty between generalists and specialists, and his local colleagues as 70 per cent generalists and 30 per cent specialists. He normally finds no problem over differing views of work or the organisation, although there is a different understanding of management. There is no job rotation in the branch yet. He evaluates British promotion prospects as fair in the branch (3) and less good outside it (2). For Japanese managers the rating is fair (3) in both cases; whereas in many instances promotion chances in Japan itself are more highly evaluated.

The manager is happy (4) with the levels of information in the company, which are 'better than in Japan', but not so satisfied with the meetings he attends (2). Contact with other departments and the cooperativeness of subordinates is good (4). Satisfaction with the climate at work is high (4).

Language difficulties crop up often but not cultural difficulties. Discussion is the way to solve them. The manager's own communication is mostly face to face (80 per cent), with written notices and so on (15 per cent), and the telephone (5 per cent) accounting for the balance.

In decision-making he either participates equally in the decision (4) or has his opinion taken into account (3), except for the appointment of a Japanese subordinate and determination of working hours, where he would be informed beforehand (2). He sees the parent company as the source of major decisions, with other levels of management in descending order of importance following the management hierarchy.

Job satisfaction is fairly high (3–4). Job security rates highest

(5). The lowest scores are opportunities for further training and development, and hours of work (2). The manager says his working week is 60 hours.[10] But the greatest cause for dissatisfaction (1) is the length of his overseas assignment: when he is recalled, he will have been abroad seven years—and that is too long. To what extent this was related to the lower than average score for promotion prospects in Japan or to children's education and other problems was not clear.

The success of the firm was highly rated (4) for quality of products and service, adaptation to the market and level of technology; and moderately rated (3) for the remaining factors of profitability, efficiency, growth and motivation.

*Marketing liaison manager 2*

| Function | Years |
| --- | --- |
| University, economics course | 4 |
| Overseas business department | 7 |
| Marketing manager, electronics, UK | 2 |
| Marketing liaison, consumer products, UK | $1\frac{1}{2}$ |

The manager stated that he had joined the company as a result of the influence of his father, an electrical engineer.[11] After four weeks' introductory training he had OJT from his seniors for one year. As part of his career development he spent some time as a union representative at department level. He considers that his development has not been typical. 'Typical development would be rotation every three years or so, to know the function of other departments. We need general career development'. How far these remarks coincide with the actuality rather than the principle of generalism in Japanese companies will be discussed in the Conclusion at the end of the book.

The manager sees himself as a generalist, although he 'did the same thing for seven years', along with 50 per cent of his Japanese colleagues. British managers he divides into 30 per cent generalists, in the general management, and 70 per cent specialists in the product areas. Although a generalist, he sees himself as more specialist in the UK; but his job is not strictly bounded—'I'm doing everything'. He pointed out that when the company started up in the UK it was small and unknown. Consequently it needed generalists. But with expansion it needs competent people who can 'communicate and carry on their business'. He regards two of his present local staff as satisfactory, five in need of development and three as unsatisfactory.

*Marketing liaison manager 3*

| Function | Years |
| --- | --- |
| University, sociology course | 4 |
| Marketing controller | 4 |
| Overseas marketing controller | 5 |
| Marketing liaison manager, UK | 1 |

The manager stated that one reason for joining the firm was that it was prepared to recruit a sociology graduate, whereas other firms required non-technical personnel to have graduated from either the economics or the law department.[12] The work is not very strictly defined, and the manager is content (3) to be a generalist. He views 20 per cent of colleagues as generalists and 80 per cent as specialists. The career profile shows that he has been in the same function since he first entered the company.

*Engineering liaison manager 1*

| Function | Years |
| --- | --- |
| Technical college, engineering course | 4 |
| Production engineer, electronics | 17 |
| Engineering liaison manager, UK | $3\frac{1}{2}$ |

In spite of the apparently specialised nature of his background, the manager is happy to classify himself as a generalist, with a flexible work area. He sees his management colleagues as 90 per cent generalists and 10 per cent specialists. He has subscribed for just over a year to two journals connected with his work, one about televisions and one about radios.

*Engineering liaison manager 2*

| Function | Years |
| --- | --- |
| Technical college, engineering course | 4 |
| Engineer, consumer products | 9 |
| Engineering liaison manager, UK | 3 |

As part of his career development, the manager has spent a period as a union official. He is happy (4) to see himself as a specialist, having spent his entire career in the company in the same product area. He sees 80 per cent of the management team as generalists and 20 per cent as specialists.

## British managers' careers

The career and the functions of the personnel manager have already been discussed above. A comparison of the career profiles in terms of job mobility and qualifications is instructive.

*Marketing manager 1*

| Function | Years |
| --- | --- |
| Technical officer, Armed Forces | 6 |
| Various sales and junior management positions* | 12 |
| Sales representative* | 11 |
| Area sales manager* | 3 |
| UK sales manager | 4 |
| Divisional manager training | 4 |
| Marketing manager 1, Japanese company* | $2\frac{1}{2}$ |

 * Change of employer.

The manager has two GCE (General Certificate of Education) A (Advanced) Levels. During his service in the Armed Forces he obtained a City and Guilds technical qualification and specialised in radar, becoming a radar officer. In his twelve years with a number of different companies he had training in retailing and attended manufacturers' courses on sales and service. During his eleven years on the job as a sales representative he was given sales training by different sales-training organisations. This type of training continued when he became an area sales manager, but at that level he also attended management courses. As a UK sales manager he attended further external management courses provided by his company. As divisional training manager he obtained a diploma from the ILEA (Inner London Education Authority) and became a full Member of the Institute of Marketing, but he does not attend the Institute's meetings. He has subscribed to *Marketing Review* for five years.

He joined the company after an initial contact in a training consultancy role. The attractions were the salary and the challenge of building a new department which would contribute to the future growth of the company, for which he already had great respect prior to being offered the position he now holds. He does not see his development in the firm as typical but is happy where he is and would not contemplate leaving. He is very satisfied (5) with the climate at work.

The functional area is quite strictly marked off and rules have to be very strictly observed (5), but the manager sees himself as neither generalist nor specialist but as a little of each. He regards 70 per cent of colleagues as generalists and 30 per cent as specialists. He rates his subordinates as moderately qualified (3). His own role in the firm is that of entrepreneur/manager. Being a manager in the firm implies a management function within the management line, as opposed to staff functions servicing the requirements of a department. Top managers require 'Leadership qualities and interactive skills—the ability to communicate and motivate'.

Differences of expectation or views about work are resolved by patient discussion and a recognition and respect for a culture which applies methods with which, in the main, the manager is in agreement—a statement that sums up the position of managers in Japanese companies in Britain who have confidence in the firm they are working for and who have gone some way towards following the new management style.

The manager attends meetings of the work team three to four times a month and finds the meetings useful (4). He is satisfied (4) with the amount of information about the company in the branch and in the wider context. Contact with other departments is quite close (3–4) and the cooperativeness of subordinates high (5). His own communication is primarily face to face (65 per cent), with 15 per cent estimated for the telephone and 10 per cent each for written messages and conferences.

Promotion prospects for local staff are high (4) in the branch, but not outside it. Prospects for Japanese managers are fairly high (3–4) in both cases. There is no job rotation in the company for managers. But if there were, the advantages, in order of importance would be:

1. Generation of a high level of managerial commitment.

2. Flexible deployment of managers as needed.
3. Opportunity for managers to become qualified in other fields.

Of the three advantages, the first two would be of most direct benefit to the company in terms of performance. The third could be expected to have the closest connection with individual managers' career development.

In the manager's view, the parent company has the greatest weight in major decisions affecting the branch, followed by the hierarchical levels of the organisations in descending order. His own decision-making consists mainly in having his opinion taken into account, outside specific business matters. Job satisfaction is uniformly high (5), except for a slighly lower rating (4+) for further opportunities for training and development. As far as working conditions and conditions for employment are concerned, 'It would be difficult to envisage improvement in these areas'. The success of the firm is highly rated (4–5).

Like many British (but fewer Japanese) managers, the manager is not a graduate, but his experience and training obviously qualify him as a specialist. In these respects he fits the pattern of Japanese companies in the UK, recruiting managers with the expertise needed to do a specific job.

### Marketing manager 2

| Function | Years |
| --- | --- |
| University, electronics course | 3 |
| n.a. | n.a. |
| Product manager, Japanese company* | 1 |
| Marketing manager 2 | $1\frac{1}{2}$ |

In addition to his university degree, in a field that is highly relevant to his present job, the manager later obtained the Diploma in Management Studies (DMS). He has been a full Member of the Institute of Marketing for a year and attends its meetings periodically. He has subscribed to *Marketing* for two years and is occasionally a speaker at external meetings, training sessions, and so on.

Recruitment to the company was by answering an advertisement in a trade journal. Reasons for joining the firm included having been impressed with the products and with the people met at the interview. Satisfaction with the climate at work is high (5), but the offer of a job elsewhere that paid 50 per cent more would probably be tempting.

The manager is content (3) to classify himself as a specialist, along with 75 per cent of the management team, only 25 per cent being perceived as generalists. There is no strict job boundary, but rules and procedures must be quite strictly observed (4–5). The term 'manager' is loosely defined in the firm, although in practice managers are considered as people who are qualified and who are decision-makers. Top managers should have the ability to deal with people, to earn respect, to be in control and to give the confidence to others that they are in control.

When differences over work crop up, the manager's policy is to challenge them once—if this is unsuccessful, then to do one's utmost to accept the situation and to work within the constraints put upon one. In line with other manager's replies, he finds that patience and discussion are the ways of overcoming linguistic and cultural difficulties.

Contact with other departments is not so close (2), but the cooperativeness of subordinates is high (5). Monthly meetings are held by the department manager and weekly meetings of the works teams are highly rated (5). Company information is good (4). Half the manager's communication is face to face, with 30 per cent on the telephone and 20 per cent written, including use of the facsimile communication system. There is no job rotation that the manager was aware of. Promotion prospects for local managers are good (4), either in the branch or outside it in his view. The prospects for Japanese managers are perceived as moderate (3) in both instances.

The top management in the branch are considered to have the greatest weight in decision-making that affects the branch, followed by the parent company and then the hierarchical levels of the branch in descending order. The manager's own decision-making consists mainly in having his opinion taken into account, outside purely business decisions in his area.

Job satisfaction is high (5), except for opportunities for further training and development, and future salary prospects (4). Present salary is the source of only moderate satisfaction (3). Company performance is rated high (4–5).

*Sales and marketing manager 1*

| Function | Years |
|---|---|
| Messenger, advertising agency | 2 |
| General office work, advertising agency* | 1 |
| Progress chaser, advertising agency* | 2 |
| Account executive, advertising agency* | 6 |
| P.R., marketing services* | 8 |
| Marketing manager, manufacturers' association* | 4 |
| Marketing manager, electric company* | 4 |
| Sales and marketing manager, Japanese company* | 2 |

The manager left school at 16 without educational qualification and worked his way up to his present position. The high degree of mobility between companies is characteristic of having a career in advertising in Britain, although it would not be in a comparable case in Japan. The second agency joined went bankrupt.

As marketing manager at the previous electric company, the manager was involved in the same type of business as the Japanese company, which he got to know in this connection. Seeing a newspaper advertisement for a job, he applied and was accepted. Comparing the two companies, he says that the British company 'had fallen behind', partly because of the recession and partly due to personnel and industrial relations problems. He is therefore relieved to be with the Japanese company. The main attractions were career prospects and job security.

He has been a Member of the Institute of Marketing for sixteen years but does not attend meetings or subscribe to a professional journal. In his first three jobs he received no training, although he was 'learning the ropes' in a practical sense. As an account executive he attended a two-day course on public speaking. In his next job he studied for the Institute of Marketing exams. After two years with the Japanese company he still has no clear conception of what training is carried out. The only session he has attended is a one-day orientation for British employees of Japanese companies at the School of Oriental and African Studies, London University. In a revealing comment, he states that during his time with the manufacturers' association he met many senior managers and realised that they were not figures on a mountain. He sees his development in the Japanese company as characteristic in the sense of being given an opportunity. He is very satisfied (5) with the climate at work and has turned down three job offers from outside.

He is happy (4) to describe himself as a generalist but could not give a definite answer about whether his colleagues were generalists or specialists, although one or two have specialist areas of work. He sees himself as having all the roles that may be ascribed to a manager. The job itself is delineated according to product areas, but there is little emphasis on rules. Sometimes unwritten rules create problems which are embarrassing. The definition of managers is vague, except for the managing director. Top managers should have drive, sensitivity and awareness. The function of the Japanese was not clear. They were really liaison people, but they made a tremendous contribution.

Different views of work and expectations on the part of the organisation were something local staff had to learn. The best solution of conflict is to avoid it and the manager says he listens to comments from the Japanese. He sees communication as generally good. He is fairly satisfied (3) with the meetings he attends and pleased with the level of information (4). Contact with other departments is very close (5) and cooperativeness high (5). Language or cultural difficulties occur on average once a week but are never a major impediment and can be settled by discussion. The manager's own communication is predominantly face to face (80 per cent), followed by conferences (10 per cent) and telephone and written memos (5 per cent each). He commented that he enjoyed the company atmosphere more than in any other company he had worked for—and he has had considerable experience.

After two years in the company he says he still knows very little of Japanese management structure. He sees promotion prospects for British managers as excellent (5) in the branch but low outside it. For Japanese managers in the branch the prospects appear good (4), but he is not able to say what they would be in Japan. He is moderately satisfied (3) with the meetings. Company information is good (4), and contact with other departments and the cooperativeness of subordinates is very good (5). Communication for the manager is 80 per cent face to face, 10 per cent conferences and 5 per cent each for telephone and written messages.

He sees the Japanese top management in the branch as the main decision-making centre, with the parent company in second place, followed by the middle management and staff or administrative departments in descending order. The manager claims to be in a position of considerable decision-making autonomy himself (4–5). Job satisfaction is high (4–5), although the friendliness of the working atmosphere is no more than moderately good (3). This is because the staff are 'mainly from the South of England'!

The success of the firm is highly rated (5), except for efficiency (3). The reason given is that the firm has outgrown its resources in the process of expansion. Although profitability is highly rated (5), the manager made a significant comment to the effect that the principal aim was to create a market for the company's products, to penetrate the market and achieve market share. The concept of the long-term growth-based strategy, where successful growth creates solidly founded profitability, is confirmed again, by a manager with a long experience of marketing. The growth rate itself was described as phenomenal.

*Sales and marketing manager 2*

| Function | Years |
|---|---|
| Apprentice, electrical engineering, chemical company | 6 |
| Research, nuclear energy industry* | 5 |
| Sales engineer, laboratory instruments* | 2 |
| Sales engineer, electronics* | 2 |
| Senior sales engineer, electronics* | 2 |
| Sales manager, Japanese company* | 2 months |
| Sales and marketing manager 2 | 2 |

The manager has several GCE O (Ordinary) Levels and in his second job he completed his HNC in electronics by part-time study. The nature of the job had led him away from electrical engineering to electronics, the field in which his subsequent career has been spent. In his third job he attended several sales training courses, having decided that he wanted to move to the commercial side. Later, as a department sales manager, he attended further courses in sales management and in finance for non-financial managers. In the Japanese company he attended a one-day sales course 'on my own initiative'. Otherwise he reports that there is no formal training for managers.

He moved to the Japanese company for the classic reason of British managers: career development. He sees the company as having great potential and was recruited through a newspaper advertisement. Good career prospects, potentiality for growth, high technology and salary were the main attractions. He sees himself as a manager and entrepreneur. Functional areas are not strictly defined but overlapping. It is a very Japanese situation— with very loose reporting routes. Procedures are very informal, with very few rules.

In the managing director's view, everyone was working for the company, but the problem was that staff were operating as two groups: there was the language and the Japanese network. The manager is not keen on the open-plan office, although the most senior managers do have separate offices. He sees the main requirements for top managers as leadership, administrative ability, market knowledge and knowing where to direct the effort. He is happy (5) to classify himself as a generalist, along with 60 per cent of the management team, but would like more autonomy, more clear definition.

In dealing with differences at work, the important thing is to try to find out the thinking behind Japanese actions. One specific case mentioned was the appointment of a Japanese sales engineer, who was qualified in engineering but in a completely different field. The Japanese were said to believe the person was important and that he could learn things, but the manager was not so satisfied. He described business objectives as ill-defined. This was typically Japanese and characteristic of a situation where staff should work for the good of the company.

But it is clear from the career profiles and the reasons given for joining the firm that the manager's own orientation is career-centred rather than organisation-centred. At present he is unsure whether promotion prospects in the branch are more than not very high (2)—and not available outside it (1). But he only rates Japanese mangers' prospects as moderate (3) in Japan and low (1) in the branch.

In his own case he has had one job change in the company but considers this due to the particular set of circumstances in a young company. There have been one or two other changes, but these cannot be seen as parts of a conscious policy of job rotation for managers.

It is significant in the present context that he differentiates between two types of advantage of job rotation, if it existed. From top management's point of view the advantage would be the freedom to deploy managers flexibly. From his own personal point of view the advantage would be to gain qualifications through experience in other fields. The differentiation sums up the distinction between organisation-centred and individual career-centred orientations referred to above.

The manager finds departmental meetings very useful (4), but not management meetings (2), which he considers too big. There is an open atmosphere in the branch, but the Japanese did not formalise communication or tell people their objectives, and information was felt to be insufficient (1). Contact with other departments is fairly close (3) and the cooperativeness of subordinates quite good (4). Satisfaction with the climate at work is moderate (3). Linguistic or other difficulties are overcome by the usual method of discussion. The manager's own communication, somewhat exceptionally, is 20 per cent face to face and 80 per cent written.

The manager sees the parent company as the main base of decision-making. His own is mostly at the level of having his opinion taken into account (3). Job satisfaction is variable. Security and conditions of employment and hours of work are highest (5): the manager works fifty hours a week but describes this as 'my decision'. Most other aspects are high (4), but the future appears uncertain, salary and career prospects being no more than moderate (3) and opportunities for further training and development being lower (2). This is because of doubts about the company's future policies.

The success of the company was highly rated (4–5), with two exceptions. Adaptation to the market was said to be moderate (3) on the grounds that it was a product-led company, with products designed in Japan and not enough liaison with factories and design groups. The other exception was profitability (2), where it was said that a big profit was not expected. Efficiency was good (4) despite the alleged lack of formal organisation and objectives. This was 'because people accept doing a job and get on and do it'.

An overall comment was that although material conditions in the company were good, there was still some way to go yet in understanding the personal satisfaction needs of local managers. The comment reflected remarks already quoted showing contentment with employment conditions and some doubt or unhappiness about work organisation.

The manager again referred to the two different structures in the company and expressed the view that they would have to be unified for the company to operate effectively in the UK in the future, a move which he considered would provide increased job satisfaction and promotion opportunities for local staff. But he saw the company as very conservative and felt that from the perspective of the head office this sort of problem in a small local branch would not be a priority. It seems likely that some of the frustration came from problems of authority, responsibility and job definition in the organisation and from corresponding doubts about career prospects. The manager's career profile shows a pattern of pursuing promotion across different organisations and it would seem to be this career aspect, rather than anything more 'cultural', that was the root of the problem.

### Sales manager 1

| Function | Years |
| --- | --- |
| Civil Service | 7 |
| Sales representative, electrical company* | 1 |
| Sales manager, electrical company | 7 |
| Marketing manager, electrical company | $\frac{1}{2}$ |
| Sales training manager, electrical company | $\frac{1}{2}$ |
| Sales director, electrical company* | 6 |
| Overseas sales manager, electrical company* | 2 |
| Sales consultant, electrical company* | 1 |
| Sales manager 1, Japanese company* | 5 |

The manager took A Levels at a grammar school and obtained the Diploma in Management Studies by part-time study. He has been a member of the British Institute of Management for six months and intends to go to meetings. With the exception of his first job, his whole career has been concerned with sales in the electrical field. In his first sales job he had formal sales training for half a day a week. In the present job he wanted to go on an external marketing course, but this would have meant an absence from work of two months, which would have been too long. Instead, he had a week's introductory training, and one week's external training run by the Institute of Marketing. There is constant training in the department. Some managers and sales people have been sent to Japan, but this was not for training.

He was recruited through a newspaper advertisement and was

attracted by career prospects, job security and high prestige; he says he has turned down several job offers but that pay was becoming a problem.

The manager's view of his role is that of manager and entrepreneur. He stated there were no restrictions within the function and that local managers were given a very free hand. Procedures have to be followed to a reasonable extent (3) and rules are very flexible. Managers in the firms are defined as people who produce results and are expected to do so. Demands are put on them, but they receive rewards on a long-term basis.

The manager is fairly happy (3) to describe himself as a generalist, along with 30 per cent of colleagues. He sees the 70 per cent of specialist managers as those who have specific, tight objectives. He does not regard his British subordinates as adequately qualified (2). They are, in any case, experienced rather than qualified—a significant remark which can be applied to managers whose career profiles have already been quoted. Regarding Japanese subordinates, he notes that he does not have any and that no one does. It is a common feature of Japanese firms in the UK that British managers are not in positions with direct authority over expatriate personnel. In the present firm and others, several Japanese managers are in a liaison capacity without direct line authority, which may be blurred.

In regard to organisational expectations, the manager finds communication difficult and requiring discussion and negotiation. He says that he is going out for his own aims but that he does this dispassionately and tries to persuade others rather than engaging in direct argument. It is an on-going discussion. He finds his own monthly departmental meetings more useful (4) than the monthly general management meeting (3); an opinion which reflects that of the last manager above. He also feels information about the company and its plans is insufficient (2), whether in the branch or outside. Contact with other departments is not so close (2), although the cooperativeness of subordinates is good (4). Unlike the majority of managers in the precision engineering company, and some of his own colleagues, the major part of the manager's own communication is written (60 per cent), with only 25 per cent face to face and 15 per cent telephone. He is quite satisfied (4) with the climate at work.

He sees the parent company in Japan as the main decision-making centre, with others following in descending hierarchical order. His own decision-making is mostly at the level of participating equally with others (4) or having his opinion taken into consideration (3).

Job satisfaction is mostly good (4) or fair (3); the latter including the possibility of realising the manager's own potential and interests, future salary and career prospects, opportunities for further training and development and working hours. Present salary gets the lowest score (2). All in all, the firm is rated as about the same as others (3).

Impressions of the success of the firm are likewise mixed. Growth, quality and technical levels score high (4), but profitability and efficiency score no more than 2. The strategy of going for growth first, followed by profitability, has already been discussed above. The score for efficiency is low in contrast with that of the last manager, for instance, who found it high despite what he perceived as a lack of formal organisation.

*Sales manager 2*

| Function | Years |
| --- | --- |
| Officer, Armed Forces | 20 |
| Sales representative, electrical company* | 5 |
| Sales training manager, electrical company | 3 |
| Area sales manager, electrical company | 6 |
| Sales representative, Japanese company* | 5 |
| Sales manager 2 | 6 |

The manager has a good educational background, having attended a commercial and technical college and university (it is not clear whether this was interrupted by the war). He was recruited through an advertisement in a trade paper, and in view of his long experience, his reasons for joining the firm are particularly striking. 'The company captivated my imagination. They are very good employers. Total job satisfaction. Makers of top quality products. A company with a tremendous future in the UK and Europe.' 'Attention to quality and world markets' was also mentioned in the questionnaire. He works seventy-two hours or more per week.

The manager's self-image is of 'entrepreneur and manager', and that of his subordinate is 'entrepreneur, manager and controller'. 'Our functional areas are clearly defined, but we work very much together as a team'; a perception that may be compared with those of the last two managers above. The manager also states that rules are to be strictly observed (5)—another point where opinions in the company are divided. There is no comment on how managers in the firm are defined, but the abilities which top managers should possess reflect characteristic British concepts of formal organisation and delegated authority. They are: 'Think clearly. Plan clearly. Delegate. Absolute knowledge of his job. Ability to make decisions'.

The list might be contrasted with the abilities to communicate, to reach decisions by consultation and to work together flexibly as a team, which might be taken as typical of the Japanese style of organisation. The manager's list of abilities is a pure example of 'individualistic' thought, which does not match the managing director's organisational principles, for example; although it is true that he refers to 'working as a team' in his department, is content to work the longest hours of any manager in the survey and has high levels of satisfaction with the climate at work (4) and with all aspects of the job (5 on all points, except 4 for opportunities for realising potential and interests, and present salary).

He is fairly content (3) to see himself fifty–fifty as a generalist or specialist. In his view, 30 per cent of colleagues are generalists and 70 per cent specialists. Promotion chances for British managers appear high (4) in both branch and outside, but there is no clear idea of what the prospects for Japanese managers are. There is no job rotation.

Communication problems do not arise. Management meetings are extremely useful (5). Information is good (4). Contact with other departments is quite close (4) and the cooperativeness of subordinates high (4). Communication is half face to face, with 20 per cent each by telephone and written memos and 10 per cent by conferences. Out of eight possible types of decision-making cases that might arise, three, in relation to appointment of a direct subordinate and other departmental staff, were classed as own decision (5). The others were left blank. The parent company in Japan was seen as the major decision-making centre affecting the branch, followed by other hierarchical levels in descending order. This coincides with the general tendency of the opinions already quoted above; although there is obviously a difference between those who see the parent company in first place and those who see the top Japanese management in the branch as playing the leading role.

The success of the firm is uniformly rated as high (4), with quality of products and service and technological levels receiving the highest marks possible (5). This emphasis on quality of products and service is the same as in the precision engineering company, as well as the same as other colleagues' in the same company's perceptions. Putting it another way, it shows the similarity of management philosophy between a manufacturing and a sales company across different product markets; the former supplying industrial customers and the latter directing its strategy at the consumer. Sales manager 1 also remarked that the company's philosophy was that 'The customer is always right', and sales manager 2's comments suggest that this is not just empty rhetoric.

### Technical manager 1

| Function | Years |
| --- | --- |
| University | 3 |
| Branch manager, software company | 2 |
| Marketing manager, computer bureau* | $3\frac{1}{2}$ |
| Software packages manager* | 2 |
| Marketing, manager* | 2 |
| Manager advance products | $1\frac{1}{2}$ |
| Software engineering manager* | 2 |
| Technical manager, Japanese company* | 2 |

The manager took A Levels in mathematics, physics and chemistry and obtained a degree from a leading university. He has been a Member of the British Computer Society for fifteen years and has taken the Society's journal for that time but does not attend meetings. In his first job he received training in general business and communications and in his last job before joining the Japanese company he attended sales training. In the jobs in between he notes that he received no training. In the present company he has attended a one-day external course and a two-day in-house session and has spent three weeks in Japan.

He joined the company by applying for an interview and was accepted after two or three interviews. He was attracted by the new business opportunity and job security. He is not particularly satisfied (2) with the climate at work and sees himself as still mobile, if salary prospects elsewhere were good. The perception of his own role is that of manager and of his subordinate as technical expert. His field is a completely separate area but with no strict boundaries. Rules have to be quite strictly followed (4). He sees himself as a specialist but in the present company feels that he is really both—a description he is moderately happy with (3). He judges that a quarter of management colleagues are generalists and three-quarters specialists. His British subordinates, in the technical field, are very highly qualified (5); Japanese subordinates once again do not come into the picture. He works thirty-five hours a week.

The problem of different expectations or different approaches are solved by discussion and persuasion. However, some Japanese views, if firmly held, were always said to prevail. Language or cultural problems crop up on average once a month and require patience and discussion. Local managers cannot always overcome them. Satisfaction with the monthly departmental meetings and the weekly work-team meetings is fair (3), but information is regarded as insufficient (1). Contact with other departments is fairly close (3) and subordinates' cooperativeness good (4). Fifty per cent of the manager's own communication is face to face, 25 per cent on the telephone, with 20 per cent for written and 5 per cent for conferences.

Promotion prospects in the branch or outside are evaluated as fair (3) and higher (4) for Japanese managers in both cases. There is no job rotation for British staff, although for Japanese managers experience in the UK is seen as part of wider job rotation. This reflects other comments and the presence of a small number of Japanese trainees in the branch, sent by the parent company to learn international business. The difference between British managers' estimates of Japanese managers' career prospects either in the branch or in the parent company again reflects local unfamiliarity with the company system, especially in Japan.

In the manager's view, the parent company has the greatest weight in decisions affecting the branch, followed by the hierarchical levels in descending order. His own decision-making consists mainly of participating equally with others in the decision (4). Job satisfaction is fair to good (3–4), although salary is rated lower (2). But on the whole the firm is rated better than others to work for (4). The growth, quality of products and service and technical levels of the firm are highly rated (4). Profitability and efficiency are moderate (3), and motivation receives the lowest score of 2.

### Technical manager 2

| Function | Years |
|---|---|
| Technical manager, software | 1 |
| Director, software | 4 |
| Manager, computer services* | 1 |
| Manager, computers* | 1 |
| Manager, data processing* | 4 |
| Technical manager 2, Japanese company* | 1 |

The manager has some O Levels and was recruited through an agency. On his side, the attractions were job and salary prospects. He refers to no training in his previous career. In the present company he has attended a one-day external course.

The job is not strictly marked off but rules and procedures are quite clearly followed (4). He is happy (4) to see himself as a specialist, along with 60 per cent of management colleagues. British subordinates are highly qualified (5). There is no job rotation and promotion prospects are not very highly rated (2). For Japanese managers the rating is also only moderate (3).

The monthly departmental meeting and the weekly work-team meetings are fairly useful (3). Information is not so adequate (2). Contact with other departments is not very close (2), but cooperativeness of subordinates is high (4). Satisfaction with the climate at work is moderate (3). Face to face and telephone contact each account for 45 per cent of communication, with the remaining 10 per cent being written.

The manager sees the parent company and then the hierarchical levels in descending order as having the weight in decision-making. His own is split between participation or consultation (3–4) and no involvement (1). Job satisfaction is moderate to high (3–5), with job security, employment conditions and the friendliness of the working atmosphere receiving the most positive evaluation (5). Salary, career prospects and the possibility of realising potential are moderate (3). Opportunities for further training and development receive the lowest score (2). The success of the firm is also assessed as moderate to high (3–5), without any further comment.

*Personnel officer*

| Function | Years |
| --- | --- |
| Personal assistant, Japanese company | 3 |
| Personnel officer | $1\frac{1}{2}$ |

The manager, who is female, has five O Levels and was recruited through a local employment agency. She was attracted by 'the interesting position which gave a reasonable amount of scope for initiative'. During her time in the company she has attended several courses on different aspects of personnel management procedures. She sees herself primarily as an administrator, with quite a clearly defined area (4) and adherence to rules and procedures (4) and is not particularly happy (2) to describe herself as a generalist. No estimation of whether colleagues are generalists or specialists is given. She is involved in different aspects of staff welfare, including the operation of the private health insurance scheme. Local managers' promotion prospects are rated as moderate (3), with no indication for Japanese managers. Job rotation is not practised.

Department meetings are rated as fairly useful (2–3), but information about the company is rated poor (1). Contact with other departments is very close (5), and the cooperativeness of subordinates is high (5). Language or cultural problems occur on average once a week, necessitating explanation and assistance. The manager's own communication is mostly face to face (60 per cent), with 20 per cent each for written memos and telephone.

The top Japanese management in the branch appears to be the main decision-maker. The manager's own decision-making is fairly limited (1–3), the main exception being the ability to appoint the direct subordinate (5). Job satisfaction is fair to high (3–5), with working conditions and salary prospects having the lowest score (2). Career prospects and opportunities for training and development are fair (3). Regarding the success of the firm, the high scores (5) for growth, quality and technology reflect a common view. Profitability is slightly lower (4), with efficiency and motivation no more than moderate (3).

*Area sales manager*

| Function | Years |
| --- | --- |
| Sales representative | n.a. |
| Sales representative, Japanese company* | 3 |
| Area sales manager 1 | 1 |

The manager's educational background consists of six O Levels and attendance at a technical college (unspecified). In the company he has had two weeks in-house training, a one-week external course on marketing and two weeks in Japan. He was recruited through direct application to the company and had three interviews. The main attractions were the good prospects in a company with high-quality products and job security.

The job is bounded by the particular sales area and compliance with rules, and procedures is high (4–5). In the manager's view, people are called managers only if they manage personnel. The manager sees his own role as 'motivator and manager' of the sales force. He is not very happy (2) to see himself as a generalist, along with 30 per cent of management colleagues. Subordinates are fairly well qualified (3–4). There is no job rotation. Promotion prospects are rated as moderate (3) and better for Japanese managers (4).

Monthly department and weekly work-team meetings are considered useful (4–5). Information in the branch appears better (4) than about the company as a whole (3). In the manager's present position there are no language or cultural problems. Satisfaction with the organisational climate is high (4). Contact with other departments and the cooperativeness of subordinates is good (4). Half the manager's communication is face to face, with 20 per cent each estimated for written memos and the telephone, and 10 per cent for conferences. His decision-making is divided between equal participation (4) and lower levels (3–1). Job satisfaction is high (4–5), except for present salary and future salary prospects (3). The lower score reflects those of several colleagues and would appear to fit in with previous findings that Japanese companies in the UK are not paying more than average salaries, though they may offer greater job security by implication.

The success of the firm is uniformly highly rated (4), except for efficiency (3). To those who are accustomed to the stereotyped images of Japanese efficiency, this may seem surprising but this is not the first case in which efficiency scored lower. It is of course likely that different people's concepts of efficiency will differ; but in Japan itself there tends to be a difference between the efficiency of blue-collar production operations and white-collar office organisations in the service sector.[13]

*Area sales manager 2*

| Function | Years |
|---|---|
| University | 3 |
| n.a. | n.a. |
| Area sales manager 2, Japanese company* | 5 |

The manager has had training in sales management both in his present job and previously. He replied to a job advertisement in a trade paper, the main attraction being the prospects offered by a growing company, including security and prestige. He has subscribed to *Electrical and Radio Trading* for nine years and to *Electrical and Electronic Trader* for four years.

The job has set boundaries. Firm company guidelines are followed (5). The manager is fairly happy (3) to see himself as a generalist, along with three-quarters of the management team. Satisfaction with the climate at work is high (4). There is no job rotation. Promotion prospects in the branch are low (2) but believed to be better outside it (3). For Japanese managers the prospects are evaluated as higher in both cases (4). Department meetings are seen as very helpful (5). Information is good (4). Contact with other departments is close (4) and the cooperativeness of subordinates fair (3). Seventy-five per cent of the manager's communication is by telephone, 15 per cent by written memos, 9 per cent face to face and 1 per cent conferences.

Top management, followed by middle management are seen as the main decision-makers. The manager's own decision-making ranges from equal participation (4) to none (1). Job satisfaction is moderate to high, with security getting the highest score (5) and opportunities for further training and development, hours of work and friendliness of the working environment getting the lowest (2). The manager works fifty hours a week or more, which is above average (Table 2.3). The success of the firm is highly rated (4), with technology and efficiency, unlike the last case, getting the highest rating (5).

*Product manager 1*

| Function | Years |
|---|---|
| Radio and TV apprentice, electrical company | 4 |
| Laboratory technician, electrical company* | 1 |
| Service engineer/service manager, electrical company* | 5 |
| Service manager, electrical company* | 1 |
| Service manager, Japanese company* | 3 |
| Product manager 1 | 3 |

The manager obtained six O Levels and three CSEs (Certificates of Secondary Education) and completed his City and Guilds qualification in radio and television servicing. He had heard about the company from a friend, and his recruitment was unusual in that his last employer before the present one had also been a Japanese company. This might have caused some embarrassment, and the Japanese managing director had had a word with a Japanese director at the other firm to confirm that it would not cause offence. At the interview the product manager stated that he had wanted to move to a company with a wider product range and he had 'gradually drifted' into his present job. The change of company was in order to further his career, since he was 'looking for better career prospects'.

After the apprenticeship at the time of his first job, he did 'some informal OJT' in his third job, changing his role from a purely technical one to one that included both technical and administrative aspects. He received no particular training in the other Japanese company, which he found unusual as a Japanese company because of the small number of expatriates. It was run as a British company. In the present company there is a small amount of training. Two-day courses, either in-house or external, are the norm, with visits to Japan for technical people and engineers.

He sees his present role as entrepreneur. There are no clear boundaries at all and no written rules. The word 'manager' is considered important, and the title is not handed out easily; but by itself it doesn't mean anything. It is not an exclusive function in the department. Top managers should coordinate the people below.

The manager has learnt over the past six years that you can't change the company's attitudes. The alternative would be to resign. Trying to resist is no good for your own career. He has already been offered another job but turned it down. Job security and other factors, such as prospects, are important and would have to be considered along with salary. He is fairly happy (3) to see himself as a generalist, together with 20 per cent of colleagues, but the majority 80 per cent do relatively specialist jobs. He regards his subordinates as fairly qualified (3).

Company policy is said to be to recruit internally for promotion whenever possible, although there have been some hirings from outside which have encouraged the competitive spirit in the organisation. Prospects in the branch are not very high (2) and lower outside it (1); for Japanese managers the figures given are 4 and 3, respectively. It was said that the company generally encourages job rotation but that little happens in practice.

The manager considered the monthly meeting of the work team useful (4), but information about the branch and the wider company context is regarded as inadequate (2, 1). Contact with other departments is not very close (2) and the cooperativeness of subordinates fair (3). Satisfaction with the climate at work was not very high (2), partly because of changes that were said to be taking place. Language and cultural difficulties arose periodically, necessitating spending a long time and hammering away at meetings. The manager's own communication was mainly face to face (55 per cent), followed by written memos (25 per cent) and telephone and conferences (10 per cent each).

The parent company is viewed as the main decision-maker, followed by the hierarchical levels. The manager's own decision-making is limited. Job satisfaction is moderate (3). Job security again gets the highest score (5). Present and future salary and hours of work get low scores (2). It was emphasised that the family were dissatisfied (1) particularly because of working hours. The manager does an average of fifty hours per week.

The evaluation of the success of the firm is more mixed than most. Growth is most highly rated (5). Technology is highly rated (4) but is not considered the highest among Japanese makers. Quality was said to range from the top end (5) for some product areas, to 4, 2 and even 1 for others. Motivation was classed as moderate (3), which was not unique, along with profitability. Here it was pointed out that the objective of profitability was related to the company as a whole rather than to the branch alone. Adaptation to the market was not rated so highly (2), because of the remoteness of the head office and ensuing delays, compounded by the small size of the UK market and the conservative organisation of the company. Efficiency was also not rated higher (2). Here there was specific reference to the advantages and also disadvantages of flexibility, the latter including overlaps. This is of course one of the commonest charges raised against flexibility, or loose job structuring, by advocates of closely defined authority and clear job descriptions—and sometimes by British managers in Japanese firms. It is a symptom of how deep the whole problem is.

### Product manager 2

| Function | Years |
|---|---|
| Product manager | 3 |
| Product manager 2, Japanese company* | 1 |

The manager has an HNC in electrical engineering and was recruited to the company through an advertisement in a trade journal. The attractions were strength of reputation overseas, product range, aggressive marketing plans, *ground-floor opportunity* and good salary. The phrase 'ground-floor opportunity' refers to the career orientation in an entrepreneurial environment. The manager has subscribed to the *Electrical Review* for five years and the *Electrical Times* for three.

He sees his role in the firm as that of promoter. There is close cooperation between specialists in areas of mutual interest. Rules and procedures are strictly followed (4) but what managers in the firm are is not strictly defined. Top managers should possess leadership, communication skills, the ability to command respect and flexibility. The use of the word 'flexibility' is perhaps significant in relation to the manager's unhappiness (1) in classifying himself as a specialist—although objectively this is what he seems to be. In his view, no more than 20 per cent of the management team are generalists. Subordinates are moderately qualified (3). He had introductory management training in his first job and in the present company has had two days in-house training and a one-week external course. He has spent a fortnight in Japan.

There is no job rotation. Promotion prospects in the branch are fair (3) but low outside it (1); for Japanese managers the perceptions are reversed. But the manager would not like to move unless the salary offered was a great deal higher.

Differing views about work are resolved by discussion, and compromise where possible. Such differences occur on average once a fortnight. Department meetings, held monthly, are considered useful (4). Information about the branch is good (4), but inadequate (1) about the company as a whole. Contact with other departments is not very close (2), but the cooperativeness of subordinates is high (5). Satisfaction with the climate at work is high (4). The manager's own communication is mainly on the telephone (40 per cent), with 30 per cent for written messages, 20 per cent face to face and 5 per cent each for conferences and training sessions. His decision-making is limited to having his opinion taken into account (3), or less (1–2). Only the appointment of his own direct subordinate is his decision (5), as in several other cases. Job satisfaction and the success of the company are uniformly evaluated as high (4–5), without particular comment.

### Product manager 3

| Function | Years |
|---|---|
| n.a. | n.a. |
| Product manager 3, Japanese company* | $2\frac{1}{2}$ |

The manager has four O Levels, no A Levels and an ONC (Ordinary National Certificate) and HNC (unspecified). He was recruited to the firm through an agency, the attractions being profit-and-loss responsibility, sales and purchasing, advertising, and so on—in short total responsibility, plus security and an adequate salary. The career orientation is clear. He works an average seventy hours a week.

The job is not strictly bounded but rules are strictly observed (5). The manager sees himself as 'manager, administrator, controller' and as neither generalist nor specialist but 'successful'. He believes the management team is split equally between generalists and specialists. Job rotation has only been practised in two examples and is not part of an explicit policy. Promotion prospects appear good (4) in the branch and fair (3) outside for both British and Japanese managers—one of the few answers of this type.

The monthly department and work-team meetings are very

useful (5), but information about the branch's plans is moderate (3) and about the company as a whole less good (2). Contact with other departments is fairly close (3). Subordinates' willingness to cooperate is high (5). There are no linguistic or cultural problems and satisfaction with the organisational climate is high (5). The manager's own communication is mostly face to face (70 per cent), followed by 14 per cent on the facsimile machine, 10 per cent written memos, 5 per cent conferences and 1 per cent telephone.

The manager sees the parent company as the dominant influence in decision-making. His own influence ranges between taking the decision himself (5) and being informed before a decision is taken (2). If accurate, this compares favourably with some previous examples. Job satisfaction is fair to high (3–5), with salary and hours of work moderately rated (3). The success of the firm receives the highest rating (5) throughout, except for adaptation to the market (4) and, again, efficiency (3). In general, the success was ascribed to 'flexibility of product, pricing and attitudes'.

### Product manager 4

| Function | Years |
|---|---|
| University, engineering course | 3 |
| Business school, MBA course | 1 |
| n.a. | n.a. |
| Product manager 4, Japanese company* | 6 |

The manager has been a Member of the Institution of Electronic and Radio Engineers and of the Council of Engineering Institutes for six years. He occasionally attends meetings. Recruitment to the company was through an agency and a consultant. The company offered the step into a general sales role, and job security, although the latter was not that important. Salary was moderate.

Definition of the functional area and of managers is not clear but rules are strictly followed (4). The abilities top managers should possess are, 'Organisational behaviour. Ability in all general business disciplines for example, MBA. Record of experience and achievement'. Here the MBA concept in particular does not fit the Japanese approach, business schools or management departments at universities having found little favour among managers in Japan to date—training and socialisation in the company itself being emphasised.

The manager is moderately happy (3) to classify himself as a generalist but is not sure how to classify his colleagues. He considers his British subordinates well qualified (4) but does not have a high opinion (2) of his expatriate colleagues' qualifications. Bearing in mind his own qualifications and his emphasis on the value of an MBA, this may reflect the difference in concepts of 'professionalism', which will be discussed further in the Conclusion at the end of the book.

Training and job rotation in the company are unclear and emphasis is put on the importance of fitting into the organisation, ahead of ability and qualifications. Promotion prospects are evaluated as moderate (3) in the branch and lower (2) outside. For Japanese managers, prospects appear brighter (4) in both places. The manager might consider a move, but only if the salary were appreciably higher and if the career path was well defined, plus other merits which could only be judged at the time. The importance of the individual 'career path', if necessary across organisations, is plain.

Regarding different approaches to work, there are difficulties. However, the manager attempts to explain his case and gain acceptance. The frustration was the number of times one had to explain things. The viewpoint echoes that of sales manager 1, quoted above. Language or cultural difficulties were said to arise on average twice a week. The manager does not find the monthly department meeting particularly useful (2) and considers company information insufficient (2). Contact with other departments and the cooperativeness of subordinates is good (4). The manager's own communication is 44 per cent face to face, 40 per cent telephone, 15 per cent written and 1 per cent conferences. His decision-making is spread between deciding equally with others (4) and no involvement (1). Satisfaction with the organisational climate is moderate (3).

Job satisfaction is moderate (3–4) with one item, job security, very highly rated (5). But the possibility of realising one's potential, opportunities for further training and development and future career prospects are less positively evaluated (2). Company performance is rated below most other respondents. Growth and technology are fairly favourably evaluated (3), but efficiency, motivation and quality of service are poorer (2).

Adaptation to the market and profitability are judged to be the weakest points (1).

### Product manager 5

| Function | Years |
| --- | --- |
| Assistant sales office manager | 2 |
| Sales management trainee* | 1 |
| Sales executive | 3 |
| Area sales manager* | 1 |
| Product manager 5, Japanese company* | 5 |

The manager has two A Levels, an OND in Business Studies and an HND in Marketing. He joined the company after replying to an advertisement in a national newspaper placed by the official organisation PER (Professional and Executive Recruitment). The attractions were career prospects, salary and job security. In his second job he attended an in-house management training course and has subscribed for five and three years, respectively, to two trade magazines.

He sees his role simply as that of manager. Flexibility is regarded as very important in the company. Adherence to rules and procedures is moderate (3). A manager is defined according to the level of his responsibilities. Top managers should possess leadership skills, dedication, conscientiousness and diplomacy.

The manager is content (3) to regard himself as a specialist, in common with 10 per cent of his colleagues. He would consider moving from the company if offered a 30 per cent higher salary elsewhere. He regards his British subordinates as well qualified (4). Job rotation is not practised. Promotion prospects do not appear high (2) for either British or Japanese managers, either in the branch or outside.

The monthly department meetings and the weekly work-team meetings are useful (4). Information about the branch's plans is adequate (3) but is less than adequate about the company as a whole (2). Contact with other departments is limited (2), but the cooperativeness of subordinates is high (5). Language or cultural difficulties rarely crop up and are solved by discussion. The manager's own communication is mainly by telephone (70 per cent), with 15 per cent face to face and 5 per cent each for written memos, conferences, and facsimile and telex. Satisfaction with the climate at work is moderate (3).

The manager sees the parent company in Japan (and then the descending hierarchical levels) as the main influence on decision-making. With the exception of the appointment of his own subordinate (5), his own authority is limited to having his opinion taken into account (3) or to being informed beforehand (2). Job satisfaction is moderate to high (3–4), with only job security securing the highest rating (5) and career prospects being lower (2). The success of the firm is also rated as moderate to good (3–4). 'The development of the company has been mainly product led'.

*Service manager*

| Function | Years |
| --- | --- |
| Apprentice toolmaker/toolmaker | 6 |
| Buyer* | 3 |
| Service administrator* | 5 |
| Production manager* | 7 |
| Service administrator* | 3 |
| Service manager, Japanese company* | $2\frac{1}{2}$ |

The manager has a City and Guilds qualification in production management, having completed his apprenticeship in his first job. This involved attendance at a technical college as well as practical experience. In all his other jobs he has had OJT.

He sees himself as a 'manager/administrator' in a job without definite boundaries but quite high adherence to rules and procedures (4–5). Managers in the company are defined according to department financial control. Top managers should set high standards and exercise control. They should have high ethical standards, flexibility, high professional expertise and knowledge of the departments. Here flexibility stands next to high professional expertise, which some managers, quoted above, might not find completely consistent. It raises the question of what 'professionalism' is. Following the discussion of management and the ROI criterion in the Introduction above, it is suggested here that there are both positive and harmful forms of professionalism, as the word is commonly understood.

The manager sees himself as a specialist, but his view of his colleagues is about the exact opposite of product manager 5 just quoted. In the service manager's view the overwhelming majority of managers in the company (80 per cent) are generalists. He sees his (British) subordinates as fairly well qualified (3–4).

In regard to differing approaches to work, the manager would make his views known but if overruled would carry out the company's wishes. The comment, like those of other managers above, contains the implied recognition that there are differences and that the manager has not been completely won over to the new system; he is making his view known on the basis of his previous working experience and custom and practice in other companies. Satisfaction with the climate at work is low to moderate (2–3). Promotion chances appear low (1–2), either for British or Japanese managers. There is no job rotation.

Departmental monthly meetings and weekly team meetings are considered fairly useful (3–4), but personal satisfaction with them is lower (2–3). Information in the branch is inadequate (2) and also about the company as a whole (1). Contact with other departments and subordinates' cooperation is good (4). Language or cultural problems occur on average once a week and are solved by careful explanation and discussion. Most of the manager's own communication is by telephone (50 per cent), with 25 per cent each for written messages and face to face.

In his view, it is the parent company (followed by the hierarchical levels in descending order) that has the greatest weight in decision-making. Regarding his own decision-making, he asserts that he participates equally in decisions with others in a majority of cases (4). Job satisfaction is moderate, or slightly less (3–2). The job itself and job security are the most positive points (4–5). Salary, salary prospects and conditions of employment are least favourably evaluated (1–2). Quality of products and service and level of technology are rated highest (4) in regard to the company's successes. Growth and adaptation to the market follow (3). But profitability, efficiency and motivation are not so highly rated (2).

*Accounts manager 1*

| Function | Years |
| --- | --- |
| University, economics course | 3 |
| Articled clerk/accountant | 5 |
| Accounts manager, Japanese company* | $1\frac{1}{2}$ |

The manager completed his three-year Articles in his first job and is qualified as a Chartered Accountant. He has subscribed to *Accountancy* for six years. His background may be contrasted with that of the Japanese financial director referred to above.

In his view, the nature of the job is distinct from other functions. However, he is expected to contribute what he may to inform or assist other colleagues. The manager sees himself as an 'administrator/controller', with high compliance (4) with rules and procedures. Managers in the company are defined, by titles, by organisation chart, by location in the office and office furniture. Managers are given a fair amount of autonomy. The perception is of a degree of formal organisation and of characteristic status differences. Top managers should have the ability to perceive problems and objectives which are crucial to the future development of the company, and the administrative ability to design and implement courses of action to solve or to achieve these—which does not sound different from what would be expected in a British company with the usual 'top down' system of delegated authority.

The manager is happy (4) to see himself as a specialist and regards 15 per cent of the management team as belonging in this category. His (British) subordinates are moderately qualified (3). He has some difficulty as an accounting professional, because of very little understanding of his role as accountant and the way the organisational structure is arranged creates unresolved problems and little job satisfaction. At a general level this refers to the differences between the accounting function in Britain and Japan in terms of qualifications, training, job mobility and professional status—interrelated aspects which create a total nexus that it is a serious mistake to split up, since this inevitably leads to interdependent factors being judged out of context. In practice, the manager feels 'severe constraints' on his job, with restricted decision-making (1–3). There is no job rotation in the firm. Promotion prospects appear low (2), although perhaps surprisingly the manager considers the prospects in the company as a whole brighter (4). For Japanese managers the prospects appear to be moderate (3) to bright (4), respectively.

Monthly department meetings and *ad hoc* work-team meetings are considered useful (4–5), although personal satisfaction is lower (2). In contrast to what many managers above reported, information in the branch is considered less adequate (1) than about the company as a whole (3). Contact with other departments is not particularly close (2) and the cooperativeness of subordinates is average (3). Communication problems with expatriates generally arise due to their philosophy with regard to the future of the company. This refers to the crucial issue of how far the branch should be an autonomous company or how far it should be an offshoot of the parent company. The respondent clearly regards this as a more serious issue than the one of language *per se*. Language problems are usually solved with no difficulty or friction. Language can be an important factor, especially at the day-to-day operational level, but it is a fallacy to suppose that if there were no language problems on either side there would be no other problems. The structure of labour markets and careers in the two countries does not depend on language. The manager's own communication is 70 per cent face to face, 25 per cent conferences and 5 per cent written. Satisfaction with the organisational climate is low (1) for reasons already given.

In the light of what has already been said, it is not surprising that job satisfaction is not high. Job security and fringe benefits, and so on, get the highest scores (4). Other aspects are rated as moderate (3), while the job itself, possibility of realising potential and opportunities for further training and development are poorly rated (1). In contrast to the cases of other managers above, the firm does not appear to be as good as others (1), although its success, except for efficiency (2), is favourably evaluated (4–5). The discrepancy is explained by the problems of job and career for an accounting professional.

### Accounts manager 2

| Function | Years |
| --- | --- |
| Accounts manager | 8 |
| Accounts manager, Japanese company* | 5 |

The manager has been a Fellow of the Institute of Chartered Accountants for ten years and an Associate of the Institute of Taxation for eight years. He has subscribed to the journals of these two professional bodies for the same number of years and sometimes attends their meetings.

He sees himself as a specialist and considers all the company's managers to be specialists but does not rate his subordinates' qualifications highly (1). He was recruited through an agency and was anxious to have experience in the company.

The expectations of the organisation are rarely (if at all) defined or communicated to local staff. Communication problems frequently arise, and expatriates largely appear to be insulated from local staff. The manager has the impression that the title of manager is abused and devalued. He himself observes job boundaries strictly but comments that expatriate managers do not. Department and work-team meetings and levels of information are not highly rated (1). Contact with other departments is adequate (3) and the cooperativeness of subordinates good (4). Satisfaction with the organisational climate is low (1). The manager's own communication is 85 per cent face to face, with 5 per cent for telephone, written memos and conferences.

The parent company appears as the main source of decision-making. In this respect the manager's own authority is limited (1), except for the appointment of his direct subordinate (5) and the claim to determine recruitment and selection procedures (5). Job satisfaction is low (1–2) except for job security (5), fringe benefits (4) and friendliness of the working atmosphere (3). As in the case of the other accounts manager, the company does not appear a better one to work for than others (1). With the exception of growth (4) and technology (3), the firm's success is not highly rated (1–2).

*Engineering manager*

| Function | Years |
| --- | --- |
| Trainee tax officer | 2 |
| Shipping and forwarding clerk* | 3 |
| Clerk, civil aviation* | 1 |
| Shipping and forwarding clerk* | 2 |
| Shipping clerk, related Japanese company* | 4 |
| Engineering manager, Japanese company* | 6 |

The manager has several O Levels and took an Open University course in computers and computing. In one of his previous jobs he was a member of the health and safety committee. He had OJT in his first two jobs and in the related Japanese company he took an IBM computer course with reference to stock control. He moved from the one Japanese company to the other after hearing about it from a friend. In the present job he has attended several IBM analyst programmer training courses, lasting between one and five days each. He describes himself as having started in the company as a general dogsbody but is becoming more specialised as a result of training and experience.

He sees himself as a 'computer expert' and is very happy (4) to classify himself as a specialist. In his view, the management team divides equally into generalists and specialists, the latter distinguished by their technical knowledge. But in spite of this specialist emphasis the job is not strictly marked off from others in the company, because the managing director's philosophy is flexibility—a point taken up by few other managers. Apart from the normal contract of employment, rules and procedures are vague, with the significant exception of time-keeping. The observation confirms the strictness of Japanese firms in the UK about time-keeping and attendance that has been referred to elsewhere.[14]

On different work expectations in the firm, the manager's standpoint is that local managers either have to grin and bear it—or leave. The interview revealed the implied recognition of a different approach. Promotion prospects are considered high (4) in the branch but low (2) outside it. For Japanese managers the small size of the branch means that promotion within it is difficult (1), while promotion in Japan looks bright (4). Job rotation is not practised in the branch.

The manager does not attend formally scheduled meetings but is frequently called in by the department manager. He is very satisfied (5) with company information about the branch, but less satisfied with information about the wider organisation (2). Contact with other departments is close (4) and satisfaction with the organisational climate high (4). Language difficulties occur on average once a week and are solved by patient repetition and simplifying English. The manager's own communication is predominantly face to face (60 per cent), with 20 per cent for conferences and 10 per cent for telephone and written memos.

The parent company, followed by the descending hierarchical levels, is regarded as the main source of decisions. The manager's own decision-making is limited (1–4). Job satisfaction is high (5–4), although there is some doubt about career prospects (3). The success of the firm is rated as moderate to high (3–4), with motivation rated highest (5). This contrasts with the scores given by the accounts managers.

### Distribution manager

| Function | Years |
|---|---|
| Administration assistant | 8 |
| Import/export clerk* | 8 |
| Import manager* | 1 |
| Shipping manager* | 1 |
| Shipping administrator, Japanese company* | 2 |
| Shipping manager | 2 |
| Distribution manager | 1 |

The manager has five O Levels and has been a Member of the Institute of Physical Distribution Management for two months. He has subscribed to *Trade and Industry* for five years. He joined the firm through an employment agency and was attracted by job security, being without a job at that time. Throughout his working life his training has been OJT.

He sees his role as that of manager, closely following rules and procedures (4). In his view, managers are defined in the firm by job titles. Senior managers should have the qualities of leadership, commanding respect, delegating and communicating. Here 'delegating' again implies delegating authority, on the normal local pattern.

The manager is content (3) to see himself as a specialist but considers 90 per cent of the management team to be generalists. Job rotation is not practised. Promotion prospects are uniformly evaluated as fair (3).

Monthly departmental and weekly team meetings are considered satisfactory (3); as are levels of information. Contact with other departments is close (4–5). Language or cultural difficulties occur on average twice a week and are overcome with patience. Satisfaction with the climate at work is high (4). The manager's own communication consists mainly of using the telephone (60 per cent), with 30 per cent face to face and 10 per cent written memos.

The parent company is considered to be the main decision-maker. The manager's own decision-making is mostly low level (1). Job satisfaction is moderate to high (3–5), though salary and salary prospects are low (2). The firm is seen as much the same to work for as others (3). The company's success is rated moderate to high (3–4), with quality of products and service very high (5).

## Transport manager

| Function | Years |
| --- | --- |
| Electrical/mechanical engineering apprentice | 2 |
| Bank clerk* | 2 |
| Transport clerk* | 2 |
| Transport supervisor* | 2 |
| Transport manager* | 1 |
| Distribution manager* | 5 |
| Distribution manager* | $\frac{1}{2}$ |
| Shipping clerk, Japanese company* | $\frac{1}{2}$ |
| Transport manager | 1 |

The manager has four O Levels and has been an Associate Member of the Chartered Institute of Transport for three years, for which time he has subscribed to the journal *Transport*. In his previous job as distribution manager he took the home study course for the RSA (Royal Society of Arts) Certificate of Professional Competence.

He joined the company to do temporary work as a stop-gap, liked it and applied for a job when another manager left. He sees himself as an 'administrator-controller', with a fairly strictly defined functional area, and is content (3) to classify himself as a specialist. In his view, the management is divided into 60 per cent generalists and 40 per cent specialists. He evaluated his (British) subordinates as fairly well qualified (3). Differences in organisational expectations are a hazard of working in a smaller offshoot of the parent company—you accept it and make the best of it.

There is no rotation of British managers but Japanese managers tend to stay in the UK for two to three years. This is an interesting observation, not made by many managers, though they are aware of the changes in personnel sent by the head office; but the normal term is four to five years. Trainees are sent for shorter periods. Promotion prospects in the branch appear good (4) but lower outside it (3); for Japanese managers the prospects appear brighter (4 and 5, respectively).

Monthly department meetings are considered satisfactory (3–4), but the amount of information available is less favourably evaluated (2). Contact with other departments is fairly close (3), and the cooperativeness of subordinates is high (5). Language or cultural difficulties occur on average ten times a month. Often it is necessary to meet face to face rather than talk on the phone. If a phone conversation becomes difficult, it is best to talk slowly and distinctly or to contact another Japanese employee who can translate. The manager uses the telephone a great deal (60 per cent of communication), followed by written memos (25 per cent), face to face meetings (10 per cent) and conferences (5 per cent). Satisfaction with the climate at work is fair (3).

The top management, and then middle management, are believed to take precedence over the parent company in important decision-making affecting the branch. The manager's own decision-making is limited (1–3). Job satisfaction is moderate to high (3–4), with job security again receiving the highest rating (5), along with the friendliness of the working atmosphere. Only opportunities for further training and development receive a lower rating (2). The success of the firm is viewed as moderate (3), with quality of product and service higher (4).

*Stock controller*

| Function | Years |
| --- | --- |
| University, environmental sciences course | 3 |
| Financial assistant, water authority* | $1\frac{1}{2}$ |
| Assistant accountant, advertising company* | 2 |
| Assistant accountant, Japanese company* | $1\frac{3}{4}$ |
| Stock controller | 2 months |

The first job after university was a stop-gap, without training. In his second job the manager studied accountancy by correspondence and learnt 'computer basics' in the company. In the Japanese company he was helped financially to continue studying accountancy in the evenings and has attended short courses on Customs clearance and other work-related subjects. He plans to take the Chartered Institute of Transport exams.

Recruitment to the company was through an advertisement in a local newspaper. The attractions were salary, nearness to home and the fact that his previous company was shedding staff. In the Japanese company he notes a tight manning policy.

He sees himself as an administrator and controller, working in a very flexible department. In spite of what was said above about the organisational principles and the lack of job descriptions, he describes having a job description with five not very tight items; but there is no standard practice manual and very little (1) adherence to formal rules or procedures. Managers in the company are defined by titles—and some individual offices and secretaries. Top managers should have communication skills, integrity and technical competence.

He sees himself as a generalist administrator, with 60 per cent of managers, including engineers and accountants being specialists. There is no job rotation, and a few managers are sent to Japan for two to three weeks. Otherwise, training in the company typically consists of short courses directly related to the job.

Promotion prospects in the branch appear high (4) and low outside (2). For Japanese managers the prospects appear very bright in the main company (5) and good in the branch (4). The manager identifies a 'technical competence' problem for them in the West in areas like finance.

He does not attend regular meetings, unlike most managers, and feels information is better on the company as a whole (3) than on the branch (2). Contact with other departments is close (4). Most of his communication is by telephone (75 per cent), with 20 per cent face to face and 5 per cent written memos. There is no experience of language or cultural problems, and satisfaction with the organisational climate is high (4). Decision-making is low level to moderate (1–3). Job satisfaction is fair to high (3–4), with job security again (the only point) receiving the highest rating (5). The success of the company is rated as moderate to good (3–4).

*Technical administration supervisor*

| Function | Years |
|---|---|
| n.a. | n.a. |
| Technical administration supervisor, Japanese company* | 2 |

The manager joined the company after replying to an advertisement in a local newspaper, the attractions being 'good working conditions, a good company with good people and products'.

He sees himself as an 'administrator' in a functional area that is not strictly defined, although adherence to rules and procedures is strict (5). He classifies himself as a specialist, along with 90 per cent of management colleagues. Subordinates are well qualified (4). Promotion prospects in the branch appear fair (3) and better

(4) in the company as a whole. In his view, Japanese managers enjoy good prospects (4) in both cases. The parts of the questionnaire referring to training and job rotation were marked 'not known'.

Monthly meetings of work teams and the health and safety committees are considered useful (4). Information on the branch's plans and situation is good (4) and on the company as a whole moderate (3). Contact with other departments is good (4) and the cooperativeness of subordinates fair (3). Language or cultural difficulties occur on average two to three times a week and are overcome 'patiently'. Satisfaction with the organisational climate is high (4). Communication is mostly by telephone (40 per cent), with 30 per cent each for written memos and face to face. The manager's decision-making is mostly limited (1–4). Job satisfaction is high to moderate (4–3). The moderate (3) items are again those concerned with salary and career prospects, but overall the firm appears much better to work for than others (5). The success of the firm is uniformly rated as high (4), with growth and the quality of products and service rated as excellent (5)—a view that reflects a common perception.

### Conclusion

The company has a task-orientated management style related to the marketing of what are generally perceived to be high quality and well-engineered products. It goes without saying that this is a different type of task from that of the precision engineering company, for instance, which is directly engaged in manufacturing in the UK. The latter is a blue-collar and engineering environment, whereas the marketing company is a white-collar and sales, distribution and service environment.

The strategy of both companies is based on growth, particularly of market share, with the need to offset investment costs and to move into profitability being part of the rationale behind the tight manning policy. Use of overtime is another part of this rationale in both cases, and the tables show the extremely long hours worked by some British managers; but other differences between the two organisations can be ascribed to their different respective tasks.

In almost all cases, British managers have been recruited through the typical local channels of newspaper advertisements and employment agencies, specifying the type of experience and expertise required. The career profiles of managers on the sales and marketing side show examples of long experience in a particular field and the accounts managers are typical of local professionals, with qualifications validated by an independent professional body of the sort not common in Japan. Where specific new expertise is required, often with regard to a particular type of product, short in-house training or OJT is provided; but training represents a cost, as can be seen from the case of the manager who was unable to absent himself for a longer external course, and in a newly established, tightly manned operation aiming at breaking into the market and becoming profitable it is to be expected that this cost would be strictly controlled. Almost without exception British managers have stayed in the jobs for which they were recruited.

The managing director's basic philosophy for the company is an extremely clear statement of organisational principles. It is in part a reaction to what are seen as organisational problems related to the normal way of doing things. As such, it has a relevance far beyond one particular organisation and is a generally valid statement of one of the main sets of organisational principles with which this inquiry is concerned. The emphasis on the advantages of flexibility and the disadvantages of tight job descriptions, and accompanying short time horizons, is similar to what is practised in the different field of the precision engineering manufacturing company, even though the 'basic philosophy' is a more explicit statement. The perceived necessity for an explicit statement is itself interesting because in organisations in Japan itself it would not be necessary to make it.

The marketing company is operating in a geographical area where unemployment is not as severe as in the engineering company's case, and in a white-collar labour market where greater mobility is the norm. But the high scores for job security given by managers in response to the questionnaire, the low quitting rate referred to by the personnel manager and the careful screening of applicants through several selection interviews, culminating in an interview with the managing director, suggest that the company is not operating a hire-and-fire policy. Although, once again, there is no formal 'life employment' system or premise, there is a policy of stability on the company's part, which has the perfectly sound rationale referred to above. In these respects, the marketing company shows little difference from the manufacturing company.

What is different, and in local conditions might well be expected to be different, is the absence of a pronounced 'egalitarian' philosophy, of the type in evidence in Japanese Company P1 in Britain described above, for instance. This is due to the basic differences in mobility, individual career orientation and status expectations as between organisations in Britain with a blue-collar workforce, on the one hand, and those with a white-collar workforce, on the other. Replies to questionnaires and the experience of the interviews suggest that identification with the company is stronger in the manufacturing than in the marketing case. Another reason for this may be the greater emphasis put on an 'egalitarian' approach by the former, although this partly begs the question of why the company opted for the strategy in the first place.

It can of course be objected that the question here is to do with managers, not shop-floor employees, but the managers in this case are not a social élite. Their career profiles show that very few have a university degree, and in terms of educational achievement they are markedly behind the Japanese managers. Many have risen to their present positions from jobs as clerks or sales representatives. Most have worked their way up 'from the ranks', and their replies show that many have had very little training in any structured or officially validated sense: they have learned their jobs by experience over the years.

The distinctive characteristics of the management style of the marketing company are rooted in the nature of its task, which is an entrepreneurial one; very different from the production management task in the manufacturing company. This can be seen, for instance, in the reasons that managers gave for joining the firm. Apart from obvious reasons like salary and security, which in the present economic climate could apply to all sectors of employment, it is significant that twenty-one out of twenty-five respondents gave 'other reasons'.

These 'other reasons' are career reasons. Career prospects, the opportunities to be found in an expanding company and the chances of advances in promotion and salary with a company with excellent products and a forward-looking growth-based marketing strategy, head the list. Two managers referred to poor prospects or experiences with previous employers. Taken

## Table 2.1 How managers see themselves in the company

*As generalists:*

Managing director (J)
Financial director (J)
Department manager, engineering (J)
Marketing liaison manager 1 (J)
Marketing liaison manager 3 (J)
Engineering liaison manager 1 (J)
Personnel manager (B)
Sales and marketing manager 1 (B)
Sales and marketing manager 2 (B)
Sales manager 1 (B)
Personnel officer (B)
Area sales manager 1 (B)
Area sales manager 2 (B)
Product manager 1 (B)
Product manager 4 (B)
Stock controller (B)

*As specialists:*

Marketing manager (J)
Marketing liaison manager 2 (J)
Engineering liaison manager 2 (J)
Marketing manager 2 (B)
Technical manager 2 (B)
Product manager 2 (B)
Product manager 5 (B)
Service manager (B)
Accounts manager 1 (B)
Accounts manager 2 (B)
Engineering manager (B)
Distribution manager (B)
Transport manager (B)
Technical administration supervisor (B)

*As both*

Marketing manager 1 (B)
Sales manager 2 (B)
Technical manager 1 (B)

*Others*

Product manager 3 (B) 'No. Successful'.

*Note:* J = Japanese, B = British.

together, the comments in the questionnaires suggest that a high proportion of managers are enterprising 'self-starters', anxious to develop the business and to benefit from developing it by progressing in their own careers. Individual career advancement, rather than 'egalitarianism', or solidarity, is what interests them. While it is hardly necessary to point to the single company careers of the Japanese managers, as revealed in their career profiles, the considerable job mobility revealed by the British managers' career profiles shows their readiness to change companies in pursuit of promotion. Conversely, some of the most frequently expressed worries were concerned with salary and promotion prospects and opportunities for further training and development. The most enthusiastic comment was, 'The company captured my imagination. Very good employers. Total job satisfaction. Makers of top quality products. A company with a tremendous future in the UK and Europe'. The comment implies an entrepreneurial orientation and the expectation of good career prospects for the individual. The managing director also stated in his 'basic philosophy' that teamwork would enable the company to grow and to increase its profitability, which in the end would be to the benefit of individuals. This may or may not appear a paradox, but it shows a recognition that it was necessary to appeal to the individual career orientation.

Tables 2.1 and 2.2 show managers' perceptions of their own functions and those of their colleagues. A comparison of the two tables shows that, unlike in the manufacturing company case, managers divide themselves almost exactly half and half into generalists and specialists. The self-perception again contrasts with that of managers' perceptions of their colleagues. Table 2.2 shows that the majority of managers (eighteen) regard the management team predominantly as specialists, compared to eight who see the team as generalists. One Japanese and two British managers regard the team as split fifty–fifty. Two managers were unable to answer and one avoided the question. Two Japanese managers expressed the view that their compatriots were divided fifty–fifty but had precisely opposite views of how their local colleagues should be classified (70 : 30 and 30 : 70, respectively). It is also significant that the actual percentages given were generally heavier on the specialist side (one 100 per cent, four 90 per cent, etc.). The managing director himself is included in the latter.

**Table 2.2** How managers see the whole management team

| Manager | | As generalists (%) | As specialists (%) |
|---|---|---|---|
| Managing director (J) | | 10 | 90 |
| Financial director (J) | | 2 | 98 |
| Department manager, engineering (J) | | 50 | 50 |
| Marketing manager (J) | | 20 | 80 |
| Marketing liaison manager 1 (J) | (Japanese) | 50 | 50 |
| | (British) | 70 | 30 |
| Marketing liaison manager 2 (J) | (Japanese) | 50 | 50 |
| | (British) | 30 | 70 |
| Marketing liaison manager 3 (J) | | 20 | 80 |
| Engineering liaison manager 1 (J) | | 90 | 10 |
| Engineering liaison manager 2 (J) | | 80 | 20 |
| Personnel manager (B) | | 40 | 60 |
| Marketing manager 1 (B) | | 70 | 30 |
| Marketing manager 2 (B) | | 25 | 75 |
| Sales and marketing manager 1 (B) | | don't know | |
| Sales and marketing manager 2 (B) | | 60 | 40 |
| Sales manager 1 (B) | | 30 | 70 |
| Sales manager 2 (B) | | 30 | 70 |
| Technical manager 1 (B) | | 25 | 75 |
| Technical manager 2 (B) | | 40 | 60 |
| Personnel officer (B) | | n.a. | n.a. |
| Area sales manager 1 (B) | | 30 | 70 |
| Area sales manager 2 (B) | | 75 | 25 |
| Product manager 1 (B) | | 20 | 80 |
| Product manager 2 (B) | | 20 | 80 |
| Product manager 3 (B) | | 50 | 50 |
| Product manager 4 (B) | | don't know | |
| Product manager 5 (B) | | 10 | 90 |
| Service manager (B) | | 80 | 20 |
| Accounts manager 1 (B) | | 15 | 85 |
| Accounts manager 2 (B) | | 0 | 100 |
| Engineering manager (B) | | 50 | 50 |
| Distribution manager (B) | | 90 | 10 |
| Transport manager (B) | | 60 | 40 |
| Stock controller (B) | | 40 | 60 |
| Technical administration supervisor (B) | | 10 | 90 |

*Note*: J = Japanese, B = British.

Three Japanese managers see themselves as specialists, in contrast to six with a generalist self-perception, and the strength of the specialist orientation in the organisation as a whole is clear. It shows that the company is less different in terms of specialisation from what a comparable local organisation would be expected to be. As far as British managers are concerned, it suggests that there has not been a major change in how they see their jobs and careers; though they may of course change their views in the future, depending on policies and practices in the company and on external factors like the state of the labour market and the state of demand.

As far as Japanese managers are concerned, it raises questions about how far Japanese organisations themselves function on a generalist or specialist management basis, which will be returned to in the final conclusion. Once again, a comparison of the career profiles of British and Japanese managers shows higher levels of educational achievement, especially at university, on the Japanese side, and careers which seem to be no less specialised than on the British side. The only significant exception is that of the accountants, where professional qualifications on the British side are linked with the ability of Chartered Accountants to move from one firm to another. In a first-class company in Japan, of the present type, mobility would not be expected either by employer or employee. Familiarity with the particular company's accounting practice would be the decisive factor. Professional qualifications of the British, American or German type would be correspondingly irrelevant in an internal labour market.

At the same time it is clear that the overwhelming specialist orientation above should not be applied to the organisation in a stereotyped manner. In fact fifteen managers regarded work as flexibly organised, while six saw clear boundaries between functional areas that had to be strictly observed. Two managers who asserted that there were clear boundaries also said that teamwork was considered crucial and another referred to the managing director's 'basic philosophy' with the comment that teamwork 'is regarded as very important in our company'. One respondent saw functional boundaries in terms of the different product areas, while another saw cooperation between different specialisms. It is therefore possible that being a competent specialist in a particular area and cooperating flexibly with other management colleagues, in order to attain overall company goals,

Table 2.3  British managers' working hours

| Manager | Hours per week |
| --- | --- |
| Personnel manager | 45 |
| Marketing manager 1 | 48 |
| Marketing manager 2 | 50 |
| Sales and marketing manager 1 | 48 |
| Sales and marketing manager 2 | 50 |
| Sales manager 1 | 52 |
| Sales manager 2 | 72 |
| Technical manager 1 | 35 |
| Technical manager 2 | 50 |
| Personnel officer | 35 |
| Area sales manager 1 | 51 |
| Area sales manager 2 | 50+ |
| Product manager 1 | 50 |
| Product manager 2 | 50 |
| Product manager 3 | 70 |
| Product manager 4 | 55 |
| Product manager 5 | 39 |
| Service manager | 43 |
| Accounts manager 1 | 45 |
| Accounts manager 2 | 60 |
| Engineering manager | 40 |
| Distribution manager | 47 |
| Transport manager | 42 |
| Stock controller | 37 |
| Technical administration supervisor | 47 |

are not as mutually exclusive as some have tended to believe. On aggregate, adherence to rules and procedures was said to be moderate, although individual perceptions ranged between five managers who saw very high compliance (5) to four who saw very little (1).

Table 2.3 shows the hours worked by local managers. When it is considered that the basic working week is thirty-five hours, the amount of overtime put in, even in comparison with the manufacturing company above, is considerable. This suggests that levels of motivation are high. Replies to the effect that motivation in the company was moderate would therefore indicate that this is a perception of the management style rather than of managers' own attitudes. The performance of overtime fits in with individual career motivation.

Training and promotion are two key elements in individual careers. The recruitment of experienced managers, who already possess the required expertise, and the need to keep training costs down, in terms of time as well as money, were mentioned above. Although three managers referred to *ad hoc* changes in other managers' job assignments, the unanimous view was that there was no job rotation for managers in the proper sense of the term. Considering the size of the firm and the recent date of its establishment, this need not cause surprise, even if job rotation has frequently been asserted to be a typically 'Japanese' organisational characteristic.

This unanimity over job rotation contrasts with the mixed view of how a manager in the company was defined, or what it meant to be a manager. Seven respondents, the greatest number to give a clear similar answer, replied 'titles'. Of these, two referred to the responsibility accompanying the title, and three referred to status symbols, such as separate offices. One saw titles as 'very arbitrary—nothing serious'. Another saw them as 'important, not handed out easily—but not an exclusive function in the department'. A different view was that 'the title of manager is abused and devalued'—a comment that reflects the definition of a manager that would be expected by managers in a British or American company. Four managers thought that being a manager in the company meant being in charge of personnel. Three saw it as being in charge of a department or as having responsibility for a function, such as marketing or finance. No fewer than six respondents gave no answer at all, and two referred to the definition as 'vague'. One respondent gave the unequivocal reply 'an achiever', reflecting the entrepreneurial character of the company and its managers already discussed.

But even if they were not agreed on what it meant to be a manager in the company, most managers had a clear idea of the qualities that senior managers should possess. The most frequently mentioned were leadership, communication and organisational skills, technical competence, familiarity with the market, business flair and pursuit of cost effectiveness—qualities which do not differ from what would be expected in a British or American company. There were several references to the ability to delegate, implying the normal system of delegated authority to individual managers rather than the 'Japanese' type of decision by consensus.

Respondents thought that their promotion chances were, on aggregate, no more than moderately good (3-) in the branch and lower outside it. Surprisingly, two British respondents thought their chances would be better in the company as a whole outside the branch, which does not suggest familiarity with staffing policies and practices for overseas operations. Fourteen British managers out of a total of twenty-five stated that they would consider moving to a comparable firm in the same locality if it offered a 30 per cent higher salary. Of these, two emphasised that having 'more autonomy, more clear definitions' and 'a well-defined career path' would be crucial. Two more also referred to the need to weigh up 'the total package' that would be on offer. Five managers stated that they would not consider moving for an increase of less than 50 per cent and four said they would not consider moving for even an increase of 50 per cent. One manager left the question blank and another expressed a readiness to move for an increase of 10 per cent 'if it was a British firm'. Opportunities for further training and development were rated moderate (3) on aggregate. The responses show a normal instrumental interest in the job.

The same question was not put to Japanese managers for two reasons that had become apparent in previous research. The first is that entry to the managerial stream of a first-class company, as in the present case, in Japan is only open to graduates who have passed through a rigorous selection process, based on educational achievement, reports from teachers and professors and the company's own tightly meshed screening and interview process. For the typical applicant who has succeeded in overcoming these considerable obstacles, the whole point is to get a job in a large corporation which offers the best material rewards and career opportunities. This is expressed in the popular Japanese phrase 'to get in the shade of a big tree'.

On the company's side, selectors and interviewers weed out applicants who are not judged to be committed to a 'permanent' career, as well as those who are in any case judged unsuitable. The company does not want to waste resources on job changers from whom it cannot expect a proper return.

Inevitably there are some mistakes on both sides but the

strictness of selection criteria and the time and care that companies put into their relations with guarantors, on whom in Japan there is a heavy obligation, and into the interview and evaluation process demonstrates how seriously such a long-term investment in human resources is taken. Since major corporations in Japan will normally not poach managers from their equals or competitors, it follows that the question of being offered more money elsewhere does not arise. It is therefore pointless to ask it.

The second reason is that in the rare cases where Japanese managers are indeed thinking of leaving of their own accord for genuine reasons, such as to set up their own business, it is not likely that they will divulge this in the process of this type of study. The two reasons underline what was already stated above about the workings of the national recruitment system for managers in Japan and the differences between the Japanese and British environments in terms of labour markets and career structures.

On aggregate, British managers' satisfaction with the regular management, department and work team meetings was quite high (4−), although information about the company's situation and plans was considered less satisfactory (2+). There was some variation in the reported occurrences of language and cultural difficulties, ranging from 'rare' to 'ten times a week', with two to three times a week being characteristic. There was some evidence that language was an underlying problem, but the connotation of words, or the context, would seem to be the more difficult problem. Japanese managers are familiar with 'management by objectives', for example, but although the words are the same, the system does not work in the same way in Japanese organisations as it does in the different business and social environment of the American organisations from which it sprang. Responses clearly showed that the most effective method found of dealing with language or communication problems was patient discussion. One respondent specifically referred to the value of speaking face to face, rather than over the telephone.

On aggregate, job security and fringe benefits, and so on, received the highest rating (4+), followed by satisfaction with the job itself (4−). Future career prospects received the least positive rating (3−), reflecting managers' concerns with their own career paths. The success of the firm was favourably evaluated (3+ to 4−) with growth identified as its strongest point (4+). This underlines managers' perceptions of pursuing their careers in an expanding entrepreneurial company, which they felt had good prospects when they joined.

## Notes

1. The intensity of this competition within such different sectors as electronics, ball bearings, automobiles, banking, trading, and so on, tends to be underestimated by some observers outside Japan. In a talk to a British audience, a Japanese manager with considerable experience of business in Britain and Germany commented that 'Even in the domestic market Japanese companies have to adjust themselves constantly to the needs of the market and keep pace with progress in technology. Otherwise they cannot survive ... I do not think there is such a high degree of competition even in the United States ... Although we have a different voltage and different wavelengths for radio and television, all the electrical appliance manufacturers have long ago built large-scale factories for export to European and other world markets. I wonder whether Japanese manufacturers adjusted themselves to the export market because they had to face competition from Japanese companies. Because Sony did this, National and Hitachi had to do the same, and because Toyota did this, so did Mazda and so on.' See Y. Funaki, 'Japanese management and management training'. The point is well expressed. Anyone who remains sceptical should consider the number of competitors in each of the sectors referred to at the beginning of the note and their aggressive pursuit of market share. Japan has, for example, eleven motor manufacturers. How many do Britain, Germany or even the United States have?

2. Or later for those who have reached director rank by the age of 55; or in an increasing number of companies, 60.

3. It should be pointed out that both types of employment system cut both ways. Japanese managers may not like the local pattern of job changing, but it does make their own recruitment of British managers easier. In Japan itself it has been well known for some time that the system of long-term employment in the major companies has made it difficult for non-Japanese companies to recruit good managers. See, for example, R. J. Ballon (ed.) *Joint Ventures and Japan*.

4. Cf. H. Mintzberg, *The Nature of Managerial Work*.

5. Cf. H. A. Simon, *The New Science of Management Decision*.

6. To take a well-known example, the word 'individualism' in its British social context refers to a positive virtue, expressing the values of self-development, maturity and self-reliance. In the Japanese social context all the connotations of 'individualism' are negative: the

word means nothing more than 'selfishness'. Since the two opposed concepts are closely linked to the respective ideas of the specialist and the generalist, this is not a linguistic quibble but evidence of the deep roots of the two approaches. It would be wrong to explain either British or Japanese types of organisation solely in terms of a stereo-typed, and static, notion of 'culture'; but in practice organisations in any society do not exist in a vacuum apart from that society. Values, whether related to the individual or to the team, respectively, found in the wider society—for example in education—family upbringing and beliefs, are present in business organisations and are at the service of organisation builders. But because society changes (cf. pre-war and post-war Britain and Japan), to see values and power relationships as permanent is to fly in the face of commonsense historical evidence.

7. See P. Doyle et al. *A Comparative Investigation of Japanese Marketing Strategies in the British Market*.

8. Japan has what might be termed an informally organised national recruitment system. Recruitment into the leading companies is only possible, with rare exceptions, directly from either university or school. Only university graduates from the first-rank universities can enter the management stream in first-class companies directly. Lesser companies take graduates from lesser universities. Graduates will not normally enter small enterprises, because the rewards, prospects and status are inferior. The Japanese man (or woman) in the street is familiar with the informal ranking of enterprises, and for that matter universities and other institutions, to a degree that has no parallel in contemporary British life. This recognition motivates parents, especially mothers, to promote their children's educational achievement. The direct link between the latter and the type of company that can be entered, on which all subsequent life chances normally depend, explains why education is such a problem for Japanese posted abroad. The point was referred to above in the context of the duration of such assignments.

9. The method and details of recruitment and the size of the group of graduate entrants reinforce the comment on the national recruitment system in the preceding note.

10. The long hours put in by Japanese managers were commented on by many British respondents, but it is not always simple to measure what is direct task performance and what is social activity related to it. Some of this social activity takes place in the office and some outside, at restaurants or on the golf course. Normally, junior Japanese managers in the UK cannot leave until the senior leaves, or possibly allows them to go first; but although the long hours, extended by a mixture of work and social activity, are obligatory in all but name, it is a moot point how far they should be included under

working hours in the sense of task performance. The hours worked by the firm's British managers are given in Table 2.3 above. The implication of long hours spent in the company for family life, and the values typically associated with it, should hardly need spelling out.

11. Engineers have better salaries and prospects in Japan than they do in Britain. The status and prestige they enjoy is more akin to that of engineers in Germany, Switzerland or Sweden. On the training of engineers in Japan, see *Journal of Japanese Trade and Industry*, September–October 1983.

12. The law in Japan is generally regarded as a last resort, after all attempts to reach a settlement by informal negotiation have failed. As such, it is rarely used and the number of lawyers per head of the population is significantly lower in Japan than it is in the UK, let alone the USA (see A. T. Von Mehren, *Law in Japan: The Legal Order in a Changing Society*). But graduates of university law departments are sought after by business firms, and the Law Department of Tokyo University is well known as a breeding ground for high fliers. Companies engaged in international business grow up their own in-house experts on the British, American (etc.) law of contract. Even if not qualified formally, they are generally far from being amateurs.

13. See, for instance, J. Woronoff, *Japan's Wasted Workers*.

14. M. White and M. H. Trevor, *Under Japanese Management*.


## 2.2 Japanese company M2: precision engineering (Germany)

The company established its first branch in Germany in the middle of the 1960s, and by the end of the 1970s it had set up six more in Europe altogether. It distributes precision engineering products through a tightly organised network. The company has four hierarchical levels, consisting of:

1. Managing director.
2. Director.
3. Manager.
4. Technical expert.

Seven people report directly to the managing director, and there are four vertical spans of control. Depending on the particular department, there are between five and sixteen employees under each first-line supervisor.

The personnel consist of 42.8 per cent German male and 39.5

female employees, with 16.4 per cent Japanese, who occupy line positions. Length of service in the firm is as follows:

| Years | % |
|-------|------|
| 0–5   | 50.8 |
| 6–10  | 28.8 |
| 11–15 | 20.4 |
| 15+   | 0    |

It is roughly estimated that half the managers are aged between 31 and 40, and half between 41 and 50. Employee's qualifications are as follows:

| Qualification | % |
|---------------|-----|
| University | 2.6 |
| Technical (etc.) university | 3–4 |
| Further training | 0 |
| Vocational training | 94 |
| Unqualified | 0 |

Holidays account for thirty days, and the annual sickness rate is 3.4 per cent. In the last three years one top manager left the company voluntarily and one was dismissed. No figures for union membership were available.

General information is distributed to all employees and each person has a copy of the organisation chart. There are job descriptions for workers and ordinary employees, for supervisors and for those in staff positions. There are also descriptions of routine procedures and work and production programmes. The top manager normally works fifty-five hours a week and takes twenty days annual leave. The middle manager works an average fifty hours a week and takes thirty days' annual holiday.

The organisational philosophy and principles are based on these concepts:

1. Participation by everyone.
2. 'Family' consciousness.
3. Feedback to everyone.
4. Maximum integration of individuals into the firm.
5. Communication and motivation.

Personnel policy is based on the principles of good rewards for good work, as little turnover as possible, and that anyone unproductive and likely to upset the team is to be dismissed. In regard to recruitment it was said that 'When I have been in the market long enough, I know everybody. If this is not the case, I would go and look for suitable employees'. Responsibility for the selection of new employees rests with the managing director alone. The selection criteria are: 'What can the applicant demonstrate? What is the sum of his achievements?' No other criteria are valid. The reward system is primarily based on nationally negotiated agreements, with a bonus that depends on the firm's profitability. The remainder is in line with local practice.

Training for managers was said by the top manager to consist of two and a half days every month, and by the middle manager to consist of one day a month in the company. Japanese staff spend approximately ten days a year in the parent company in Japan for training. The selection of staff for training in Japan depends on three criteria. First, the person must be interested in receiving training. Secondly, he must be the person whose task it is to present a new product on the German market. Thirdly, it must be absolutely necessary for him to receive training in Japan.

Job rotation was tried in European branches but failed. Japanese managers are rotated between Japan and the branch approximately every five years. The most important advantages of job rotation are said to be flexibility, the avoidance of bottlenecks and not having to provide managers with temporary assistance. In the field of sales and distribution, job rotation seems to make good sense. The example was given of the warehouse manager who had come to understand the fulfilment of the organisation's task as a whole better by being transferred for a time to other functions.

Promotion is based 100 per cent performance. The promotion chances for German managers were estimated to be very low, but for Japanese managers the chances were said to be very high, both in the branch and in the company as a whole. As regards management discipline, training is used as far as possible. There has only been one dismissal in the last seven years, and none in the last three years. In one case all the European managers spent an entire weekend training a colleague in order to support him in his difficulties. The pension scheme is administered through a special account.

Department managers' meetings and work-group meetings are held once a month. Other groups, such as sales and administration, meet once a fortnight. In contrast to the other German branches described above, it was confirmed for the first time that there was a considerable difference between formal and informal communication. In this case, department managers lunch together every day. Satisfaction with meetings was also higher: the top manager evaluated them at 4.4 and the middle manager at 4 (on the scale of 1 to 5).

The following communication channels are used:

|  | Middle manager (%) | Top manager (%) |
|---|---|---|
| Telephone | 20 | 15 |
| Written messages/notes | 20 | 10 |
| Face to face | 50 | 25 |
| Conferences | 10 | 25 |
| Others (incl. computer) | 0 | 25 |

A formally organised suggestion scheme had been established in the past, but it is no longer in use. The situation in regard to suggestions is considered satisfactory: the important thing is to meet annual targets.

The top manager and the middle manager gave different evaluations of the weight of the respective hierarchical levels in decision-making affecting the branch:

|  | Middle manager (ranking) | Top manager (ranking) |
|---|---|---|
| Parent company | 2 | 3 |
| Top management | 1 | 1 |
| Middle management | 3 | 2 |
| Works council | 5 | 5 |
| Staff or administrative departments | 4 | 4 |

Individual decision-making showed a degree of integration into decision-making processes. The top manager scored 3.9 and the middle manager 3.3.

The top manager sees himself as a generalist and is neither

happy nor unhappy about it. The middle manager sees himself as a specialist and is happy about it. The top manager sees between 60 and 70 per cent of management colleagues as generalists, but the middle manager sees no more than 34 per cent in this category. The top manager evaluates the work climate at 4.2 (on the scale of 1 to 5) and the middle manager at 3.8, and the employer–employee relationship was said to be a very cooperative one. The top manager evaluated the success of the firm at 4.6—almost at the top of the scale.

### Conclusion

The company provided the first example of a top manager who stated that he used the computer as a means of information. Both the company's internal meetings and its degree of success were very high evaluated, and the company showed an extremely high performance level; as demanded by the top management. This success seems to demonstrate that information as a motivating factor has proved itself in practice.

## 2.3 Japanese company M3: precision products (Germany)

At the end of the 1960s an import–export firm made contact with the present branch's parent company in Japan, and at the end of the 1970s it received the concession for the distribution of the company's products. When it became impossible for the import–export firm to continue, on financial grounds, the Japanese parent company took over the German operation and established a branch. The latter started trading in the first half of the 1970s.

There are five hierarchical levels (the English terms are used):

1. President.
2. Department manager.
3. Group leader.
4. Foreman.
5. Employee.

The vertical spans of control consist of four to five levels. Nine people report directly to the managing director. Depending on the department, between five and ten employees are under the

first line of management. The personnel consist of 72.9 per cent
male and 22.8 per cent female employees, with 2.2 per cent
Japanese staff. Length of service in the firm is as follows:

| Years | % |
|-------|-----|
| 0–5   | 58 |
| 6–10  | 31 |
| 11–15 | 10 |
| 15+   | 1 |

The age distribution of the management is:

| Age   | % |
|-------|-----|
| 21–30 | 35 |
| 31–40 | 30 |
| 41–50 | 26 |
| 51–60 | 8 |
| 60+   | 1 |

It was roughly estimated that 1 per cent of staff were university
graduates and that a further 10 per cent were graduates of a
technical or other commercial etc. university.

Absence is accounted for by an average 22.4 days annual leave
and a sickness rate of 4.6 per cent. In the last three years three
senior managers and four middle managers have left the firm.
Thirty per cent of production workers and 20 per cent of office
staff are union members. According to the formal organisation,
general information is communicated to all employees but
specific information is only passed to department managers, and
the organisation chart is only available to the general manager.
Job descriptions are only for ordinary workers and employees.
The senior manager interviewed works an average of sixty hours
a week and takes two weeks holiday a year.

The organisation's philosophy has not yet been worked out and
the company's plan and its marketing philosophy must be set out
in the near future. In detail, the organisation has three principles.
The first is to have a large number of satisfied customers; which
will in turn produce satisfied retailers. These two principles will
then have a direct effect on the manufacturing company. Three
aspects are considered crucial for the development of the

company. They are product development, the development of the dealer network and the training of sales and technical staff.

Personnel policy is similar to that of the other German operations described above. Staff are only recruited when absolutely necessary; there is a six months probation period; and special training and language courses are available. For quick feedback, monthly and annual production and sales statistics are given to employees by their respective superiors.

Recruitment is based on the two main concepts of technical knowledge and education level. Several interviews are held—first with the personnel manager and then a second interview to allow more in-depth observation. For more senior management posts interviews are held with the German and the Japanese top manager. The phrase 'He is the best person in relation to our group in the company', means that the relationship as a whole is considered and not just the individual, abstracted from his social context. There are no intelligence or knowledge tests, although both factors are taken into consideration. When people are recruited externally, recruitment agencies are used. The final decision is made by the president in consultation with the personnel manager. The criterion for selecting the successful applicant is that he is 'of high calibre', a criterion that refers to job-specific as well as personal competence. After an applicant joins the firm, he or she is observed for the first four or five months, after which another interview is held.

The reward system is primarily based on individual performance and the basic minimum negotiated with the trade union. Beyond this there is an extra increment, paid because the company is conscious of its position as a foreign and as a small firm. In certain cases a bonus is paid at the end of the year depending on company profitability.

Training largely consists of language courses. There are three-day seminars for department managers and special courses for ordinary workers and employees. Japanese staff are sent to Japan about twice a year for training lasting two weeks. The top management decides who shall attend which type of course. A good knowledge of English and good motivation are preconditions. Training can serve as a kind of reward for employees who 'work well', and there is also the hope that it will lead to increased output. There is no job rotation in the German branch.

Promotion depends 95 per cent on performance and greatly

differs in this respect from the salary structure in the parent company in Japan. As regards management discipline, training is normally used if a manager does not come up to expectations. There is no pension provision beyond what is statutorily laid down. Formally organised communication consists of monthly meetings for department managers. Work groups meet as and when necessary and other meetings are held without any fixed schedule. The subjective degree of satisfaction with meetings and communication in the company scored an average of 3.1.

The various types of communication are used as follows:

| Means | % |
| --- | --- |
| Telephone | 10 |
| Written messages/notes | 10 |
| Face to face | 60 |
| Conferences | 20 |
| Others | 0 |

There is no formally organised suggestions scheme.

According to the senior manager interviewed, major decisions affecting the branch involve the different hierarchical levels in the following order:

| Level | Ranking |
| --- | --- |
| Parent company | 3 |
| Top management | 1 |
| Middle management | 2 |
| Works council | 4 |
| Staff or administrative departments | 5 |

Individual decision-making scored an average 3.5 on a scale of 1 to 5.

The senior manager interviewed sees himself as a generalist and is fairly satisfied to be one. He sees his management team as 20 per cent generalists and 80 per cent specialists. The work climate scored an average of 3.9, although no information was available about the employer–employee relationship. As an average, the success of the firm was rated as 3.4 out of 5.

## Conclusion

The company maintains very close contact with its parent in Japan, and the president flies back three or four times a year. He telephones the head office about twice a week and the same goes for the middle management. Every day a Japanese manager specifically responsible for coordination telephones Japan—and this ensures a fast reaction on the part of the head office management.

Apart from job descriptions for ordinary workers and employees, there are no written company documents. A one-year and a five-year business plan were mentioned with reference to turnover but no further specific details were alluded to. It was not possible to identify any overall company philosophy, a lack which the top management were aware of and which they will probably take steps to rectify in the near future.

## 2.4 Japanese company M4: engineering (Germany)

The company established a branch in Germany in the mid-1980s with the aim of increasing its market coverage and supporting direct customer sales. The service network is intended to be closely connected with the sales network, and particular emphasis is placed on prompt service to the customer.

The three hierarchical levels in the company are:

1. Managing director.
2. General manager and controller.
3. Employee.

As far as the spans of control are concerned, two people report directly to the managing director, and there are three levels between the top and bottom levels of the organisation. The personnel consists of 70 per cent male and 30 per cent female employees. Japanese staff account for 10 per cent of the total personnel, but because operations have only recently started it is not possible to give a definitive figure for the numbers employed.

The age distribution of the management is:

| Age | % |
|-----|-----|
| 21–30 | 10 |
| 31–40 | 40 |
| 41–50 | 50 |
| 51–60 | 0 |

Employees' qualifications are as follows:

| Qualification | % |
|---------------|-----|
| University | 10 |
| Technical (etc.) university | 20 |
| Further training, such as '*Meister*' technician or economist (*Fachwirt*) | 30 |
| Vocational training | 40 |
| Unqualified | 0 |

No figures for absence or turnover were available and union membership was probably low.

Each employee has a copy of the organisation chart and receives all general company information. Each person has a job description, which is fixed for each person. The senior manager interviewed works about fifty hours a week and has taken three days' leave since August 1983.

The organisation's philosophy and principles can only be deduced from a number of statements that were made. In the German, as in other European branches, there should only be nationals of the country concerned working. Direct sales to the customer should guarantee a quicker turnover and the service network should be extended as far as possible. Management's aims should be closely adapted to the German market. As far as in-house relations are concerned, there should be swift communication between the top and the middle management.

Personnel policy is based on three fundamental concepts. The first is, what is the best way to cooperate at any given time? The second is performance, and the third is that there is no 'lifetime' employment. Recruitment to the company is either through newspaper advertising or through internal announcement of a vacancy. The personnel manager interviews applicants once or twice. Responsibility for selection rests with the department manager concerned, and for senior positions with the general manager. The reward system is primarily based on adaptation to local salary structures, plus a general increment which makes the company's salary levels slightly higher than those of its competitors. In addition, a year-end bonus based on the profitability of the firm can be counted on.

Training only takes place in Japan, for periods of three weeks each, from which German managers are excluded. There is no job rotation in the branch. Promotion is based 100 per cent on performance. If a manager fails to live up to expectations, he may be transferred internally, or retrained for a different function: or he may have to brush up his knowledge. There is no company pension scheme in addition to the normal statutory one.

Department managers meet regularly once a week and work groups were said to meet 'very often'. Frequent communication between top and middle managers and between managers and their subordinates takes place daily. The subjective perception of communication in the company gave it the high average score of 4.3 out of 5. The different means of communication are used as follows:

| Means | % |
| --- | --- |
| Telephone | 17.5 |
| Written messages/notes | 50.0 |
| Conferences | 15.0 |
| Others | 0 |

There is no formal suggestions scheme.

The respective weight of the different hierarchical levels in making decisions that affect the branch are as follows:

| Level | Ranking |
| --- | --- |
| Parent company | 3 |
| Top management | 1 |
| Middle management | 2 |
| Works council | 4 |
| Staff or administrative departments | 0 |

The senior manager interviewed sees himself predominantly as a generalist, or, to put it more precisely, as 70 per cent generalist and 30 per cent specialist: a perception that he is neither happy nor unhappy with. He estimates that 10 per cent of the managers subordinate to him are generalists and 90 per cent specialists. The work climate scored 3.6 out of 5. Little can be said about the employer–employee relationship, as the degree of unionisation is low; but the success of the firm is very highly evaluated (4.5).

## Conclusion

The organisatioi s ordered in strictly hierarchical fashion and the decision-making process rarely seems to involve middle managers. However, great emphasis is placed on quick communication, and the head office in Japan is telephoned every other day, even though the influence of the parent company on decisions affecting the branch is said to be no higher than 10 per cent (third place among the hierarchical levels listed above).

The fact that each employee has a job description, made out individually for him or her, is in striking contrast to the other German branches described above.

# 3. Commercial and financial sector

## 3.1 Japanese company C1: general trading (Britain)

Japanese commercial and financial companies opened branches in the City of London up to twenty years before the establishment of the first Japanese manufacturing operations in Britain. As an international financial centre, with established institutions and high levels of expertise, the City has attracted some thirty Japanese banks, a similar number of general trading companies and the leading securities and finance companies. For several Japanese commercial and financial companies it is the regional headquarters not only for Europe but also for the Middle East and Africa, for which it functions as the coordinating centre for such important business as plant exports and major construction projects.

A small number of Japanese companies in the City have had a long experience in the UK, and their opening in the 1950s and 1960s has been a re-establishment after the war rather than the beginning of a fresh experience. The first trading company, Mitsui, opened its London branch in 1880 and reopened it after the war in 1957. The forerunner of the Bank of Tokyo opened its branch in 1881 and reopened after the war in 1952. Mitsubishi Trading Company, now Mitsubishi Corporation, opened in 1915. With the growth of the Japanese economy and the consequent loosening of Japanese foreign exchange and other government controls, the City has grown in importance as a centre for the commercial and financial companies.[1]

### Personnel management

The trading company is the same size as the UK electrical marketing company, with something under 200 staff, but is located in the City of London and is in a different type of business. The marketing company's activities relate to a range of products in one area, whereas the major Japanese general trading companies handle all types of products, from steel to textiles and lumber. They engage in commodity trading and play significant roles in organising projects and arranging financial backing. The trading company therefore has a large number of departments dealing with quite separate types of business.

In the context of the generalist/specialist discussion, the trading companies are interesting because they are often held up as a good example of generalist organisation. As managers, they recruit language, economics and arts graduates and assign them to the different business areas. In principle, they should be ready to tackle anything and be ready to be sent anywhere. The major trading companies have a system of branches covering the world and a highly developed communications network, as also became apparent during the German part of the study. This network carries business intelligence from the branches to the headquarters in Japan and strategic policy decisions from the headquarters to the branches. The business of the trading companies in centres like London, Düsseldorf and Amsterdam is more centralised than that of the marketing companies or manufacturers, but the difference is one of degree rather than kind.

The personnel manager of the trading company's London branch is Japanese. He is assisted by a British personnel officer. This is not the unvarying pattern. A number of commercial and financial companies have put personnel affairs, along with general affairs, office administration and other tasks, such as relations with the local authority, legal matters, and so on, in the hands of 'generalist' British personnel managers. The latter are not usually personnel specialists, in the sense that they are not IPM qualified professionals, but several have extremely long service with the company and have 'learned the ropes' by experience on the job. As older, experienced and more senior people, they enjoy a certain position in the eyes of expatriate managers. Many are considered 'loyal', or trusted. Their responsibility is to carry out the broad directives of the Japanese top management, generally through a senior Japanese manager who is appointed to oversee local personnel. As in other companies, Japanese personnel administration is separate. The reasons for this type of arrangement are not difficult to understand. Employment legislation, the contractual employment system, custom and practice, and employee attitudes and expectations in Britain are not what Japanese managers are accustomed to in the normal company environment. It saves time and trouble to engage a local manager familiar with local conditions and to give him a policy to implement. This particularly applies to specific problems, such as unfair dismissal cases, where laws and procedures are unfamiliar to expatriates and where potentially embarrassing direct confrontations between manager and employee can be avoided by deploying an experienced local manager. It is a system of remote control.

In the trading company's case it was not made explicit what the reason for having a Japanese personnel manager for local staff was; although it is possible that his assignment was part of a policy to tighten up the organisation and improve business performance to cope with the recession. Day-to-day problems have in any case been left to the local personnel officer.

The personnel manager's own career and assignment are especially interesting in the light of the present discussion. Although he wanted to work in a business department, he was assigned early in his career to personnel and spent ten years in Japan doing recruitment. He also had experience in other aspects of the personnel function, such as salary administration, assessment, training and promotion. He himself considers ten years in recruitment as an unusually long assignment.

His job in Japan was to evaluate the educational and general background of applicants and to assess their potentiality according to their ability to clear the many entry barriers. The scale of the task can be understood from the number of applicants, about 2,000 university graduates in a normal year, and the number of interviews, five or six per applicant.

For graduate applicants to enter the company's management stream, the first interview was conducted by junior personnel department staff, followed by screening out and an interview in a business department. The third interview was with business department middle management and the fourth with middle management in the personnel department, followed by another screening out. The remaining applicants then went forward to a group discussion, attended by three to four assessors, the main purpose of which was to identify 'leadership qualities'.[2] Lastly, there was an interview with a director of the company, with three to four people from the personnel department, at which the final decision would be reached. The care in vetting applicants for long-term hiring by the company contrasts with normal practice in the British labour market, to which Japanese companies in Britain must accommodate themselves in hiring local managers, and underlines why Japanese and local personnel administration in the UK branches should be a separate responsibility.

The manager was insistent that the questions were the same throughout the graduate recruitment process in Japan. They were aimed, for example, at finding out the applicant's 'intention in the company'. Companies in Japan are well aware that applicants prepare carefully for interviews and that they apply to several companies at the same time, although it is usual practice to accept the first company that makes a job offer after the tests and interviews. The manager asserted that the company was not so interested in what applicants had done. It was interested in more individual things, like their reactions to university life. A company needs many types of characters—not all leaders. Many types of leadership are valuable, but the most valuable type is to pick up power from the team. The company did not like a loud voice, but natural behaviour—then others willingly follow. That was said to be a very good type of leadership. The remark about needing many types of characters, not all leaders, is reminiscent of the English phrase 'horses for courses' and suggests that in spite of the generalist ethos there is already an idea among the selectors of fitting new entrants into suitable positions in the organisation.

The manager stated that the induction training for management stream entrants in Japan was one week. It was followed by assignment to a department and training every day by senior people. This is based on the 'companion system', in which each junior (*kohai*) is allotted to a senior (*sempai*) who is responsible for his training and general development,[3] and who passes on 'the spirit of the company'; in other words, its management philosophy. The manager himself was allotted two to three juniors within the comparatively short time of entering the company of five years. In his view, the personnel department in Japan was important but could only do 20 to 30 per cent of things, such as formulating policies or systems. This left considerable freedom to line departments: a point that will be returned to in the Conclusion at the end of the book.

The personnel manager stated that the top management in Japan were worried about the danger of losing flexibility as companies become too big and the attitude of young people changed. He saw two main aspects in the different approaches to flexibility in Japan and Britain. The first was at the recruitment stage. 'In the UK the *post* is advertised first but in Japan *people* are recruited'; in other words, advertisements in British newspapers or at recruitment agencies are for 'a marketing manager', 'a production engineer' or 'a cost accountant'; while in Japan the recruitment process that he himself described is aimed at recruiting suitable people into the organisation who can then be assigned to specific tasks. The difference reflects the two different hiring patterns, whereby in Britain hiring is theoretically possible at any stage, while in Japan in first-class companies like the trading company it is only possible for graduate applicants at the time of graduation—theoretically and also to a very high degree in practice. The labour markets for British and Japanese managers, respectively, are very different, a fact that has profound implications for managers' attitudes towards their job, their career path and their employer.

The second aspect identified by the personnel manager was in the underlying attitudes towards flexibility. He considered that the sense of the borderline of the job was quite different in Japan from that of European people; in Japan, team play not individual play was liked. Use of the word 'European' suggests that this is seen as a basic difference between the approach in Western European countries as a whole and that prevalent in Japan; it is not restricted to British managers and might be equally applicable to American managers.

From an analytical point of view the two aspects identified refer, first, to the structural factor of the labour market: the contrast between the Japanese national recruitment system, with the preference in the major corporations for recruitment on completion of education, and the atomistic character of the labour market in Britain, with its less regular initial hiring patterns and greater emphasis on previous experience and job-related qualifications.

The remarks about the second aspect—the attitudes towards flexibility—represent the ideological factor (the word is used in the sense of a consistent pattern of beliefs or values). Clearly the two belong together: belief in the individual career being a reflection of labour market realities in a country like the UK just as much as belief in 'team play' is a reflection of the labour market realities in the major corporations in Japan. It is futile to indulge in a chicken-and-egg argument as to which came first, the structure or the ideology. The origins of both types of labour market can be traced in the history of industrial development, although people have disagreed about the Japanese case.[4] At the present time the reality is that the structure and the beliefs and values interact on one another, although on both sides most of the actors are too much part of the situation to analyse it objectively.

Recruitment is different from the starting point, was the personnel manager's view in regard to the two different points of departure from which expatriate and local staff in the London branch start. He had suggested an internal move to several local staff in depressed business departments; some accepted, but some refused. In the UK there is a hiring contract and a detailed job description, so the company had to get the individual employee's agreement if it wanted them to change. But in Japan it would be no problem. The company could order them to move. Local staff were not so flexible. They would ask for more money for additional tasks or changes, while Japanese would be *happy* to have an important job or added responsibility. They would feel they had to work harder to show the general manager etc. that they were highly reliable, even though their salary would not be changed. They had a long-term view. In Japan people would do the job without being asked, and if this led to trouble then the senior manager would decide who should do it. Trading companies must create new areas and get new business; so different sections may compete for the same target—but they couldn't do this if they were strictly demarcated—they couldn't do business on a borderline. But many Japanese employees would like to do more jobs. Some local staff were more flexible than others. When the London branch recruited young local staff it always explained the flexible business system and covering other people's work. If the applicant did not agree, he could not enter. But the manager's impression was many young people would like to have broad experience.

The emphasis on the development of new ideas and new business by encouraging more than one group to work on them is an interesting instrumental reason for what to some people would appear to be duplication, but it is made clear that the senior manager is responsible for stopping this getting out of hand. In an internal labour market of this type, extra work or responsibility is usually a mark of favour, typically followed by upgrading or promotion after the manager has proved himself and there is therefore every reason why Japanese employees should be happy with it. But, like other Japanese managers with sufficient experience in the UK, the personnel manager can see why this may not be the same for local staff, who have 'hiring contracts and a detailed job description'.

His own experience is an interesting one because although he has spent altogether twelve years in personnel, this was not, as it would be expected in the UK, his own choice. While serving the company loyally, he still wants to realise his original ambition of being in sales or buying, not administration, and is cultivating contacts in the business departments. Given the type of business of the trading companies, it is natural that the business departments are the most important—and where the best career chances are generally found.

Japanese managers spend an average of five years in the London branch, to which they are assigned by the head office. This is characteristic of the Japanese companies in the City in general. Local staff are recruited through the usual method of newspaper advertising, with local practice again being followed in the recruitment of junior staff through agencies.

From the personnel manager's remarks above, it is clear that local staff are selected as carefully as possible. While there is no formal long-term employment system, or formal long-term pay structure, for local staff, the details of the selection process suggest that the company is looking for people likely to work flexibly and to stay, provided of course that their performance is satisfactory. This is not necessarily easy in the City, where job opportunities are comparatively good in spite of the recession—and certainly much better than in the old industrial area where the precision-engineering company built its factory, for instance. In the past this has meant that there has been a core of long-serving local staff and a 'floating population' of transients.

## Japanese managers' careers

*Department manager, product area A*

| Function | Years |
| --- | --- |
| University, technical design course | 4 |
| Product area A | 7 |
| Manager, product area A, London | 5 |
| Section manager, product area A | 10 |
| Department manager, product area A, London | ½ |

The manager joined the company straight from university, did the initial week-long induction training and has since then been trained according to the senior–junior system, all according to the prescribed pattern. His university subject is directly relevant to his work, and he has spent his entire company career of over twenty-two years to date in the same field. He sees his development in the company as typical.

Although he has a technical background, he was attracted to the company because he wanted to enter commerce and his expertise has apparently served him well. 'I can work at my pace and insist on my ideas. If I have the capacity and capability, I can take the initiative in a project or anything'. Perhaps not surprisingly, he sees himself as a specialist and points out that there is no one else in the London office who has the same knowledge and experience. Since his arrival in London he has been reading three technical journals related to his business field, paid for by the company. He sees 30 per cent of colleagues as generalists. They include department managers. The 70 per cent who are specialists are those with expertise in a particular product area, such as machinery, ships and aircraft.

He thought the terms 'generalist' and 'specialist' were 'too logical'. A manager had to be professional, and at the same time a flexible generalist. 'But the good football player is not necessarily the best captain'—a remark that expresses a problem in British organisations where the specialist expert, perhaps an engineer for example, is not felt to have the other skills or interests that will make him suitable for general management. Here the manager referred to a big problem of many frustrated people not being promoted according to their expectations. His own career had suffered because of the effects of the recession on his product area.

He explained that some capable people may try to change from a specialist sales area to the president's general staff, for example. They are always thinking of the company structure, and staff in that department know what is going on. They get a broad view. The company always says you have the possibility of promotion— which is explained as a spur to performance. The company's slogan means that you have to get round obstacles, to be flexible. In Japan senior people are always boss. No excuses are accepted! You must do things outside your (normal) job. This is his second assignment to London, but he does not see any change among the local staff in relation to flexibility compared to the first time. In his own job he has no job description and deals with all aspects, whether technical, financial or legal.

He feels that an overseas assignment used to be an advantage for promotion but that this is no longer necessarily the case. What is more significant is the state of the market and the size of the intake that joined the company in the same year.

*Department manager, product area B*

| Function | Years |
| --- | --- |
| University, legal course | 4 |
| Product area B, domestic | $7\frac{1}{2}$ |
| Product area B, export | $1\frac{1}{2}$ |
| Product area B, export, overseas | $5\frac{3}{4}$ |
| Product area B, export | $2\frac{1}{2}$ |
| Department manager, product area B, London | 3 |

The manager had been interested in working overseas and therefore thought of either banking or trading. As a student, he had not known so much about the different companies, but he had a friend who had entered this company three years earlier and he also had the (fifty-page) company brochure.

He did the one-week induction training course on basic business, accounting, credit control, and so on. After being assigned to the field in which he has so far spent his entire career in the company, he made two- or three-day visits to plants producing the goods he was to handle. He has done a considerable amount of self study, using books produced in the series with the English initials CSDP (Course of Self Development and Progress). The subjects he covered were law, commerce, labour relations, personnel and finance. He also spent a period as a union committee member, which was a useful experience in the light of his study of labour law.[5] He sees his development in the company as typical.

The manager found the question of generalists and specialists 'difficult'. His job is flexible. Although the career profile appears completely specialised, he said that he was not a specialist, except for the time being, and in a sense he had to be both generalist and specialist—which may sound rather like the kind of ambiguity that local staff who want a clear job definition dislike. In their view, the two concepts would tend to be mutually exclusive at both an intellectual and a practical level.

Generally, he sees top management as generalists and lower-level managers as specialists, which does not seem to be very different from what one would expect in a British organisation. He also sees the Japanese education system, which does not have the British degree of specialisation at A level and university, as a generalist system and infers that there is a carry-over in the approach between the educational system and the company system.[6] On the other hand, he classifies only 5 per cent of managers in the London branch as generalists. They are the branch manager and the department managers; in other words, the senior management team. The overwhelming majority (95 per cent) are specialists.

In his opinion, whether a person is a generalist or a specialist depends on the job he is doing. Trading companies are especially specialised. Manufacturing companies practise more rotation so as to know many sides of the business. Banks require specialised knowledge, but it is all related to money. In this company, the business departments are more specialised than the administrative departments. The company handles many industries, and each has its own way of business and its own commodities. Therefore specialist knowledge is required. *Unless something happens, people don't move to other departments.* This seems quite clear, and consistent with the view of other Japanese managers in the study, with the exception of the assertion that there was more job rotation in manufacturing companies. The assertion falls outside the manager's experience and is in any case unproven.

*Department manager, product area C*

| Function | Years |
| --- | --- |
| University, economics course | 4 |
| Product area C | 9 |
| Assistant section chief, product area C | 1 |
| Department manager, product area C, overseas | 3 |
| Manager, product area C | 1 |
| Department manager, product area C, London | 6 |

The manager entered a trading company because he wanted to go abroad and to do foreign business. His general induction training lasted three days, since which all his training has been OJT. He sees his career in the company, in the same product area for twenty years, as typical of the organisation.

He stated that the job had a boundary but not a very strict one. There was no job description. People had to be involved in everything. He sees himself as a generalist and even though he has specialised for twenty years in the same product area, this area is very wide and deep. He expects to be sent overseas again but does not expect to move out of his product area. Although apparently quite content in his job, he has an enterprising attitude and volunteers the information that he would be prepared to move to another company if there was a good chance.

His view of his colleagues makes an interesting contrast with that of the last manager above. He sees 97 per cent as generalists and 3 per cent as specialists; but the former have special knowledge. In his interpretation, specialists are found in areas such as law, computers and accounts. He sees trading company people basically as generalists, though outsiders regard them as specialists. Manufacturers are more specialised, but trading companies take up any product that is good. For managers there may be one move, for rationalisation or profitability, but two or more would be unusual. The general pattern is always to stay in one department. Local staff are more clear-cut, with clearer job descriptions and so on, but the Japanese try to increase flexibility and stress teamwork. British staff like to put a limit on the job and on working hours. Japanese managers must teach and guide them and must create a good atmosphere and get them involved in the job. As far as management development for Japanese senior managers is concerned, basically they have to learn themselves and develop a sense of wide view, balance, how to manage political and human relations—something that cannot be promoted only on technical grounds.

It is significant that an experienced manager, with what looks like twenty years' specialisation in the same product area, which if he were British would certainly qualify him as a specialist or professional, should put such emphasis on the classic generalist approach. The lack of job rotation and the importance of self study or self-development in the manager's own time are clear. Even the moves that are referred to are said to occur because of 'rationalisation or profitability'; in other words, because of business imperatives which require the company to trim unprofitable departments and to expand those that can make money.

But the manager defines what he sees as the difference between the flexible Japanese system and the 'demarcated' attitude of local staff. It is significant that he refers to 'a limit on the job and on working hours' in the same breath. This clearly shows the connection between the two and that Japanese management regards both as open-ended. It is also interesting that he points out that although 'outsiders regard them as specialists . . . trading company people are basically generalists'. This characteristic is applied to trading company managers as a whole. For senior managers, the need to develop a broad generalist view of the business as a whole, and to develop skill in 'political and human relations' within the organisation, is clear. 'That can't be promoted only on technical grounds'. In other words, to be top management material it is not enough to be expert at a particular job: wide knowledge and the all-important human relations skills are essential. How far this differs from what is normal at general management level in the UK will be discussed in the final Conclusion below.

*Department manager, product area D*

| Function | Years |
| --- | --- |
| University, foreign language course | 4 |
| Product area D | $2\frac{1}{2}$ |
| Product area D, overseas | 3 |
| Product area D | 9 |
| Department manager, product area D, London | $2\frac{1}{4}$ |

The manager entered the company from one of the foreign-language universities, a common source of recruitment for trading companies. In addition to his degree in English and French, he had a first-class qualification in the Japanese abacus—a quick and effective means of calculation until the arrival of pocket calculators. He entered the company because of what he saw as its potential and its entrepreneurial orientation. He claimed that the comany was less bureaucratic than some of its rivals, with correspondingly better chances for junior managers to promote business. He sees himself mainly as an entrepreneur.

Originally he had wanted to enter a different, if related, business field but had stayed in product area D for nearly nineteen years. Once again, he would be classed as a specialist in the British system. He sees his development as typical of the company.

According to his information, new entrants with some accounting skill were assigned to trading departments, while those without were put in the accounting department to acquire it. His own introductory training of one month consisted of management, basic knowledge of trading, accounting and communications, and so on. Over a period of three months the group of about fifty-five new entrants received an average of two training sessions a week in-house. This consisted of instruction in accounting, credit control and financing and occasionally two to three hours of English conversation. The training on the financial side was evidently intended to support managers in business departments; in other words, it was seen as an integral part of the business function of all departments.

The manager's first overseas assignment was to a branch office in the Pacific area, where he was the only manager. The office had been opened because of the area's connection with the product he had been handling, but he was also responsible for selling totally different products.

After recruitment, the different departments in the company apply for the number of new entrants that they require and influence their assignment. Business and administrative departments, rather than the personnel department itself, have the decisive influence. The manager emphasised that some people were transferred to other departments; but being transferred, as the manager in product area C above pointed out, is not the same thing as a job rotation system.

His own job in London is flexibly organised, not least because business such as plant exports require the cooperation of other departments. He found the question of whether he saw himself more as a specialist or as a generalist 'very difficult'. In his view, business needs financial, management and other skills and a knowledge of the geographical territory, and so on. Finally, he decided that he was 35 per cent generalist and 65 per cent specialist, but was not very happy about it (2). He thought Japanese managers wanted to be generalists and specialists as well. He also sees the management team as a whole divided

35 : 65. The company needs specialists for particular types of business.

The remarks again raise questions how far the differences between generalists and specialists in Japanese organisations are semantic, perceptual or real. The issue will be dealt with in the Conclusion at the end of the book.

### Coordination manager

| Function | Years |
| --- | --- |
| University, political science course | 4 |
| Overseas department, corporate planning | 1 |
| Overseas department, international strategic planning | 7 |
| Overseas department, European section | 2 |
| Coordination manager, London | 3 |

The manager wanted to join a trading company and go abroad and applied to more than one company. Like the preceding managers, he felt that the company offered better chances to young managers than some others. He sees his development during thirteen years in the same overall function of corporate planning as typical for the company; but he did not originally want to be assigned to it. He would have preferred a business department.

Initial training consisted of a two days' residential course, where there was general training, group discussion, sports, and so on. The purpose was to get to know the other new entrants to the company. Exceptionally, he was sent on a twelve-week course for simultaneous translators in large organisations, in spite of his university degree not being in languages. He described himself as the first one from the company to attend—and the last. He has subscribed to *The Financial Times* (London) for eight years.

He says he was not conscious of the automatic promotion through the first junior ranks which was based on service, or time with the company. He spent two years as a union official, as part of his management development, and was quick to point out that this was not anti-management. He was responsible for publishing union news sheets and reports on salary negotiations. The union had its left and right wings, although these are relative terms. The main concern of the most left-wing members was apparently job security.

He sees his job in London as a bit of everything, without definite boundaries. It was like being a kind of freelance. Sometimes he tries to make his own barrier so as not to be overloaded. In his job as coordinator he sees himself as a generalist with no particular expertise (which may be too modest). But he knows what everyone is doing and has a little knowledge about *all* the products. The job is half information gathering, including the investigation of new business possibilities, new technology, and so on, and half planning and administration. Although he describes himself as a generalist, referring to his generalist staff type of work, he sees 100 per cent of his colleagues as specialists in his terms; in other words, as managers who handle separate product ranges.

He was willing to discuss the problem in more detail and quoted a company training manual that states, 'You must have eyes like a dragonfly to see all areas—and at the same time specialise in a particular business'. This expresses the need to be at the same time both a generalist, with a broad view of the interlocking aspects of the business and its overall strategy, and a specialist, with knowledge of a particular product area that enables the manager to achieve professional levels of achievement. He gave the example of a textile man who must sell trucks to the customer or, for that matter, land for the customer's new premises. In reply to a question about the purposive system of job rotation aimed at producing generalist mangers, which is frequently alleged to be practised by Japanese companies as part of their overall management system, he was dismissive. This was no more than an ideological theory.

In his view, there are three sorts of people who join trading companies. In an intake of 270 new entrants he estimated that there would be:

1. Thirty to forty with parents who have their own firm. They then send their son to learn about a large organisation, returning to the family firm after ten years or so. The son may then, for example, enter manufacturing through a business connection.
2. Two hundred 'company men' who want security and a company career.
3. A small minority aiming to set up their own business after experience in the company—'Small is beautiful'—and they would be working for themselves.

He believed that trading company entrants are keen to go abroad, selling, for example, all over the world. They did not really think that they were going to be in the company in ten or twenty years time. Doubtless this does not apply literally to ambitious high-fliers, but at a time of rapidly changing technology, rapidly changing markets, the rise of keen competitors, such as the NIC's, trade disputes and political instability, it is difficult for company managers to foresee accurately what they may be doing in ten to twenty years time.

In this connection the manager made one crucial point that is highly relevant to the main discussion. In 1975 Ataka & Co., 'Japan's ninth largest trading company at the time and presumably indestructible',[7] was in acute financial difficulty because of a venture in Alaska that had not worked out. Ataka's difficulties, the various merger proposals and its eventual merger with another leading trading company received considerably publicity—the threat of bankruptcy and the fate of Ataka's employees likewise. 'President Komatsu told union leaders that Ataka wanted 1,000 early retirements within three weeks', to reduce the 3,600 staff by about a third. 'By the three-week deadline, 850 employees had applied for early retirement on preferential terms. More than a third of the applicants were over forty, a sign that a substantial number of older employees had decided to abandon ship despite the difficulties many would encounter when finding new jobs. '*No matter what their skills, they would lose all seniority when they moved*'. In fact no more than 1,000 Ataka employees were retained at the time of the merger.[8]

The Japanese writer of the above account draws attention to the problems for company personnel, including managers, in such a situation. In Japanese companies of this type, which would not normally be expected to get into such severe diffi-culty, the premise of long-term employment bears directly on the generalist–specialist issue. When difficulty does occur, it can have a traumatic effect on employees in competing companies as well.

In the present instance, the interviewee asserted that the Ataka case had indeed sent a shockwave through the company and that young people especially thought that you needed expertise in order to survive—you never knew when your turn would come. Slower economic growth in the post oil shock period has serious implications for promotion in Japanese corporations that took in large intakes of managerial trainees in the boom years. But the Ataka case and the words just quoted show that managers regard the possession of specialist expertise as a defence measure. It does not (yet, at any rate) amount to job mobility in the European or American sense. In the manager's opinion, his colleagues are still more amoeba-like than British staff. They tend to stick together in the work group, with diffuse generalised job responsibility.

His point about the importance of having one's own expertise is that, if anything does happen to the company, the possession of expertise and ability may enable the manager to remain with the company after it merges. In the Ataka case, it was only the 1,000 out of 3,600 in this position who 'received equal treatment' or retained their seniority. The rest lost it.

The Japanese writer makes it clear that by itself their expertise did not have the value in the external labour market that would be expected in Britain, Germany or the USA. Mergers, particularly in large Japanese organisations with long-term employment, tend to have the same problems as they do in other countries but in a more acute form. A well-known case was that of Nissan and Prince in 1966.[9]

### Credit manager

| Function | Years |
|---|---|
| University, business economics course | 4 |
| Credit department (for product X) | 6 |
| Credit department (for product Y) | 2 |
| Credit department (for product Z) | 1 |
| Credit department (exports) | $1\frac{1}{2}$ |
| Credit manager, London | $3\frac{3}{4}$ |

The manager joined the company directly from university because he was interested in international trade and finance. At university, his business economics course had included subjects such as decision-making in Japanese and American companies. He sees his development, with eighteen years in the same function, as typical and thought that he would probably stay in credit control and go abroad again.

His initial company training consisted of one week of general and basic knowledge, but with no sports, hiking, and so on. Functional training consisted of thirteen weeks on cost accounting and credit control. As part of his management development, the manager spent one year as a union official at one of the company's branch offices. This assignment was 'half voluntary'. It took approximately half of the manager's working time, and he found it useful for management development and for seeing the employee viewpoint. He pointed out that, because there was one union for the whole company, the union was less powerful in the branch than at the head office. His duties consisted of negotiations with the latter as well as at branch level.

The job in London has a boundary, but is not strictly marked off. The manager sees himself as a specialist, along with 40 per cent of management colleagues in the branch. He sees trading as split between generalists and specialists. The former cover such areas as steel, textiles, chemicals and general merchandise. The latter cover electronics, building and specific product areas in some of the former categories. Greasy wool was mentioned as a particular example of a highly specialised area, which had resulted in one manager being assigned to Australia for over ten years—an exceptionally long overseas posting in the same place. In the administrative departments, legal work, credit control, auditing and accounting were mentioned as specialist areas, giving the impression that in trading companies specialists were more to be found in the administrative or 'support' departments than in the business departments. It was also pointed out that managers become more generalised as they are promoted, which is not so dissimilar to what happens elsewhere in Europe or America.

Like two other managers already referred to, the manager had originally wanted to be assigned to a different department. Like the personel manager, he had wanted to be assigned to a business, not an administrative, department. He stated that new entrants were able to express either a broad or a narrow preference but that less than half got their preference, and his own request had been unsuccessful. This was because, as already mentioned by another Japanese manager above, the different departments put in their demands for staff. Personnel were then allocated on the basis of consultation, or negotiations, between the personnel department and the other departments. Some people might be moved, but this was not intended, because the company got greater efficiency from specialists. With a slow rate of growth and rationalisation there were some changes, resulting in increasing, decreasing or abolishing departments.

If this is the case, is there then any difference between being a specialist in the UK, USA or Germany and in Japan? In this manager's view, Japanese specialists are more flexible and loyal than British specialists. They specialise for the company. Attitudes in the UK are very different, and it is hard to educate local staff in flexibility. Ten per cent of a manager's knowledge is specific to the company, although 90 per cent could be used in other companies. He thought that special skill was important as a marketable insurance against company collapse, as in the Ataka case, but that most people still had to rely on the usual Japanese employment system, which was unlikely to change in the medium term. The emphasis here, exactly as with the last manager above, is on the essentially defensive nature of acquiring specialist expertise against a rainy day. Because different trading companies have to an extent their own organisational forms and procedures, knowledge is less easily transferable than it would be with most British, German or American firms.

From all that has been said, it is obvious that in cases in the trading or other companies where there is an emphasis on a generalist approach, there is a business rationale; it is not just a question of ideology or some so-called cultural trait, even if this is frequently given as an over-generalised explanation. 'Look at the job not only from the inside but also from the outside', was the advice given to the credit manager at an earlier stage in his career. He then quoted the advantage of deliberately leaving, and encouraging, grey areas. 'The area between the steel department and the machinery department, for example, is to be covered by flexibility. We can get new orders here, in the gap'. Cross-fertilisation and the possibility of spotting openings for new orders in a different but related field are seen as valuable. 'In trading companies most employees have flexibility, though credit management is very specialised on a particular product area', as the manager's own career profile amply demonstrates. Because the London branch is smaller than the one in Japan, his job is not as specialised here. He has to deal with all sorts of related queries from the trading departments, though he has no objection to doing so.

In his view, the organisation had a pyramid structure until the time of the oil crisis and slower economic growth in Japan in the mid-1970s. Now he sees it as diamond-shaped, with fewer entrants and a bulge in the middle. In this context the number of people specialised in his function who can be sent overseas is an important determinant of job assignments. There is pressure on the hierarchical level in the bulge of the diamond.

In his opinion there is a possibility that two types of manager might develop: the 'home-employed type' and the 'overseas-employed type'. The latter may represent a considerable training investment for the company, and it may be more cost-effective to reassign such managers abroad. This would increase the tendency towards specialisation. It would also have other serious consequences for Japanese organisations, given that the unity of the management team is a major organisational principle. In view of career and family problems, such as that of children's education already referred to above, it is interesting to speculate on how many Japanese managers would in any case by happy to be assigned abroad for long periods, some quite prominent examples notwithstanding. These speculations fall outside the scope of the present study, but they do underline how important the organisational principles are with which the generalist–specialist issue is connected. But in the present case the view was that managers needed both speciality and generality for promotion.

*Department manager, product area E*

| Function | Years |
| --- | --- |
| University, economics course | 4 |
| Product area E | 6 |
| Department manager, product area E, London | 6 |

There were five people in the manager's class at university who wanted to join a big trading company, and it was decided that he should join this particular company. The students knew that each trading house would accept one person from the class. The manager attended one of the top universities, and his remarks provide further insight into the type of recruiting links that exist between the major companies and universities.

He says he missed the company's induction training, because of severe disturbances at the university which caused the course to finish late, but that he was always training. While they were doing business, employees were always learning; but there was no special training. He sees his development, with twelve years in the same function, as typical and finds nothing unusual in people staying ten to fifteen years in the same department. In his view, job changes are *ad hoc*, depending on the state of the market.

The generalist–specialist issue is 'a difficult question'. He is quite happy (4) to see himself as a specialist but the job itself is wide. It involves purchasing, selling, shipping, payment and banking. In Japan employees had to know all sides of the business. He regards 20 per cent of managers in the branch as generalists. They are principally the senior executives. The specialists, who make up the remaining 80 per cent, include all the British managers. In this context he notes that job changing, between firms, is their normal pattern. He pointed out that while in Japan it was necessary to be good friends with the customers and invite them out very often, in the UK, business was on less of a personal basis. The comment puts the different way of doing business into perspective: job changing, and a more purely contractual approach to business, make it difficult to cultivate long-term business relations on a Japanese model, which aim at establishing a certain level of trust. Trust is intangible, and defined differently in Britain and Japan, for instance, but it can be crucial. The manager of a Japanese firm in Britain that wanted to enter into a particular deal with a British firm was in a quandary. 'I know you and trust you. I will still be with my company in ten or fifteen years time, but where will you be?'

*Department manager, product area F*

| Function | Years |
|---|---|
| University, legal course | 4 |
| Product area F, imports | 10 |
| Department manager, product area F, exports, London | 3 |

The manager wanted to join an international trading company and believed that this company offered more independent scope than others. He had six days' induction training, after which there was continual OJT. New company entrants were supposed to do self study, but working hours were too long.

The manager had thought there was job rotation but found actually that there was not. Staff had to have a close connection with the customer and be competent in one field. They had to keep the connection with the customer as both progressed through the company ranks. When he returns to Japan he expects to change places with a manager in the same department who will then be assigned to the London branch. In his view, the change of people is not continuous, but the organisation is continuous. It is like a family organisation. The reference is to 'presumed perpetuity', one of the distinguishing characteristics of corporations,[10] especially in Japan, where corporations tend to be viewed as organic bodies rather than as man-made.[11]

The manager sees himself more as a specialist, along with 60 per cent of managers in the London branch. It was explained to him during his first six days in the company about specialists and generalists. Specialists work in the business departments. Generalists in the legal, personnel, accounting and foreign-exchange departments. In this definition, specialists are line managers; generalists are in the staff departments. The definition does not quite tally with those given by other departments but it will be remembered that the personnel manager himself and others were keen to work, not in the staff, administrative or 'support' departments, but in a business department. They saw this as the real function of the trading company; and the one with the greatest prestige and best career opportunities, although some administrative managers might disagree.

The manager commented that the Ataka case had caused a considerable motivation problem and that the post-war baby boom had had an effect on the seniority aspect of the promotion system. This factor, together with slower economic growth, meant that, in his view, the first criterion for promotion was potential for the future, and the second was age. By 'potential for the future' was meant a wide view, human relations skills and leadership qualities.

He emphasised that the general manager did general work but is promoted from a specific department. He has been through the section chief and department manager stages, and so on. The latter includes the development of subordinates and how to use section chiefs. His major concern is the company; his own department is second. Then he may become a director, and so on. In his development, continual OJT and self-motivation were said to be crucial.

The manager defined rank as the number of years service in the company. Titles may reflect the actual function performed but status may be different. Sometimes there might be intentional confusion of titles; particularly during the period of slower growth after the oil crisis. The remark underlines some of the problems in coming to grips with organisational reality, not just with what is on the organisation chart or a manager's business card.

The manager had obviously thought a great deal about the differences between British and Japanese career patterns and organisational styles during his three years in London. He and his compatriots had to stay in one company, he believed. For Japanese, belonging to the company was their entire life. Local staff devoted part of their life to the company, and there was a different approach to overtime. Local staff were more specialised and developed their own careers. Some, however, were more generalist, in this particular firm, due to the company's influence. The manager had expected people locally to be narrower, but it was not so much of a problem. British specialists and Japanese were the same, in his view, but the British were more mobile.

The manager also referred to another important consideration for Japanese companies in the City that employed local staff: cost. He thought it would cost the company a lot to employ a qualified metals dealer, for instance—a problem that would hardly arise in Japan. In other words, part of a policy of keeping wage costs down in order to improve profitability may be to prefer hiring generalists to specialists in the City, except where absolutely necessary. The latter case would include British foreign-exchange professionals in Japanese banks, for example, where the consequences of employing amateurs could be disastrous.

The manager stated that competition for promotion is generally keener in companies in Japan than in British companies, a proposition that many would agree with. Managerial trainees in a Japanese company who belong to the same annual intake all start at the same point; and the majority know that they must make their careers in the same company. This was 'the survival of the fittest'. By contrast, the manager saw British managers joining the firms as specialists who expected promotion within their specialism and who could change companies in pursuit of promotion. This makes them less flexible, or more fixed, and also gives them an easier life which is less competitive. Conversations with many other Japanese managers in different types of companies in Britain expressed the same basic ideas. As a generalisation, it can be claimed that career competition in Japanese companies is often fiercer than in comparable British companies; while competition between companies in almost all sectors is harder than in the UK, or USA—as the examples of automobiles, electronics, bearings, trading, banking and insurance testify.

Having stressed that Japanese managers, especially those in business departments and those below senior management level, were specialists, the manager then emphasised the importance of another fundamental organisational principle. This was coordination between the specialisms, a problem frequently discussed in British, American and other organisations.

*Finance manager*

| Function | Years |
|---|---|
| University, economics course | 4 |
| Cashiers section | 1 |
| Export documents credit section | 2 |
| Import bills section | $\frac{1}{2}$ |
| Finance department | $1\frac{1}{2}$ |
| International finance section | 2 |
| Assistant manager, accounts section, London | $3\frac{1}{2}$ |
| Finance manager, London | $\frac{1}{2}$ |

The manager had wanted to enter a trading company in order to work abroad and had been attracted by the company's profitability. Unlike some managers, he was in the department of his choice, having volunteered for it before entering the company. He described this as a very rare occurrence.

His general orientation training included a run, hike, and so on, and lasted two weeks.[12] After that there had been some OJT and self study. He expects to return to the same department when he is assigned to Japan again. Rotation would be unusual. Staff normally stay in one area. The career profile shows ten years spent covering various aspects of the same area: finance. The time spent in the export documents credit section and the import bills section was as a member of 'the foreign-exchange finance team'.

The boundary of the job in the London branch is quite clear, but although the manager sees himself as a generalist, he would like to be a specialist. This is because of his belief that even if a company goes bankrupt, specialists can still be employed. He stated that Ataka specialists were accepted by the other company, but not generalists. In the past, Japanese trading companies could make a profit, but they are now becoming increasingly specialised. Profit is in the specialised areas. He sees 60 per cent of the management team as generalists. These include the business department managers who have a wide range, but not in depth. The 40 per cent who are specialists include managers in commodity trading, where familiarity with the market, individual judgement and speed are essential, and those in financial areas such as the bond market and foreign-exchange dealing.

Like the credit manager above, he saw a difference between Japanese and British specialists. His opinion was that Japanese specialists are still flexible, but British specialists are not so flexible. In his view, there was no formal management development system leading to general management. Personality and characteristics such as flexibility and leadership were described as dominant. Contacts and internal politics would also play a role. The remarks underline what was already said above about the harmful nature of narrow conceptions of 'professionalism' often met within the UK.

The interview again drew attention to the variety of definitions of 'generalist' and 'specialist' among Japanese managers and to the lack of uniformity among their ideas on the subject. This problem, and its significance for the whole study, will be taken up again in the Conclusion at the end of the book.

## British managers' careers

### Personnel officer

| Function | Years |
| --- | --- |
| Office junior, engineering company | 1 |
| Clerk, exports | 5 |
| Clerk, legal firm* | 9 |
| Property manager, insurance company* | 5 |
| Manager, quantity surveying company* | 12 |
| Manager, patent agency* | 2 |
| Office manager, Japanese company* | 4 |
| Personnel officer | 7 |

\* Change of employer.

The manager has had little formal training in previous jobs, but the interview suggested that he had picked up a fair amount informally, particularly in the legal company and the quality surveyor's. In the last job he had informally started to do office administration and had learned a lot by experience.

Recruitment to the company was through a job advertisement. Security and the prospect of a broad job were the main attractions. He had a liking for variety—not doing the same thing all the time, which he saw as characteristic of a Japanese firm, where they rely on you for all sorts of things. As well as being personnel officer, the manager has responsibility for general affairs. He is not a qualified IPM personnel specialist, or 'personnel professional', but conforms to the generalist pattern of British managers assigned to oversee all personnel and general administration, as already discussed in the case of Japanese trading and other companies in London above. This is welcome to the Japanese management. The manager's self-perception is that of 'administrator'.

He is very happy (5) to see himself as a generalist but when asked to say what proportion of the management team were generalists or specialists replied that this was 'a difficult question'. He believed the Japanese went where they were put, not necessarily reflecting their qualifications. They were specialists while they were in London, but they could also be assigned to different types of business without having any previous experience. This is a reference to a small number of cases, also reported in other commercial and financial companies, where Japanese managers in a London branch have been assigned to a product area without previous experience. Where this occurs when there is a longer-serving local assistant manager who has had experience of the business, it inevitably tends to create problems.

The personnel officer had not been to Japan and did not seem to have a clear idea of organisation in the head office. He thought that most British managers in the London branch, such as traders in a specific product area, were specialists but was unable to put a percentage on the respective proportions of generalists and specialists. The manager described the definition of his own job as fairly blurred. Adherence to rules and procedures was moderate (3), except in regard to pay systems, and so on, where it was very high (5).

In the personnel officer's view, managers in the firm were defined as people in charge of sections dealing with trade. Here it is necessary to point out that although the London branch is a major regional centre for Europe, it is small compared to the head office. In terms of size a 'department' in London is equivalent to a 'section' in Japan, which can cause confusion over the meaning of titles. A Japanese manager who has the title of department manager in London is unlikely to have the same title in Japan. Some departments, or sections, in London are inevitably smaller than would normally be expected in the head office. A section in the head office would consist of ten to a dozen people. Regarding top managers, the personnel manager thought that they should have insight into personalities, and the ability to handle people.

Promotion prospects in the branch were not evaluated as very high (2–3) and outside it as low (1). Because the company is so large, the prospects for Japanese managers outside the branch were high (4), although there were few moves within it (1). This description of opposite promotion prospects for the two groups follows that identified by many local managers in this study.

There is no job rotation in the branch, although the personnel officer thought expatriates might be moved after they had returned to Japan. OJT was said to be the main form of training for local staff.

The manager found the quarterly personnel meeting and the joint (expatriate and local) managers meeting every two months fairly useful (3). There is a company news sheet, but levels of information about the company and its plans were not seen as very high (2). Contact with other departments, on personnel matters but not business matters, was high (4), and the cooperativeness of subordinates was favourably evaluated (5). Satisfaction with the climate at work was fair (3).

The manager's own communication was equally divided between telephone, written memos and face-to-face communication. Language was not seen as a serious problem and the difficulties that did arise could be ironed out by discussion. In the manager's view the problem was slightly different. His opinion was that the Japanese had to work themselves in, especially on their first tour, and that there were more personality clashes than cultural clashes.

It is sometimes overlooked that, in spite of the 'company man' style fostered by the large corporations, there can be considerable differences of personality and style between Japanese managers. Speaking to their local subordinates, it is clear that these differences are reflected in the day-to-day running of a department. One

Japanese manager, for example, will put a high priority on speed, while another will put the emphasis on documentation. The differences are a factor in the problem of continuity; in other words, the need for local staff to accustom themselves to a different personality and possible changes in management style approximately every five years, when expatriates are reassigned by the head office. Local staff perceptions of the company are to some extent influenced by what sort of Japanese department manager they have. The assessment system in the company is based on department manager's reports and is not in the hands of the personnel department.

The personnel officer believed that the major decisions affecting the branch were taken jointly by the parent company and the London top management. The levels of middle management and staff or administrative departments were concerned with implementation rather than the decision-making process. If correct, this would mean that control of the London branch was highly centralised and that communication between head office and the London general manager would be close. During this and previous studies, many managers in commercial and financial firms in the City confirmed that there is daily and heavy use of the telephone and telex between London and Japan, although no figures are available. The personnel officer's own decision-making was limited (1–3) and he stated that the appointment of his own subordinate (3) would have to be authorised by the Japanese personnel manager. The greatest influence (5) would be in determining recruitment and selection procedures for junior local staff.

Job satisfaction was fair to high (3–5), with job security and employment conditions topping the list. The lowest rating (2) was for the possibility of realising potentiality and interests. Overall, the company was seen as being about the same as others to work for (3). Not being directly connected with the business side, the personnel officer found it difficult to give an evaluation of the company's business success. He rated quality of service, adaptation to the market and level of technology highest (4). Profitability, growth and motivation were said to be fair (3). Efficiency was not so highly rated (2). This concerned the waste of time in committee decisions, the alleged lack of understanding of the local business climate and the use of unsuitable business methods.

Other problems mentioned were difficulties in 'organising' Japanese managers, which were said to result in phone calls to Japan being missed and inquiries not being followed up; although in the last case there was a suggestion that they might be too small. In common with local generalist personnel or general affairs managers in other Japanese companies in the City, the personnel officer has an open-ended responsibility for helping Japanese managers after their arrival in the UK with housing contracts, car insurance, doctor's appointments, and so on. It was said to be difficult to make these arrangements efficiently, which cost the company time and money.

There was said to be a certain rigidity in company organisation and a reluctance to consider anyone else's ideas. He thought it was amazing that the company worked as well as it did. Most of the Japanese had never been abroad before and were thrown in off the deep end. But the remark was not unmixed with admiration, and he saw the way in which the Japanese were willing to move as a lesson. Local staff were more inflexible. He admired Japanese who were prepared to go anywhere and do anything for the company. Interviews with managers in other companies also suggested that orientation or other training for Japanese managers before going overseas was minimal and reference was made above to the type of career pattern found in large Japanese companies, in contrast to British companies with the background of a more active external labour market.

*Marketing manager, product area G*

| Function | Years |
| --- | --- |
| Clerk, insurance company | $\frac{3}{4}$ |
| National Service* | 2 |
| Trader, product area G, foreign company* | 5 |
| Clerk, product area G, Japanese company* | 7 |
| Assistant manager, product area G | 2 |
| Marketing manager, product area G | 8 |

The manager has five O Levels. During his National Service he did a ten-week technical course in an area unconnected with his present work. He first learnt trading in product area G by OJT in the foreign company and spent two years abroad in the region that the product comes from. In the Japanese company he had OJT as a clerk and as assistant manager. As marketing manager he spent two weeks in the head office in Japan, mostly getting to know people and procedures, but with some lectures. He now visits Japan annually and sits in at *ad hoc* board meetings of a sister company, discussing the strategy for the year.

He does not see his development in the firm as typical. According to him, it is not difficult to get to assistant manager level but to get further requires durability, effort and acceptance of the system. It is not just a job for a whiz kid, who would be frustrated by the bureaucracy. The reference here, and in the personnel officer's case, to what is perceived as rigidity in the system contrasts with the comments of the Japanese managers quoted, several of whom saw the company as more entrepreneurial and as giving greater opportunity to junior staff than some other trading companies. The companies operate global networks, deal in huge sums and employ several thousand people. The task requires formal organisation and systems to monitor profitability, but the local perceptions are evidently something different.

The manager sees trading, based on his twenty-two years' experience in the product area, as the most important part of the job and one whose expertise he should pass on to his juniors. He feels it is important not to fall into the Japanese way. He works with a Japanese liaison manager, who is in constant touch with Japan, and classifies him as a subordinate; though it was not possible to discover whether this was the same from the Japanese management's point of view.

The functional area of the job is not strictly marked off at all but very flexible. Adherence to rules and procedures is moderate (3). He sees people lower down as more involved in bureaucracy, relating to accounts, reports, returns, and so on. The frustration comes because the procedures are not always clear. There are Civil Service type rules for applying for tickets and so on.

As far as local staff are concerned, how managers are defined depends primarily on the general manager. It all depends on the top man, in his view. Though this may to some extent depend on the top manager's outlook and experience, it probably depends a great deal more on the policy that the head office wants him to implement. The problem of how much autonomy general managers of overseas branches in the UK, Germany or elsewhere have is an interesting one. It can vary both between and within sectors. The marketing manager pointed to the centralised organisation of the company. 'This is a Japanese company—we are not a multinational', was the expatriate view quoted.

The manager had joined the company through hearing about it from a friend who was the company's agent in the same overseas area. He had been obliged to change jobs when the previous firm closed down. Job security was important, but he had joined the Japanese company 'as an expedient' and then stayed. During the interview it became plain that he saw himself first and foremost as a trader, with a long experience in the field that provided a solid basis of expertise, and although promotion was important, job security was more important. He did not think the possibility of moving was a serious consideration and pointed out that there were, in any case, no British firms comparable to the trading company that he could move to.

In spite of his specialised experience and expertise in a particular type of trading, he saw himself as more of a generalist, but the job itself is very specialist. Everybody became an expert. The Japanese liked to have one job and one job only. This pattern was said to be imposed on local staff, and the manager himself had been promoted within the same function during his long service with the company. The focus on the 'one job' was also said to be sometimes at the expense of 'the overall view', a statement which, with that below on communication between departments, differs from the conventional wisdom, or the theory of Japanese company organisation.

It might have been expected that more managers, especially British managers, would have questioned the terms 'generalist' and 'specialist'. In fact, this was practically never the case. The marketing manager was one of very few who did so. According to him, the terms used were not very useful or very clear, and he declined to classify the members of the management team as one or the other. In his interpretation, the company theory was to be an expert, but the practice was to take on bits and pieces; in other words, different aspects of a particular job. In his own case, he was involved in the administrative, personnel and legal aspects of the job as well as its main concern, trading; hence the self-perception as a generalist. The personnel department has clear rules regarding company loans and concessions over working hours in case of illness in the family, and so on, but the manager sees it as his responsibility to meet staff individually about any other problem they wish to raise.

The department works well, in spite of what is seen as a rigid environment, and satisfaction with the climate at work is high (4). The manager claims to be quite forceful in pushing his view of how business should be done and asserted that you could make the system work for you but that you had to know when to concede and when to be firm.

Language and the fact that this was definitely a Japanese company, not a multinational, led to some communication problems. The company rule is that all communication should be in English, but this is not always followed. There was an education process on both sides. The solution to language and cultural problems is to try and make allowances and periodically to go out to dinner at a Chinese restaurant and talk things over. Sometimes the differences between the approaches to business problems are irreconcilable. In general, the manager sees older managers as less dogmatic, because they remember the post-war reconstruction period in Japan. Younger managers may only see the Japanese company 'on the up and up'. The British personnel manager in another trading company and other informants made similar comments. The remarks suggest that younger managers are not necessarily more international in outlook, as some supporters of a simplistic notion of 'internationalisation' appear to believe. In practical terms this means that there is likely to be greater emphasis on 'Japanese' organisational principles rather than the reverse. The marketing manager commented that one function of the London branch was to serve as a training ground in international business for Japanese managers, again following the principle of OJT. He did not see that the London experience would otherwise make much difference to them when they were back in the organisation in Japan. Supporters of 'convergence theories' may believe that the increasing pressures of economic interdependence and the spread of an international management style will gradually result in the national origins of the large corporations that operate internationally becoming blurred. The multinational issue is outside the present subject, except insofar as it influences the prevalence of either generalists or specialists in Japanese overseas operations; but the marketing manager's viewpoint is that the company will remain 'Japanese' in the foreseeable future.

He attends the joint management meeting every two months, at which the work of each department is discussed. The meetings are fairly useful (3), but he is personally less satisfied (1). He feels information about the branch is fairly adequate (3), but not about the company as a whole (1).

Contact between departments is limited (1), and they were seen as very isolated—like separate companies. 'Interlopers' are not welcome. Here again, the view expressed runs counter to much of the received wisdom about Japanese organisations. On the other hand, the cooperativeness of subordinates and the flow of information within the department are good (4). Most of the marketing manager's own communication is face to face, with 25 per cent by telephone.

Bearing in mind that the department's business is day-to-day trading, the manager sees the middle management as having a strong influence on decision-making, although he is conscious that the opinion is different from that generally expressed. The parent company and the top management in the branch together plan the company's long-term strategy. His own decision-making is limited (1–3), and he did not know what the payment for staff was. He has no involvement in the assessment of Japanese staff. Organisational changes seldom occur, because everything is laid down. On the determination of working hours, the policy is to work until the job is done. Department people are very loyal to their department.

Promotion prospects in the branch are fair (3) and low outside it (1). The manager sees a problem in assessments being carried out by expatriates who typically stay no longer than five years. For Japanese managers, prospects in the branch are fair (3), and sometimes there is a sudden change if someone is posted away. In the company as a whole, Japanese prospects are higher (4). Some of those in London were felt to be marked for something better— and to be on the ladder. There is no job rotation in the branch.

Job satisfaction is moderate to high (3–4). The promotion that the manager has received has disproved an earlier warning that he would get nowhere, but the rating for further opportunities for training and development is not high (2). Satisfaction with job security is high (4), although he describes the received wisdom about 'lifetime employment' as 'a myth'. If there was a big mistake, the man at the top would be likely to go. He knew of some Japanese who had been eased out of the company into jobs with sub-contractors. The manager is quite happy where he is, in regard to future prospects for instance (3). Working in the firm is on balance about the same as working for others (3), but he has not thought about it for ten years. He is content (3) to put in the time necessary to get the job done, but the long hours are not appreciated by his family (1).

He rates the success of the firm as fair (3) in almost all respects. Motivation is higher (4), partly because he 'loves problems', or a challenge. Quality of service in his own department is high (4) because of its 'professionalism'; for other departments the rating is fair (3), but this is based on hearsay. Once again the departments appear somewhat isolated. The only lower rating (2) is for profitability, where he considers the margins in his own product area are too small. In contrast to the precision engineering company and the electrical marketing company, where growth received enthusiastic comment, it receives a 'don't know' answer in this case.

*Assistant manager, finance*

| Function | Years |
| --- | --- |
| Data processing clerk | $1\frac{1}{2}$ |
| Secretary, sports association* | $\frac{1}{2}$ |
| English teacher, Japan* | 6 |
| Clerk, legal department, Japanese company* | 3 |
| Clerk, credit control department | 3 |
| Clerk, finance department | 1 |
| Assistant manager, finance | 4 |

The manager has five O Levels and one A Level, in law. He had some OJT in his first job and studied the law further by himself as a clerk in the legal department. Among all the managers interviewed during the study, his stay of six years in Japan is exceptional: the vast majority have never been. In his view, his development in the company is not typical, because the majority of local staff only worked in one department, and transfers were unusual. Recruitment to the company was through a contact made with a related firm in Japan. Having lived in Japan and acquired a knowledge of the language, employment in a Japanese firm was a logical step. Job security was also an important reason. Overtime makes the salary attractive but prestige was not a factor. The manager is aware that the company is almost totally unknown in the UK, even though it is among the top nine trading houses in Japan and correspondingly famous.

He sees his role as that of administrator and controller. The job is strictly bounded, although there is a grey area between long-term and short-term contracts. In theory rules have to be strictly observed, but not always in practice; adherence is moderate (3).

Managers in the firm are defined as those who deal with their own customers. Few managers control an entire department. This is related to the small size of departments in the London branch. Top managers should have a good grasp of the business and the state of the market and be able to get information from the staff. They should be decisive. In the context of the present study, the most interesting comment was that they should be able to deal with the political aspects of departmental rivalry. When the question is 'Who should get the business?', the top management must settle it. This refers back to the comment of the Japanese credit manager above, who pointed out that leaving a blurred area between departments would encourage more than one to go after new business. Here the interviewee emphasises the aspect of the top management as the authority that should 'hold the ring' and adjudicate in what in a British context might be termed a 'demarcation dispute'.

The manager is moderately happy (3) to be a specialist in his work, although he feels more of a generalist by inclination—an important recommendation in a Japanese company. He estimates that 20 per cent of the London management are generalists. The 80 per cent who are specialists work for one department over the whole of their working lives. He experiences no conflicts over objectives. If something goes wrong, it may have to be cleared up over the telex, or if there is a failure of communication, it will be discussed with the department concerned, to prevent misunder-standings in the future.

The regular joint management meetings and the daily finance liaison meetings are satisfactory (4) from the manager's personal viewpoint. Information about the branch is good (4) but less good (2) about the company as a whole. Contact with other depart-ments is close (4) and the flow of information downwards good (4). The cooperativeness of subordinates is average (3).

The manager's knowledge of Japanese is exceptional among local staff interviewed, not only in this but also in preceding studies. He uses it for reading telexes and documents from Japan, but there is almost no opportunity to write in Japanese. He personally finds almost no language or cultural difficulties in communicating with the Japanese staff, though he is naturally aware that others do. The English of some expatriates is also said to be poor. The way of solving these difficulties is to explain the other standpoint to both sides and get a compromise. Ninety per cent of the manager's communication is face to face, with 5 per cent each for conferences and written memos.

The impression was that his use of Japanese and his role as an unofficial mediator or 'go-between' is more a piece of individual initiative than part of company policy. A number of Japanese companies in the City do organise subsidised Japanese classes for local staff, but, given the complexity of the written language and the time factor, the classes are peripheral to the business itself. To train company employees, few of whom are linguists, to the point where they could use the language in business would require an immense investment of time and money. Not all expatriates would think this a good idea, and it is unlikely that many staff would have sufficient motivation; but so far there has been little role for the handful of local graduates in Japanese or others who are proficient in either the spoken or the written language.

The manager regarded promotion prospects in the branch as fair (3) and low (1) in the company as a whole. He saw his prospects as good, but in the long term it all depended on him. Since Japanese managers are assigned to the branch by the head office in Japan, it was impossible to know how good their prospects in the branch were—an indication of the centralised control of expatriate personnel. In the company as a whole he regarded Japanese managers' prospects as good (4). In regard to job rotation, there was some between finance and accounts, to understand both sides of the business; otherwise not. The manager himself takes a broad responsibility for staff welfare in his department.

In his view, the important decisions affecting the branch are taken jointly by the head office in Japan and the top Japanese management in London. The remaining influence is wielded by the hierarchical levels in descending order. In his own department his decision-making is divided fifty–fifty between cases where his opinion is taken into account (3) and cases where he participates equally with others (4).

Job satisfaction is high (5) to fair (3). Job security, friendliness of the working atmosphere, the possibility of realising potentiality and interests and employment conditions were most highly rated (5). Conditions were described as very good, particularly after the introduction of a new pension scheme. Physical working conditions, hours of work (fifty-five a week!) and the job itself were rated as fair (3). The only low score (2) was for further opportunities for training and development. There was said to be no comparison possible with working in another firm. As in some other cases, the replies may not appear entirely consistent—for example, the low score for further opportunities for training and development, the moderate score for the job itself and the high score for the possibility of realising potentiality and interests. On the other hand, the manager's remarks about his future prospects during the discussion of promotion referred to above are fairly optimistic. Job security, good conditions of employment, the friendly atmosphere and factors connected with his stay in Japan and knowledge of the language also form part of the positive side of the picture.

The success of the firm was rated as fair to high (3–5). Technology and adaptation to the market were the most highly rated (5), followed by growth, quality of service and profitability (4), though the latter was said to have experienced 'ups and downs'. Efficiency was rated as no more than moderate (3), while motivation received the lowest score (2), reflecting the same score for opportunities for further training and development already mentioned above.

### Assistant manager, accounts

| Function | Years |
| --- | --- |
| University, general degree course | 3 |
| Accounts clerk, Japanese company | 5 |
| Accounts executive | 1 |
| Assistant manager, accounts | 4 |

Before going up to university the manager spent a year working in a hospital for handicapped children. Apart from that, he is the rare case of a British manager in a Japanese company who has not worked for other employers. He had been learning Japanese by himself and happened to see the advertisement in a national newspaper for a job with a Japanese company and applied for it.

As with the assistant manager (finance) just mentioned, the fact of it being a Japanese company was an attraction. The other main points were job security, trust, loyalty and the expected 'family' atmosphere of the organisation—the characteristics popularly ascribed to companies of this type.

During his career with the company, the manager has had no formal training but sees his development as typical of the organisation. He discussed the idea of becoming a chartered accountant or certified accountant but could not get the time off to study and could not study under a chartered accountant. For the last year he has subscribed to *Accountancy Magazine* and remains largely self-taught. In this respect he resembles the Japanese accounts manager already referred to in the marketing company case rather than British accountants, who would normally have a professional qualification. He sometimes worries about not having one and the work itself is specialised. The Japanese, in his view, are generalists but in a British company you would be expected to be a specialist. He thought the Japanese education system was generalised, unlike the British. The idea of being a generalist is so you can fit in and be used in different places. Japanese generalists should be capable of everything!

Like the assistant manager (finance), the manager sees himself to a certain extent as a mediator, or a buffer on the personnel side as he put it. The responsibility of his directly subordinate manager is general accounting work. The Japanese did not like job descriptions and job assessments. They disliked boundaries intensely. Secretaries were pooled. One person's promotion was blocked because of their inflexibility. The Japanese had this idea of being flexible.

Adherence to rules was said to be moderate (3), with a considerable lack of clarity over procedures. Although the company itself has rules, how they were enforced was said to vary between departments. Timekeeping was very strict in accounts but not in all other departments. Managers were seen as people locked into the system. Local managers were said to need an understanding of the Japanese way of doing things, and their outlook should be cooperative. Like his colleague in finance, the manager works long hours, on average fifty-five a week. The holiday entitlement is four weeks, but he normally takes eighteen days. This is because of the need to meet accounting deadlines and because taking too many holidays 'is not liked'.

The manager sees himself as a specialist, in the sense that his entire ten years in the company have been in the same function and that he deals with complexities like VAT; but he is aware that he would not be considered a professional from the outside point of view. He notes that expatriates in accounting are similarly not qualified, although they have university degrees in economics, which would be less normal in an equivalent British case. He sees 100 per cent of the management in the branch as specialists, in spite of the remarks already quoted about the idea of the generalist. According to him, expatriates are not specialised by background but by experience—a principle that could equally well be applied to many of the British managers in the study.

Promotion prospects in the branch do not appear very high (2) and are lower (1) outside it. There is a similar observation to others already quoted on the difference between business and administrative departments in trading companies: he thought the accounts department was a bit looked down on by the business departments. There was also a feeling that the promotion system was too strongly geared to age—not for high fliers. For Japanese managers, promotion prospects are not very highly rated (2), either in the branch or outside it, although this is not a typical judgement. Job rotation is rarely practised. You could not be effective without specialisation. Assessments in the department are carried out jointly by expatriate and local managers and communicated directly to staff.

The manager finds the regular joint management meetings useful (4). Information about the company is adequate (3) and better now that the manager is older and more trusted. Contact with other departments is close (4), and the flow of information downwards within the department good (5). The cooperativeness of subordinates is no more than fair (3). Language and cultural difficulties crop up daily. The manager's solution is to accept certain things, and forget others because you cannot do anything about them—a more pessimistic viewpoint than that of the manager in the preceding case who had been six years in Japan. In spite of these problems, satisfaction with the climate at work is high. The reason is that the Japanese department manager has a genuine open-door policy. Once again, the importance of the department, rather than of the organisation as a whole, is brought out. Seventy per cent of the manager's communication is face to face, with 28 per cent for the telephone and 2 per cent for written memos. At a general level, the main problem with communication is the replacement of expatriate managers approximately every five years. This can lead to the phenomenon of the 'new broom' syndrome, whereby all desks, phones, and so on, have to be moved and the staff have to build up a relationship and become accustomed to a new style. This is seen as taking place in the context of expatriate managers having to report their activities and achievements to the head office.

The manager believes that important decisions originate in the parent company, with the hierarchical levels playing their roles in descending order. With the exception of the authority to appoint his own direct subordinate (5), the manager's decision-making is very limited (1), although his opinion will be taken into account (3) in changes in his own department.

Job satisfaction is varied (2–5). Security and conditions are best (5). Other aspects are fair to good (3–4), except for opportunities for further training and development and physical working conditions (2). The problem is the crowded open-plan office. On balance, the manager sees the company as better to work for than others (4), but because he has not worked in other firms, says that he cannot really make a comparison. Satisfaction with working hours (fifty-five a week) scores high (4) on the manager's part but on the family's part satisfaction is no more than moderate (3).

The success of the firm is judged to be fair to high (3–5), with the exception of efficiency (2), where the view was expressed that the company could be better organised and save costs. Service was actually said to be too generous (5), because customers were 'spoilt'. Profitability was seen as fairly good (3), but the Japanese were more keen on turnover because of the need to compete with the other trading companies. Sometimes a presence is more important than productivity *per se*. Even so, growth was not rated as more than fair (3), although the generally depressed state of the market outside the company must be taken into consideration.

### *Assistant manager, EDPS*

| Function | Years |
| --- | --- |
| Clerk, Law Society | 4 |
| Clerk, accounts department, Japanese company* | $3\frac{1}{2}$ |
| EDPS department | 4 |
| Assistant manager, EDPS | 2 |

The manager has four O Levels and four CSE's. He applied for a job with the company that was advertised by an employment agency as being for an accountant, although he thinks what was really meant was an accounts clerk. He said he was young, not so fussy, and looking for something new at the time and was attracted by the salary and the prospect of job security.

In his first job, with the Law Society, he received no training at all. After entering the Japanese company he began a correspondence course in accounting but did not complete it. He then requested a transfer to the EDPS department, where he felt the prospects were better, although he had no previous experience of EDPS. He attended two to three courses on IBM machines. As assistant manager, he attended further IBM courses, the longest being three days. He does not see his development in the company as typical. He feels the Japanese regard him as very young (he is 30). Since joining the EDPS department he has subscribed to three computer magazines.

He sees his role in the company as a bit of everything—administration, troubleshooting, and so on. The area of the job is quite strictly marked off and compliance with rules and procedures is very high (5). Management titles are not very relevant because people still do the same job as before but he believes the company has adopted a policy of 'localisation' and that this will give better prospects for British staff. British managers, who aspire to senior positions, should get used to it being a Japanese company, different from a British company. They should have spent some time in Japan and speak Japanese. They need a great understanding of Japanese culture and to be patient.

The manager sees himself as a specialist. He considers it would be very difficult to take what has been learned in the company somewhere else; even accounting is very particular. The point underlines the system of in-house learning on the job in Japanese companies, and what is learned may well be company-specific procedures that cannot be transferred straight to a different corporate environment. The image of the 'Hitachi man' or the 'Mitsubishi man' may sometimes be exaggerated, but there can be considerable differences between how things are done in the different companies.[13]

The manager stated that he had 'not heard' of the generalist approach in Japanese companies or among Japanese managers. He did not know the details of other people's jobs but considered that each person had to be specialised in what they were doing. People were assigned to a job and generally stayed there. He quite often disagreed with the way of working, which was described as very frustrating. In the end people gave up. There were set ways and no way of changing them, though some managers would listen. Others did not see the problem.

Present promotion prospects in the branch were not highly rated (2), but like the last manager above, the manager believed that the localisation policy was coming in, which would benefit him. Prospects outside the branch were rated as low (1). He sees the promotion system as 'age related' and not depending so much on what a person knew about the job. The emphasis on age perhaps explains why he thought prospects were not good for Japanese managers either (1). Neither this last point nor the point about the importance of age were typical of other informants' comments. They show the underlying local unfamiliarity with the company's systems, particularly in Japan. The manager stated that there was no job rotation in the London branch.

Satisfaction with the regular joint management meetings was high (4–5) but information about the company and its plans, either in the branch or in the wider context, was felt to be insufficient (1). Contact with other departments was close (5), but this was 'mainly with local staff'. Because of personality problems in the department, satisfaction with the climate at work was very low (1)—an exceptionally low score for the whole study. Reflecting the same difficulties, it was said that there was nothing much you could do about language and cultural problems. The telephone was the main channel for the manager's communication (60 per cent), with 25 per cent was face to face and 15 per cent by written memos.

The manager thought that the parent company was the main source of decisions affecting the branch, followed by the Japanese top management. He was unsure how far the authority of the London general manager extended and thought that he would be likely to communicate with the head office first and get agreement before implementing any major decision.

Job satisfaction varied (2–5). The job itself and conditions of employment received the best rating (5). Job security and opportunities for further training and development were also highly rated (4). Future career prospects were rated as very high (5) if localised, and as fair (3) if the present structure continued.

Salary and the possibility of realising potentiality and interests were rated as fair (3). The lowest scores (2) went to the friendliness of the working atmosphere and to hours of work (sixty a week). The latter had created dissatisfaction at home. Because of the lack of experience of other firms, the manager was unable to say how the company compared with others.

The evaluation of the success of the firm was varied (2–5). The highest rating was for the quality of service of the manager's own department (5)—but he did not know about the company in general. Technical levels in the department and the growth of the company were good (4). Profitability, adaptation to the market and technical standards in other departments were fair (3). The lowest score (2) was again for efficiency; but in spite of internal inefficiencies, he thought the company was achieving very good results.

## Conclusion

As a general trading company, the firm deals with an extremely wide range of products in comparison with either the UK precision engineering company or the electrical marketing company. As one British manager in particular noted, turnover is important, equivalent to the importance of growth in the other two cases.

The City of London environment is different from that of either of the two other companies, and the company is operating in a job market where expertise is expensive. In spite of the recession, there is still considerable confidence in the ability to change jobs in pursuit of earnings and career on the part of younger staff. But two managers referred to older British managers with long service in the company and one interviewee had twenty-two years' service. Four out of the five British managers interviewed worked long hours.

The company is a large white-collar organisation, staffed by Japanese managers who are university graduates and whose tour in London is normally five years. Only one of the British managers interviewed was a graduate, with a general degree, and the level of educational achievement was not high.

Apart from one British manager who had spent six years in Japan and approached the company through a contact, recruitment of local managers was through the usual channels of advertisements and agencies. The advertisements specified the posts that were to be filled. It goes without saying that Japanese managers had been recruited to the company after passing through the fine mesh of the selection process already described. There is no formal 'life employment' system for local managers, although the company is looking for stability among suitable people and the longest-serving local manager interviewed is an example.

Four managers out of the five interviewed stated that the prospect of job security was a reason for joining the firm, and one especially referred to this as characteristic of Japanese corporations. Apart from this, the reasons for joining the firm varied and did not present such a uniform pattern as the reasons given by the managers in the UK marketing company. The recruitment of the manager who had been in Japan and who had a knowledge of the language was exceptional, and was his initiative rather than the company's.

**Table 3.1** How managers see themselves in the company

---

*As generalists:*

Department manager, product area C (J)
Finance manager (J)
Personnel officer (B)
Marketing manager, product area G (B)

*As specialists:*

Department manager, product area A (J)
Credit manager (J)
Department manager, product area E (J)
Department manager, product area F (J)
Assistant manager, finance (B)
Assistant manager, accounts (B)
Assistant manager, EDPS (B)

*As both*

Department manager, product area B (J)
Department manager, product area D (J) — 35% generalist
65% specialist

---

*Note*: J — Japanese, B — British.

Table 3.2 How managers see the whole management team

| | As generalists % | As specialists % |
|---|---|---|
| Department manager, product area A (J) | 30 | 70 |
| Department manager, product area B (J) | 5 | 95 |
| Department manager, product area C (J) | 97 | 3 |
| Department manager, product area D (J) | 35 | 65 |
| Credit manager (J) | 40 | 60 |
| Department manager, product area E (J) | 20 | 80 |
| Department manager, product area F (J) | 40 | 60 |
| Finance manager (J) | 60 | 40 |
| Personnel officer (B) | don't know | |
| Marketing manager, product area G (B) | not clear | |
| Assistant manager, finance (B) | 20 | 80 |
| Assistant manager, accounts (B) | 0 | 100 |
| Assistant manager, EDPS (B) | don't know | |

*Note*: J = Japanese, B = British.

Like the marketing company, but with a higher degree of formal organisation and evidently greater separation into departments, the trading company had hierarchical levels which none of the interviewees commented on as being different from what would be expected in British organisations. The company had no formal policy of 'egalitarianism', in the sense that it was found in the manufacturing environment of Japanese Company P1 above, for instance, and the managers were orientated towards their own careers, and their departments, rather than towards the organisation as a whole. In this sense the company could be said to be fitting in with local practice in the City of London environment.

Tables 3.1 and 3.2 show how managers see themselves and how they see their colleagues in the company. Table 3.1 shows that, in spite of the generalist principle, half the managers, including Japanese managers, see themselves as specialists. Two Japanese managers see themselves as both, but one of them sees himself as nevertheless 65 per cent specialist.

A comparison shows that although in Table 3.1 only half the Japanese managers see themselves as specialists, in Table 3.2 six out of eight Japanese managers see the majority of the management team as specialists, and with quite clear percentages. The British managers are split between two who are decisively in favour of classifying the majority as specialists, two who don't know, and one who regarded the terms as neither very clear nor very useful. The conclusion as to whether managers are generalists or specialists in local eyes may not be clear, but the result shows that they are not automatically seen as generalists according to the received wisdom. It will be recalled that one manager had not heard of the generalist principle in Japanese trading companies or other large white-collar corporations and in the context of these results, and the interview comments already quoted, it seems clear that the generalist principle was not one that was being actively promoted by the company.

Apart from the one British manager quoted who did not approve of the terms, there was no difficulty on the part of interviewees in understanding them. This was particularly true for the Japanese managers, one of whom stated that he had believed that such a principle was applied and then found that it was a 'myth'.

This does not, of course, imply that flexibility within certain limits was not an organisational principle, in spite of the degree of specialisation shown by the evidence of the actual career profiles, and the point was indeed recognised by several British respondents. Three saw work as flexibly organised, without strict boundaries between different tasks. One had become conscious that Japanese managers 'dislike boundaries intensely and don't like job descriptions'. Two thought that work was quite strictly marked off according to function, although one qualified this with a reference to 'grey areas'. It is difficult to tell how far these differences of perception referred to the differences and distance between departments that were frequently mentioned.

The remarks of the Japanese managers with reference to specialisation will be taken up again in the Conclusion at the end of the book. Local managers confirmed that it was normal to stay in the same department or function once a person had been recruited to it, and the absence of a job rotation system was clear from their comments. One manager classified 80 per cent of the management team as specialists because they worked for one department throughout their careers. Another classified all managers as specialists according to work experience, if not background, formal qualifications or training. A third manager,

Table 3.3 British managers' working hours

| Manager | Hours |
| --- | --- |
| Personnel officer | 39 |
| Marketing manager, product area G | 50 |
| Assistant manager, finance | 55 |
| Assistant manager, accounts | 55 |
| Assistant manager, EDPS | 60 |

who described himself as a generalist, saw the job itself as specialised and believed that everybody was supposed to become an expert. He was at the same time critical of what he saw as a tendency to lose the overall view. One respondent said he assumed each manager had to be specialised in whatever he was doing, though he said he did not know the details of other jobs. The extremely long hours worked by local managers suggested considerable pressure, tight staffing levels and a policy of restricting training to what was strictly necessary for the job. In practice this meant predominantly OJT.

Table 3.3 shows the hours worked by the British interviewees. Two respondents thought that the definition of a manager in the company was someone who dealt with his own customers, or who was in charge of a department. One saw 'a definite line of responsibility'. Another saw managers as 'locked into' a formally organised and rigid bureaucratic system, in which they performed basically routine tasks according to company procedures.

No one commented on whether there were status differences between managers and other employees, which suggests that the status system was comparable to what managers would have expected in other companies in the City and that there were no particular innovations in this area. Two managers commented that titles were not very relevant, while two expressed the hope that the company would proceed with a policy of 'localisation' that would assist the promotion of local staff.

The abilities that interviewees felt top managers in the firm would need were divided into two types: those required in any firm and those specifically required in a Japanese firm. The former included such standard abilities as a good grasp of the business and the market, human relations skills and the ability to lead and motivate people. Three respondents in particular had a definite view that working for a Japanese company was not the same as working for a British, American or European firm and that it required special awareness and adaptation on the part of British managers. One manager felt it was necessary to have spent some time in Japan and to have a knowledge of the language—something that was not mentioned in the other companies. Others felt that it was necessary to understand and follow 'the Japanese way of doing business'. It was considered essential to recognise that the company is 'a Japanese company—not a multinational'.

Promotion prospects in the London branch were seen as fair to not very high (2+), with no real prospects in the company as a whole. The youngest manager interviewed was very conscious of the age-related aspect of the company's approach to promotion and felt too much attention was paid to age, at the expense of skill or ability. Another comment was that the annual assessment was a good idea in principle, provided that it was carried out correctly, preferably by local managers, because they remained longer, and in some cases considerably longer, in the branch. Two respondents expressed the view that the senior Japanese management were now more in favour of 'localisation'. They were therefore looking forward to improved opportunities for promotion.

The withdrawal by the Inland Revenue of the 50 per cent tax concession for expatriate employees temporarily based in the UK was said to be a factor, rather than any other organisational change. Given the present structure of Japanese business and the web of relationships between the trading firms, their customers, suppliers and related firms, increased 'localisation' could be inconvenient for the companies. At present few British managers are familiar at first hand with business relationships in Japan and to change this would cost time and money. Some people would argue either that this would not be possible or that it would not be worth it. On the other hand, British managers have the edge in business in the UK, including the manner of conducting relations with government and official bodies, and in traditional British markets in Africa and the Middle East. The underlying problem would appear to be the high cost of expertise in the City and the career expectations of 'high flying' British managers.

In spite of this, four out of the five managers interviewed said they would not consider moving. One manager stressed the importance of job security and another pointed to the long time that he had spent in building up to his present position. 'I wouldn't like to start all over again. Development in the company is based on salary rather than anything else'; in other words, years of service, or 'age' as one manager put it is a factor, and promotion cannot be expected quickly.

There is a contrast of degree with the perceptions of British managers in the marketing company, with its more straightforwardly entrepreneurial orientation. An interesting comment on the part of the manager who emphasised the time it had taken him to advance in the company was that 'If I left, I would feel that I had betrayed the company. I have been well treated, in spite of the complaints'. This is a very 'Japanese' reaction. It suggests, firstly, that in this case the company, or the department, had been successful in putting across its idea of 'loyalty' and, secondly, that this quality is less culture-bound than some have claimed. The manager who was least satisfied with his present career replied that future prospects, rather than the amount of salary *per se*, would be the decisive factor. In contrast to the preceding manager, he was evidently thinking of a career path, using his particular transferable expertise, along British lines. He did not feel loyalty of the above type towards the present organisation.

For reasons already explained in the case of the electrical marketing company, the hypothetical question of job changing was not directly discussed with Japanese managers. Nevertheless, several expressed anxiety over the Ataka case, which seemed to have sent a shock wave through the trading companies. The point was made that the Ataka staff who were obliged to retire or to seek other jobs were largely those who did not possess the necessary level of individual expertise, although they may have included staff in product areas that did not fit into the new organisation and those whose performance was not felt to be adequate.

Except in the case of one Japanese manager, who was openminded about moving if it had been a real possibility, it was clear that thoughts of employment in another company were essentially defensive and unwelcome. When the efforts to enter the company and to make a career of it are considered, together with the disadvantages under the Japanese system faced by mid-term recruits to another company, it is not difficult to understand the rationality of 'loyalty' from a Japanese manager's point of view. He may have invested enormous time and effort in personal relations in one company, which cannot be transferred to another, where those who are already in place have an advantage that he may never be able to overtake.[14]

Individual satisfaction with meetings varied considerably, from one manager who was very dissatisfied (1) to another who was completely satisfied (5). The former manager also saw the different departments as 'very isolated' and as not welcoming 'interlopers'. Another manager commented that relations with other departments were 'on a personal basis only' and a third comment was that contact was 'mainly with other British managers'. On aggregate, meetings and inter-departmental communication were felt to be satisfactory (3–4) but information about the London branch (2–3) and about the company as a whole was felt to be less adequate (1–2). One person mentioned the company news sheet as a source of information, while another considered that local staff should be sent to Japan to see how the company worked and in order to understand the wider picture.

The British managers were fairly satisfied (3–4) with the cooperativeness of their subordinates and with the climate at work, although once again one was very dissatisfied (1) and another completely satisfied (5).

Language or cultural difficulties were said to occur very frequently. Exceptionally, there was one British manager with a knowledge of Japanese and another who had started to learn the language. In both cases this was a private initiative and there was no structure in the company for teaching local staff Japanese for business purposes or for using whatever skill the first manager mentioned possessed. There was also some suggestion that the language skills of a number of Japanese managers required further development. As in the case of the other companies discussed above, the way of solving communication problems and other difficulties was generally seen as a process of patient and painstaking discussion, described by one manager as 'an education process on both sides'. 'This is a Japanese company', was a general perception, and this, with a recognition of the degree of formal organisation in the company, resulted in an acceptance of the need for compromise with 'the system'. A comparison of the comments and perceptions of managers in the trading company with those in the electrical marketing company show that the former is perceived to have a more 'Japanese' style than the latter. Reflecting this, the trading company has a greater proportion of expatriates, and there was more comment on the problem of continuity, connected with the head office system of assigning managers to London for five-year periods.

Together with job security, conditions of employment, such as the pension scheme, fringe benefits, and so on, received very favourable comment (4–5). Provision of these advantages is an aspect of the company's policy of encouraging long service among suitable local staff. Housing loans, for instance, would not be consistent with a hire-and-fire policy. The long hours worked by some local staff indicate a considerable level of commitment. The pattern is for good performance and long service to be rewarded by progression up the salary scale and by title, though there was some doubt as to the meaning of titles. Opportunities for further training and development received the lowest rating (2–3) of all the items in the part of the questionnaire dealing with job satisfaction.

The success of the firm was considered greatest in the area of quality of service and levels of technology (4–5). One manager thought that customers were actually 'spoilt'; a reference to the high degree of attention that customers in Japan would naturally expect—and get. Comments on growth (3–4) were less conspicuous than in the electrical marketing company case, but there are two significant factors in this respect. The first is that the UK branch of the marketing company dates from the 1970s, while the London branch of the trading company dates from the 1950s; they are therefore at different stages of development. The second is that the marketing company is specialising in one main product area, in which the market for certain goods continues to be lively, while the trading company is dealing with the widest possible range of products and services, some of which are depressed because of external market conditions. Profitability in the trading company was rated as fair (3) and one comment was that, because of the nature of competition between the trading companies, turnover was considered more important.

Of the items discussed in the context of the firm's success, efficiency was seen in the least positive light (2–3). The gist of comments was that the size of the company and its degree of formal organisation made quick response to the market difficult; a common critique of large organisations. The continual circulation of managers between Japan and the London office and the process of familiarisation were also said to create problems.

Differences between the perceptions of the friendliness of the working atmosphere, levels of information about the company's plans for the branch, or motivation, and so on, may be partly ascribed to the distance and differences between departments. Other factors are length of service, type of function and position, and of course, differences of expectation and outlook. Some of the perceptions—for example, of Japanese managers' promotion prospects or particular items in the sucess of the firm—may not be accurate reflections of the situation; they may not be based on sufficient knowledge or experience. But what managers feel will to a large extent reflect the message they are getting from the company and will influence how they behave and how they perform their tasks. The informal system, especially in a company of this type where the relations between the senior Japanese managers and department managers is crucial, outweighs the formal system expressed in the organisation chart. The latter can therefore be misleading, even in a situation where compliance with rules and procedures at department level is high.[15]

The issues related to generalist or specialist job and career orientations raised by the Japanese managers will be taken further in the Conclusion at the end of the book.[16]

## Notes

1. See M. H. Trevor, *Japan's Reluctant Multinationals*, on the development of Japanese firms in the UK.
2. The procedure resembles that used in the British Army, Civil Service and police for officer or graduate-stream recruitment.
3. The relationship can persist informally for many years after training is over, personal and hierarchical relations being important (and often useful) according to Japanese social and organisational norms. On the other hand, many companies have strict rules against the employment of relatives, since nepotism is seen as a threat to teamwork and performance.
4. See K. Taira, *Economic Development and the Labour Market in Japan*.
5. The practical importance of labour law is not as great as it is in Britain or Germany. Following what was already said in note 12 of section 2.1, above, use of the law in Japan is generally a confession of failure after all attempts at reaching a solution through informal negotiations have failed. Because this is tantamount to a breakdown in relations, it is seen as shameful, particularly when management cannot conduct proper relations with the union of its own company. But labour law does exist in Japan. Much of the legislation, such as

that modelled on the Wagner Act of 1935 and the Taft–Hartley Act of 1947, is of American inspiration. See A. M. Whitehill and S. Takezawa, *The Other Worker*.

6. Again following the American model, the range of subjects which are compulsory for Japanese students during the four years of their university education is wider than in Britain.

7. See S. Zushi, 'The Ataka Affair', in *Politics and Economics in Contemporary Japan*, ed. H. Murakami and J. Hirschmeier, pp. 204, 212–14, on the crucial issue of job security.

8. Ibid., pp. 213, 216.

9. C. Nakane, *Japanese Society*, p. 113.

10. Cf. M. G. Smith, *Corporations and Society*.

11. Cf. Nakane.

12. On the significance of this type of orientation training in large Japanese organisations and the form that it can take, see T. P. Rohlen, *For Harmony and Strength: Japanese White-Collar Organisations in Anthropological Perspective*. See also Rohlen, 'Spiritual training in a Japanese bank'.

13. This applies to trading companies, among others, where each of the Big Nine has developed in its own way, and where there are still considerable differences in their comparative strengths in the various product areas. A glance at the organisation chart can be revealing. At Mitsui the department in first place is steel, in C. Itoh it is textiles. Traditionally, Mitsui focused on commodities, Mitsubishi on finished products and Sumitomo on unfinished products. Traces of the different emphases can still be found. A Japanese saying is '*Soshiki no Mitsubishi, ningen no Mitsui*', which might be translated as 'Mitsubishi is a company of organisation, Mitsui is a company of people': an allusion to the greater degree of formal organisation said to exist at Mitsubishi, to deal with finished products, and the greater emphasis said to be put on traders at Mitsui, in order to deal with the more volatile commodity markets. The saying is well-known in Japan, but it is doubtful whether it reflects the impressions of most local staff in London.

14. Two experienced Japanese managers in the commercial and financial sectors respectively in the City of London have explained these points for the benefit of local people, who would not be expected to understand them fully. 'Mitsui & Co. Ltd is the only company in which I have worked in my life . . . A manager's function is related primarily to his relationship with the people whom he is to manage. Inevitably, even if a manager has outstanding capability, if he is imported from outside he cannot display his capability until he has gained the confidence of people . . . Managers are almost inevitably to be developed inside . . . This situation applies almost without any exception to any of the large Japanese corporations' (Y.

Funaki, 'Japanese management and management training'). 'Your real position which makes your strength in the company is based very much on how many and how well you know people inside and outside the company. These personal relationships which I accumulated in my career in Mitsui are probably the most important asset for me to be successful in the company' (Y. Funaki, 'Cross culture management'). The former general manager of the Sumitomo Bank in London, Mr T. Ono, explained that 'In large companies in Japan you tend to stay till retirement—you get very little choice to do anything else, though theoretically you have the right to leave. In fact, you're forced to stay because it's the only place to work once you start. So the only way to improve your life is to improve the company'. The difference between Japanese socialising with colleagues after official working hours and local staff socialising with people who have nothing to do with their work was also mentioned. Up to now, this has been an important part of a Japanese manager's duties. It is characteristic of the blurred distinction between working hours and the manager's own time and between socialising and work in the strict sense of the word. See J. McLoughlin, 'Comfort in Suntory's happy song'.

15. The general manager of the branch of a Japanese trading company in London, Düsseldorf, and so on, normally has a level of authority, revised annually by the head office to compensate for currency fluctuations. Within the branch there are established criteria and procedures, laid down in company regulations, for credit control. They are designed to reduce the financial risks in organisations with complex activities and high turnover. The situation is the same in the branches of Japanese banks, where attention to detail in correcting small mistakes is aimed at preventing more serious losses. Both trading companies and banks have high levels of formal organisation and are staffed by a greater proportion of expatriates than either manufacturing or marketing companies. Cf. Trevor, *Japan's Reluctant Multinationals*.

16. The many similarities between management in commercial and other companies in Britain and Germany can also be seen from B. Kumar, H. Steinmann and Y. Nagamura, *Japanische Führungskräfte in Deutschland*.

## 3.2 Japanese company C2: banking (Germany)

The bank is among the twenty-five largest banks in the world and is one of Japan's largest international banks. Several branches of Japanese banks in the main commercial and financial centres in

Germany have their own specialities, with the emphasis on the import of cars, electrical and consumer goods.

The middle and senior management levels account for approximately a quarter of all employees in the main branch studied. Staff departments are manned entirely by Japanese, who also occupy 70 per cent of line management positions. The key function of personnel is administered by a Japanese manager and a German manager together. The hierarchical levels are:

1. General manager.
2. Deputy general manager.
3. Manager of a group of departments.
4. Department manager.
5. Employee.

Two deputy general managers report to the general manager, and the vertical span of control consists of three to four levels. The density of control is between four and twenty, with eleven employees being the average. There is one Japanese working as a technical advisor.

The composition of the staff is as follows:

|          | Male (%) | Female (%) | Total (%) |
|----------|----------|------------|-----------|
| German   | 30       | 49         | 79        |
| Japanese | 14       | 2          | 16        |
| Others   | 5        | 0          | 5         |

The middle and upper management levels are exclusively occupied by male staff.

The length of service of staff is as follows:

|                      | Years 0–5 (%) | 6–10 (%) | 11–15 (%) | 15+ (%) |
|----------------------|---------------|----------|-----------|---------|
| German               | 34            | 20       | 15        | 10      |
| Japanese and others  | 0             | 15       | 5         | 1       |

The age distribution of employees is:

| Age | % |
| --- | --- |
| under 20 | 5 |
| 21–30 | 63 |
| 31–45 | 20 |
| 46–60 | 10 |
| 60+ | 2 |

The percentages for employee qualifications are:

| Qualification | % |
| --- | --- |
| University | 3 |
| Commercial (etc.) college | 2 |
| Economist (*Fachwirt*) | 6 |
| Vocational training | 89 |

The average annual holiday entitlement for Germans and Japanese is twenty-five days, and the average sickness rate is 2.4 per cent. In practice, German employees take thirty days' leave, and Japanese staff only ten days. In the last three years no managers left the bank voluntarily but 2 per cent of the senior managers were dismissed by the bank. According to the top management, there are no union members and the only employee organisation is the works council.

Information, whether general or specific, is only given to department managers and above. The managing director and top managers have the organisation plan. Job descriptions and working instructions become progressively less specific as one goes down the hierarchy, but for staff 'in authority' they are extremely precise. The two managers interviewed, belonging to the top and middle management respectively, work between fifty and sixty hours a week and take a maximum of two weeks' holiday a year. This is the normal rule for Japanese staff in Germany and for German managers in Japan.

The bank has one cardinal principle that pervades its operations: the spirit of service to the customer, or as they say in Japan, 'the customer is king'.

Personnel policy is primarily based on performance. Managers assess their subordinates annually according to a number of criteria and the merit ratings are passed up through a deputy general manager to the general manager. They are then submitted to the head of personnel in Tokyo. The assessment is not based on length of service but on performance and potential ability. Staff generally remain loyal to the bank until the age of fifty-five, when they must look for another job. A harmonious relationship with the organisation is considered very important.

The Japanese personnel manager is responsible for local recruitment in the first instance and reaches decisions with the help of his German assistant on the basis of applicants' papers and the impression that they make. The higher the hierarchical level at which there is a vacancy the greater the likelihood that it will be filled in consultation with the general manager. Assuming that applicants are competent at a specific job, what is looked for is the ability to be flexible and to persevere—qualities that German staff, like British staff, are often said to lack. Orderliness, discipline and output are likewise important.

For Japanese staff, training consists of an annual two-day course, with an average of ten days every three years for managers. Transfer to a new function takes place after about five years, so that younger employees can be assigned to the branch; but job rotation is not practised within the branch. Personnel planning for the rotation of Japanese staff is carried out centrally by the head office personnel department for the bank's branches throughout the world.

The promotion criteria are performance, which accounts for 80 per cent of the weight, and seniority, which makes up the remaining 20 per cent. German managers are perceived to have very good promotion chances in the branch (4) but very poor outside it (1). For Japanese staff the situation appears rather different. They are perceived to have good chances in the branch (4) and even better chances outside it in the bank as a whole (5), where 'the sky is the limit'. For those who do not perform as expected, the system appears to be quite rigid: German staff would be threatened with dismissal and Japanese staff sent home immediately. The statutory pension scheme is only supplemented by the bank for staff with more than ten years' service.

The European regional head office in London is telephoned every day and visits between London and Germany generally take place every three months. The only formally organised meeting mentioned was that of the monthly conference of all department managers: a meeting whose value was assessed by the middle manager interviewed at 3.8 and, at a higher level, by the top manager interviewed at 4.5.

The following communication channels are used:

| | Middle manager (%) | Top manager ranking |
|---|---|---|
| Telephone | 20 | 2 |
| Written messages/notes | 5 | 3 |
| Face to face | 70 | 1 |
| Conferences | 5 | 4 |
| Others | 0 | 0 |

There is no formally organised suggestions scheme.

As far as decision-making is concerned, the degree of authority of the top manager was rated as 4.1 and that of the middle manager as 3.5 on average. The ranking of the respective hierarchical levels in major decision-making affecting the branch of the bank was perceived as follows:

| Level | Ranking |
|---|---|
| Parent company | 2 |
| Top management | 1 |
| Middle management | 3 |
| Works council | 5 |
| Staff or administrative departments | 4 |

The senior manager made it clear that, in his opinion, 'All senior managers are generalists. Specialists are not respected': a view that was shared by the middle manager, who was quite content (4) to see himself as a generalist.

The company climate and the degree of identification with the bank were assessed by both managers at 4.7 and the employee–employer relationship was said to be very cooperative and productive. There had been no disputes, but if there were the general manager and deputy general managers would be responsible for solving the problem. The success of the firm received the highest possible evaluation (5).

# Conclusion

1. The density of control, which ranged from four to twenty, is extremely variable.
2. Even in Germany, Japanese only take ten days' leave, and the sickness rate of 2.4 per cent is less than half that in comparable German organisations.
3. Written instructions become increasingly less specific the further one goes down the hierarchy. Personnel policy is very strongly based on performance, and if Japanese staff do not meet expectations they are liable to be sent home immediately. So far, this has not happened, but everyone is aware of the possibility.
4. A harmonious relation between staff and the bank and within the organisation is considered important.
5. German staff are not seen either as being sufficiently flexible or as having sufficient ability to persevere. The reward system is supposed to be based on performance; in reality it largely reflects the usual type of negotiated salary agreement, although the actual level of salary is slightly lower. Additional pension provisions only apply to staff with more than ten years service.
6. The training of Japanese staff generally follows the pattern: OJT, transfer to another function after five years, an annual two-day course, and every three years a ten-day course. Subordinates are assessed annually by their superiors and the results are passed up the line to the head of personnel in Tokyo. The assessment is based primarily on performance.
7. The rotation of staff throughout the bank's global network is centrally controlled by the parent company and staff seldom know where they will be assigned next. Individual wishes are said to be taken into consideration, but there is no guarantee of being assigned to, for example, the Paris office.
8. Active or passive membership in professional organisations is mostly restricted to Japanese associations. Membership in German–Japanese organisations is rare and is found only at senior management level. Language difficulties are said to be the reason for the low level of participation.
9. The success of the firm received the highest rating (5).

### 3.3 Japanese company C3: banking (Germany)

The bank opened its first branch in Germany in the early 1960s. At that time its customers were Japanese companies who required finance and insurance for their imports into Germany. Even now they make up the majority of the bank's customers, although business with German companies has been pursued in the meantime.

The bank's hierarchical levels are:

1. General manager.
2. Department manager.
3. Assistant manager.
4. Accountant.                    the English terms are used
5. Checker.
6. Ordinary employee.

It is estimated that the vertical span of control consists of five levels on average. It is not possible to give any details on the numbers of employees. The German middle manager who was interviewed works an average of fifty hours a week and takes thirty-two days' holiday a year.

The organisation's philosophy could only be partially gathered, although servicing Japanese companies and expanding the bank's activities to include more German companies were two of the main components of the bank's strategy for growth. No details were available about recruitment, reward or personnel management systems. Training seemed to be a weak point, and development was left to individuals, although measures to improve the situation were under discussion.

Job rotation only applies to Japanese staff, in the sense that they are likely to change their jobs three or four times during their five-year assignment in Germany. In consequence, the German middle manager has a critical view of this type of job rotation, which he sees as leading inevitably to a certain degree of superficiality.

The following regular meetings were said to be held:

| | |
|---|---|
| Department managers: | 5+ per month |
| Work groups: | 1–2 per month |
| Planning conferences (general manager and department managers): | 1 per month |
| General management meeting on company goals: | 1–2 per year. |

Satisfaction with these meetings was rated as 3.7 out of 5.

The channels of communication used are:

| Means | % |
| --- | --- |
| Telephone | 50 |
| Written messages/notes | 10 |
| Face to face | 10 |
| Conferences | 30 |
| Others | 0 |

There was no reference to a suggestions scheme.

Management decision-making authority was evaluated at 1.9 out of 5. The weight of the various company levels in decisions with a significant effect on the branch was perceived in the following order:

| Level | Ranking |
| --- | --- |
| Parent company | 2 |
| Top management | 3 |
| Middle management | 1 |
| Works council | 0 |
| Staff or administrative departments | 4 |

The German middle manager interviewed sees himself as a generalist and specialist at the same time, which may suggest some adoption of the Japanese style, and is neither happy nor unhappy on that account. He sees 70 per cent of his colleagues in the branch as generalists and 30 per cent as specialists. The atmosphere at work scored 2.7 on a scale of 1 to 5. No details of employee relations were available, but the success of the organisation was evaluated at 3.9 out of 5 on average.

## Conclusion

1. The percentage of managers perceived as generalists is very high.
2. Training programmes are not developed and individuals are responsible for acquiring further job-specific knowledge where necessary.
3. Satisfaction with the considerable number of meetings is quite

high, but the participation in decision-making of the middle manager interviewed is extremely low in comparison with other firms.

4. The perception of the influence of the middle management on major decisions affecting the branch, apparently seen as more crucial than that of the parent company, is extraordinary.
5. With a score of no more than 2.7, satisfaction with the climate at work is below average.


## 3.4 Japanese company C4: transport (Germany)

The company is a world-wide transport organisation. It established its first branch in Germany in the early 1960s, although it was not, as is usually the case with Japanese companies in Germany, incorporated as a limited liability company. Because there are few Japanese transport companies in Germany, the firm cannot be described more closely on grounds of anonymity.

The hierarchical levels are:

1. Managing director.
2. Manager.
3. Assistant manager and supervisor.
4. Employee.

Eight staff report directly to the managing director, and there are four levels between the highest and lowest levels. In general there are four employees for each first-line supervisor.

The firm is composed of employees as follows:

|          | Male % | Female % | Total % |
|----------|--------|----------|---------|
| German   | 48     | 32       | 80      |
| Japanese | 20     | 0        | 20      |

One per cent of line management positions and 9 per cent of staff positions are occupied by Japanese.

The following table analyses length of service.

| Age | % |
| --- | --- |
| 0–5 | 25.0 |
| 6–10 | 14.3 |
| 11–15 | 39.3 |
| 15+ | 21.4 |

The top manager is the only member of the management team more than 50 years old. It is estimated that only 1 per cent of the staff have a university degree, but all have received further training in the firm. On average, staff take twenty-eight days a year holiday, and the sickness rate is between 4 and 5 per cent. In the last three years one manager left the firm voluntarily and one was dismissed. About 30 per cent of the employees are union members.

Information is passed by managers to all employees, although due to the small size of the firm, only managers have the organisation chart. There are written guidelines for company policy, as well as detailed working procedures. Line and staff personnel, including even the managing director, have job descriptions, although these are being reviewed. The senior manager interviewed works over fifty hours a week and takes between five and ten days annual leave.

The philosophy of the organisation is based on the principles of concentrating on providing good service, fast company growth, 'becoming Number One in the international transport business' and having a small headquarters and keeping the system as simple as possible.

Personnel policy is based predominantly on performance, and the seniority principle is relatively unimportant. The external recruitment of new managers seldom occurs (so far only once) and all managers have been promoted from within. Salary levels are very slightly above those of competitors. Following the company's personnel philosophy, there is only internal training. OJT plays a considerable role and staff are not offered either external courses or training apart from the job. Every two years, a week's training in Japan is allocated to one manager, through the European regional headquarters in London.

There is definitely no job rotation in the German branch, although the principle may be applied in the company in Japan. Promotion is firmly based on performance. Promotion chances for local staff are seen as very good in the branch but very limited outside it. Japanese staff do not receive promotion in Germany. They can only be promoted outside the branch, but their prospects in the company as a whole are very bright. If a manager fails to perform satisfactorily he will either be provided with an assistant or told that he may be dismissed. The statutory pension scheme is not supplemented by the company.

Department managers hold a monthly conference, and there is a marketing conference every two months. Satisfaction with communication is high (4.3). The different means of communication used are as follows:

| Means | % |
|---|---|
| Telephone | 40 |
| Written messages/notes | 10 |
| Face to face | 40 |
| Conferences | 10 |
| Others | 0 |

As far as the administration is concerned, there is no particular structure for suggestions, but Quality Circles have been working very effectively in the sub-offices since January 1984.

Managers' individual participation in decision-making scored 3.9 and the relative importance of the different levels in major decisions affecting the branch was evaluated as follows:

| Level | Ranking |
|---|---|
| Parent company | 2 |
| Top management | 1 |
| Middle management | 3 |
| Works council | 5 |
| Staff or administrative departments | 4 |

The top manager interviewed sees himself as a generalist and is content with the description. He sees 20 per cent of his management colleagues as generalists and evaluates the company climate quite highly (3.8). Relations with the works council (*Betriebsrat*) are perceived as good. 'We talk to them and they agree—then we can get on with the job'. The success of the company is highly evaluated (4.1).

Conclusion

1. The branch operation has a clear and simple structure.
2. Sixty per cent of the staff have been longer than ten years with the company, and almost all the managers have been promoted internally. The 30 per cent rate of union membership is exceptionally high for a Japanese enterprise in Germany.
3. Formal communication has not been developed very far: the emphasis is on informal communication, and this is one of the few firms that has involved its local staff in Quality Circles.

## 3.5 Japanese company C5: transport (Germany)

The German branch was established at the beginning of the 1980s as an independent company, and not as a 'representative office' as is usual with this sort of firm. The rationale for the German operation is the provision of better and faster service and a tightly organised 'door to door' network.

The hierarchy is structured as follows:

1. Managing director.
2. General manager.
3. Manager.
4. Employee.

Six managers report directly to the managing director. There are three levels between employees at the lowest level and the managing director and on average there are between six and ten subordinates for each first-line manager.

The personnel of the branch are composed as follows:

|          | Male (%) | Female (%) | Total (%) |
| -------- | -------- | ---------- | --------- |
| German   | 77       | 8          | 85        |
| Japanese | 13.5     | 1.5        | 15        |

Twenty per cent of both line and staff positions are occupied by Japanese, and there are two German 'technical advisors'. Since the firm is quite newly established, all employees have been with it for less than five years. All middle managers are between 31 and 40 years old and all senior managers between 41 and 50.

The following were the qualifications of the staff:

| Qualification | % |
| --- | --- |
| University | 1 |
| Technical (etc.) university | 0 |
| Further training | 90 |
| Vocational training | 0 |
| Unqualified | 2 |

The average annual holiday was between twenty and twenty-three days, and the sickness rate was 5 per cent. In the last three years one middle manager left the firm voluntarily and one senior manager was dismissed. There were apparently no union members. All managers have the organisation chart and staff will have formal job descriptions. At present each person receives a job description as part of the contract of employment instead. The top manager works between forty-five and fifty hours a week and takes ten days annual leave. The German middle manager who was interviewed works fifty hours a week and takes fifteen days' leave.

The organisation's philosophy is expressed in the four following concepts: serving the company by serving the community; door-to-door service; further development of techniques and service; keeping healthy.

Personnel policy in Germany is guided by the same principles as in the Japanese parent company. Recruitment is initiated by newspaper advertising or recruitment agencies, and in some cases by use of assessment centre procedures. The applicant's personality is an important factor right from the start. The reward system is based on union agreements plus an increment reflecting individual performance, bearing in mind competitors' salary levels so that rewards offered are competitive.

In the Japanese parent company, training and development are initiated by a department with responsibility for this area, but this practice is not followed in Germany. There is no job rotation in the German branch, whereas in Japan managers change jobs every two to three years. Staff in the German branch have to help out with different types of tasks, but this is not 'rotation' in the real sense of the word.

Promotion depends 80 per cent on performance, productivity

and leadership qualities. The prospects for German managers are perceived to be very high in the branch and in the company as a whole, outside Japan. For Japanese managers there is no real prospect of promotion in the German branch, but overall their chances are better than those of German managers, because they can expect promotion at home. If a manager does not fulfil expectations, he may be transferred to another department or function; but 'It is not so easy to dismiss someone'. Extra pension provisions are under discussion.

Formally organised meetings for department managers take place fortnightly and for work groups every week. All staff meet two or three times a year, when the overall company situation is discussed. Satisfaction with these meetings is high (4.4), although the middle manager's score was somewhat lower (3.6).

The different means of communication are used as follows:

| Means | Middle manager (German) (%) | Top manager (Japanese) (%) |
|---|---|---|
| Telephone | 40 | 20 |
| Written messages/notes | 10 | 50 |
| Face to face | 40 | 20 |
| Conferences | 10 | 10 |
| Others | 0 | 0 |

Suggestions procedures are built into the regular conferences, obviating the need for a separate scheme.

Neither the top manager nor the middle manager appear to have extensive decision-making authority (2.4 and 2.5, respectively). Both managers perceive the weight of the different hierarchical levels on major decisions affecting the branch in the following order:

| Level | Ranking |
|---|---|
| Parent company | 2 |
| Top management | 1 |
| Middle management | 3 |
| Works council | 0 |
| Staff or administrative departments | 4 |

Both managers are content to see themselves as generalists. The Japanese top manager sees 20 per cent of the management team as generalists, but the German middle manager sees 80 per cent in this category. The work climate is evaluated by the top manager at 3.8 and by the middle manager at 3.2. There is no union or works council activity. Both the managers interviewed evaluated the success of the firm very favourably (top manager 4, middle manager 4.5).

## Conclusion

1. The staff are highly qualified, 90 per cent being said to have completed extended training, but there is no training in the German branch at all. Nor is there any union activity.
2. Each employee has a precise job description in the contract of employment. There are few conferences.
3. Although both managers expressed the view that the top management preceded the parent company in making major decisions affecting the branch, they themselves did not appear to possess much decision-making authority.
4. The concept of the 'generalist' seems to have very different meanings for Japanese and German staff and the two managers' perceptions of whether their management colleagues should be classified as 'generalists' or 'specialists' differed widely.

# 4. German and Japanese companies compared

The context in which management development can take place was studied under three main headings: organisational structure, personnel policies and practices, and communication in both the wider and narrower senses of the word. In what follows, the differences between the German companies studied and the branches of Japanese companies in Germany are set out in accordance with these three main concepts.

## Organisational structure

Japanese companies in Germany have as flat an organisational structure as possible, and this was a declared goal of one of the transport companies above. It also results from the comparatively small size of most of the companies.

Because of Japanese technological and competitive advantage, there are no *Meister* (lit. 'master') in Japanese companies in Germany, although *Meister* are apparently a source of pride to German employers (cf. Nixdorf, 1984). Complete production and service programmes are provided by the Japanese parent company, and on the technical side, adaptation to local conditions is the responsibility of 'technical advisors'. In the personnel field, a German manager normally works side by side with the Japanese personnel chief or assists as a subordinate.

Although Japanese firms' business strategy of expanding production and the range of services offered is well known, only three of the Japanese firms studied specifically mentioned this aim. The strategy of growth was particularly noticeable in the transport sector, where the aim of German firms by contrast was one of 'moderate expansion'. In the production sector, the business philosophy of the Japanese firms was determined by the situation concerning exports and turnover. Quick, efficient distribution and better cooperation with German firms were important for them. On the other hand, the aim of the German production companies was to be the market leader in their own sector and to offer top-quality products. Most had a regional organisation structure.

Japanese managers stressed the importance of a strong 'service orientation', covering such aspects as obligation to the customer, speedy distribution of goods, satisfied customers, a good service network, direct sales, serving the community and the principle that 'the customer is king'. By contrast, only three out of seven German companies made specific references to service, stressing good technical advice, quality of service and the highest quality possible. One of the German production firms stated that its goal was to become 'Number One' in its field, but these aims are generally more typical of Japanese than of British or German companies.

It is sometimes claimed that Japanese companies do not constrain their staff with tight job descriptions and instructions, and that they expect a high degree of flexibility and mobility, together with a well-developed sense of responsibility; but the study showed that as far as formal organisation is concerned there was little difference between German and Japanese companies. There were job descriptions for almost all the hierarchical levels, although in the German production companies there were no job descriptions for ordinary workers or employees. Of the two Japanese transport companies, one had tight and the other loose job descriptions. One German transport company had tight job descriptions but used them in a loose way. It is, of course, a crucial question how tightly formal job descriptions are followed in actual practice.

German and Japanese companies also seem to use the organisation chart in the same way: generally it is only circulated to managers and only in a few cases is it given to all staff.

## Personnel policies and practices

Almost all Japanese companies operating internationally prefer the principle of 'lifetime' employment, but only four out of the ten Japanese companies studied mentioned it: they were the three production companies and one of the transport companies. One Japanese firm specifically stated that performance and not 'lifetime' employment was the basis of its personnel policy, and Table 4.1 shows that long service was more typical of German than of Japanese firms, even where some of the latter had been in Germany for over twenty years.

Five of the seven German companies studied follow the

Table 4.1  Staff with more than ten years'
service

| Company | % |
| --- | --- |
| Japanese company P2 | 20 |
| Japanese company P3 | 45 |
| German production company 1 | 62 |
| German production company 2 | 45 |
| German production company 3 | 41 |

principle of 'permanent' employment, in fact if not in name, and try to retain their staff as long as possible, although German industry does not like to see this practice taken as a guarantee of 'lifetime' employment. While seven out of ten senior Japanese managers interviewed emphasised the significance of the performance element in personnel policy, only two out of six German managers saw the situation in their own firms in the same way. The data on resignations and dismissals over the last three years given in the case studies showed that in these instances German top managers in German firms were less mobile than German middle managers, and that the latter were less likely to move from Japanese than from German firms.

German firms in the production sector were found to employ considerably more male staff (almost all of whom had completed vocational training) than female. Although the companies were not perfectly matched cases, the proportions of male and female employees were related to the type of production process. In the Japanese companies where production was based mainly on the assembly line, the percentage of female employees was between 53 and 85. In the German companies the percentage was said to be between 17 and 40.

In the banking sector half of all employees were female in both Japanese and German organisations, but in the German transport firms there was a considerably larger proportion of female staff than in the Japanese firms (68.6 per cent and 30 per cent, respectively, compared to 32 per cent and 8 per cent).

On average, fewer than 10 per cent of all line management positions in the Japanese branches were occupied by Japanese, the main exception being one of the banks, where 70 per cent of line positions were occupied by Japanese managers. Japanese occupation of staff positions varied between 10 and 100 per cent, the latter figure applying to one bank and one production company.

As far as education and training in the production sector are concerned, local staff with university degrees are represented by approximately the same proportions in both German and Japanese companies. Those who attended a technical university are particularly well represented: in Japanese firms between 4 and 12 per cent of staff, and in German firms between 1.1 and 30 per cent. On the other hand, those with training up to *Meister* or equivalent level are less well represented in the Japanese companies: between 0 and 6 per cent, compared with 7.4 and 10 per cent in the German cases. Two of the Japanese production firms outlined previously have especially high proportions of employees without qualifications (87 and 70 per cent, respectively) and across all the sectors studied the average for unqualified employees is four times as high in Japanese firms as in German firms (46 per cent, compared to 11.8 per cent). Higher vocational qualifications, such as those of *Meister* or of graduates of banking institutes and other external training institutions, seem to be outside the purview of Japanese managers. In all sectors, Japanese companies hire either university or technical and commercial university graduates or those who have completed ordinary vocational training, such as an apprenticeship.

The purpose of comparing managers' ages in German and Japanese companies was to see whether Japanese managers were younger than their German colleagues. The results showed that, while there is very little difference between the proportions in the 41 to 50 age group (Japanese 31 per cent, German 30 per cent), there are more German managers in the 51 to 60 age group and more Japanese in the younger groups (ages 21 to 40). This contrast may be compared with the findings for the Japanese companies in Britain, which also provided examples of younger Japanese managers on overseas assignments.

The concept of the 'generalist' seemed to be interpreted in a great many different ways by German as much as by Japanese managers. Interviews also showed that at upper hierarchical levels, especially in German firms, the emphasis tended to be on 'generalist' orientations.

Japanese and German career structures normally differ. The career development of Japanese managers has a horizontal as well as a vertical component, through development in specific yet broadly defined areas, and an overseas assignment is often a normal part of this process rather than a promotion *per se*. But German managers, whether university graduates or specialists in a particular field, mostly concentrate on a narrow range of tasks. On account of their sense of responsibility towards the firm, they may nevertheless have a self-perception of themselves as generalists.

The majority of managers in the companies studied, including the German managers, see themselves as generalists. The Japanese managers also see 60 per cent of their colleagues as generalists, while the Germans see 40 per cent of colleagues in this way. In the Japanese production and banking sectors the percentages of generalists are higher, while the transport sector is the only one on the German side where there are perceived to be more generalists.

The interviews showed that the senior German managers in the German firms were less mobile than their middle management colleagues but that the latter are less likely to leave Japanese than German firms. The relatively high number of managers leaving one of the German banks needs to be seen in the light of the total number of personnel.

Absence from work is accounted for by two different reasons: annual holidays and illness. A comparison of the results shows that holidays in Japanese firms are short and no more than ten days on average. What may be surprising is that some German managers declared they would be quite happy to take shorter holidays, were it not for the regulations. As far as sickness rates are concerned, there is little difference between Germans and Japanese. Only one of the Japanese banks mentioned a lower than average rate of 2.4 per cent.

Vacancies in both German and Japanese companies are normally filled as a result of internal announcements. When specialists are required, advertisements are placed in local or regional newspapers. Two Japanese firms use recruitment agencies or assessment centre techniques in addition. Japanese managers emphasised that an applicant's personality is particularly important and that professional qualifications are often secondary. On the other hand, two of the Japanese marketing companies stated that the applicant's personality was unimportant and that what counted was performance alone.

Job rotation played no part in three of the German firms and only a minor role in the few others, nor was it found to apply to Japanese companies in Germany. Japanese managers were assigned to Germany for between four and five years, although in the case of one of the banks the duration of the assignments was no more than eighteen months to two years. Their German colleagues commented that this was too short a period in which to become an expert. In one of the production companies the Japanese comment was that 'Germans do not seem to like job rotation'. Japanese transport company C4 rotates managers around its global network, occasionally including German managers. One of the German transport companies expects each manager to spend a period abroad, and to date this has included 80 per cent of all managers.

The climate at work was judged to be slightly better in German than in Japanese firms, although the expectations of German and Japanese managers may have differed on this point. The cumulative results for all companies on the scale of 1 to 5 (5 high) are shown in Table 4.2.

Evaluation of the company climate, together with motivation, are often linked with rewards, but how do Japanese firms in Germany pay? One-third of the Japanese firms do not pay more than the nationally negotiated wage, and the remaining two-thirds are at least comparable to local firms, even if half the Japanese firms pay slightly more than the local firms. The reason given for paying average or slightly higher salaries is that 'We are a small firm in Germany'. Two of the Japanese companies, both in the marketing sector, pay a bonus based on the successful or otherwise performance of the firm. At one of the German banks it was surprising to learn that 15 per cent of the salary consisted of a special individual increment (based on individual performance).

Company pension schemes are closely linked to pay systems. All the German companies studied had comprehensive, and in

Table 4.2 Perceptions of the climate at work (scale 1–5)

| Perceived by | German companies | Japanese companies |
| --- | --- | --- |
| Top managers | 4.1 | 3.9 |
| Middle managers | 3.9 | 3.4 |

some cases very comprehensive, arrangements in addition to the statutory minima, but two-thirds of the Japanese companies did not have any pension scheme going beyond the statutory old-age pension provisions, although the possibility of a company pension scheme was under discussion at two Japanese firms. Two of the three Japanese firms that did have a pension scheme stipulated requirements of ten and thirty years' service, respectively. In the banking sector it was clear that staff were more generously rewarded in German than in Japanese banks.

As far as decision-making was concerned, a topic of major interest was the influence of the parent companies in Japan over their branches in Germany. The other important aspect of decision-making was the degree of authority enjoyed by individual managers within the company. In the production sector, the influence of the parent company on major decisions affecting the branch was perceived to be extremely strong. In one case this was denied by the Japanese top manager, but his German middle manager expressed the same view as all other managers interviewed.

In the marketing sector the top management were said to have the major role in making important decisions, and this was also the case in the transport companies and one of the Japanese banks. One Japanese middle manager at the other Japanese bank expressed the view that the middle management were of decisive importance, but since his own decision-making score was only 1.9 his remarks should be treated with caution.

In the German companies the pattern of major company decision-making followed the hierarchical levels in the way that might be expected, but there was one surprising exception. At one of the transport companies the works council was said to be highly influential and was put in second place, after the top management. The middle management were only in fourth place, after the staff or administrative departments.

Managers' individual decision-making authority was perceived to be slightly less in Japanese than in German companies, although the difference may be less than might have been expected, given the differences in decision-making styles that are frequently said to exist. The averages show only a slight difference (Table 4.3).

Japanese top managers have to take the influence of the parent company into account when making decisions, which makes it

Table 4.3  Extent of decision-making authority
(scale 1–5)

| Japanese top managers | German top managers | Japanese middle managers | German middle managers |
|---|---|---|---|
| 3.6 | 3.9 | 3.2 | 3.5 |

understandable that they should score lower than their German opposite numbers. German managers also appear to be marginally more involved in decision-making than their counterparts in Japanese companies. At one of the Japanese transport companies, the score of the top manager was as low as 2.4. This could be interpreted in at least two ways: either it was the result of a conscious policy to adopt a highly participative style of management, or it was the consequence of the parent company allowing him only limited decision-making authority. Further study of the company situation would be required in order to reach a definitive conclusion.

In almost all the Japanese and German companies studied, the criteria for promotion are based almost exclusively on performance. One Japanese firm explicitly stated that it did not follow the seniority principle and in the two Japanese enterprises, one bank and one transport company, where seniority was a recognised criterion for promotion it accounted for no more than 20 and 15 per cent, respectively, when compared with achievement. Typically, the promotion prospects of German managers in local branches of Japanese firms are restricted to the branch, and there have been no reported instances of German managers being promoted in the company in Japan. For Japanese managers the situation is virtually reversed, with promotion chances in the wider organisation, as might be expected.

If managers fail to perform as required, their treatment is similar in both German and Japanese organisation. Transfers to other functions or branches are usual, or some form of further training—'patient instruction' as Japanese production company P2 termed it. In the case of one Japanese bank, more extreme measures could be taken: unsatisfactory Japanese managers would be sent back to Japan and German managers would be dismissed.

In order to meet company and career demands it is usual, at least in German firms, to send managers on seminars and different training systems are in use. One German transport firm, for instance, has set itself the task of raising its managers to a level equivalent to that of a technical university graduate by a progression of in-house management development seminars in eight stages.

German banks have equally comprehensive training systems, and in general they outshine the branches of Japanese banks in Germany that were studied as far as training and development are concerned. At the apprentice or trainee stage, employees are interviewed about their training and careers. Provided they perform well, they are then given experience in several different jobs, with the consent of the manager responsible, although being assigned to another post in this way is not necessarily accompanied by an increase in salary. An overseas assignment is desirable and helps career development. Progression from apprentice to board level is not common, but there are some examples. Japanese banks in Germany cannot, or perhaps do not want to, provide this sort of training or development, and the complaints from German managers were unmistakable. In some cases even journals that were concerned with the company's own line of business had to be bought privately.

The personnel departments of German banks carry out long-term personnel planning and counselling, using some computerised systems, and it may be the case that Japanese managers are looked after in the same way by the parent company. On the other hand, they never know what their next assignment will be, and this situation remains the same until they retire.

Japanese management is exported to Germany like a complete service programme. A few companies send their staff beforehand to the Goethe Institute in Japan to learn German, or to London to learn English. In Germany the Japanese firms that were studied did not send their Japanese staff on external seminars for training or development. An informal means of development is provided by the continuous exchange of information via personal contacts in Japan and/or Germany. Japanese technicians visit the parent company in order to learn the latest production methods, so as to be able to introduce them into the German branch. Depending on their size, German firms mostly have their own centres for training and development, where staff attend courses for an average of one or two weeks a year.

## Communication: 1

Communication here refers primarily to institutionalised forms of communication and cooperation, rather than to individual contact.

It may seem surprising that only two Japanese companies, in production and transport, respectively, have introduced Quality Circles. Suggestions schemes are also relatively underdeveloped, although one of the German production companies and one of the German transport companies have the usual type of suggestions box.

It was not easy to obtain information on the degree of unionisation of employees and three-quarters of the companies studied could only provide estimates of union membership. None of the companies reached the average unionisation figure for German industry as a whole of 43 per cent. The highest figure among the companies studied was an estimated 30 to 40 per cent in one of the German production companies. Among the Japanese companies, production company P2 had a low unionisation rate of 4.3 per cent. Production company P3 had a rate of 10 per cent among first-line supervisors and 30 per cent among ordinary employees. No figures were available for company P4. In the marketing sector, Japanese company M3 had a rate of 30 per cent on the service side and 20 per cent on the sales side. Figures for the other two Japanese marketing companies were not available. Japanese transport company C4 estimated union membership at 30 per cent, while the other Japanese transport company reported no union members.

In the production sector, relations with the statutory works council (*Betriebsrat*) were said by Japanese managers to be 'good' or 'very positive'. On the German side, comments were that relations with the works council were 'important' and that 'we wouldn't want to be without it'. But there was also a note of caution and the comment that 'We are sceptical of the political influence on the works council'; in other words, of the irruption of external political concerns into employee relations in the company, where they had no proper place.

From the management point of view, employee relations in the firms studied were generally good, and there were no significant differences between the Japanese and the German firms.

Regarding the span of control, a number of differences between

Japanese and German firms were observed. On average, more people (9.2) reported to the top manager in German than in Japanese firms (6.1). This can be interpreted in two ways. On the one hand, the higher number of people receiving information means a higher rate of diffusion, while on the other hand, the recipients of information are dependent on just one person at any given time.

It was also observed that the Japanese firms studied had one less hierarchical level than the German firms, which can serve to provide quicker communication and better control. At the lowest level of the organisation there are indeed on average more subordinates reporting to a superior in the Japanese firms, but the significance of this finding should not be exaggerated.

## Communication: 2

Here communication refers to direct contact between individuals and groups and to the medium for exchanging information.

The data on the frequency of institutionalised meetings showed that regular meetings take place as often in German as in Japanese companies, both at management and at work-group levels. As far as informal communication was concerned, Japanese managers who were interviewed mentioned that this was very frequent, although a survey of this type cannot state definitively whether there is more informal personal communication in Japanese than in German enterprises.

Satisfaction with the quality of communication was based on answers to questions on a scale of 1 to 5 in regard to the usefulness of meetings, information about the company's plans in the branch and outside it, closeness of contact with other departments, the flow of information down through the direct subordinate and the willingness of subordinates to cooperate. The results did not show any significant differences between the perceptions of managers in German firms and Japanese managers in branches in Germany, although the average result for Japanese middle managers was slightly above that of German middle managers. The cumulative results for all companies are shown in Table 4.4. As with the climate at work, these are quite positive results, although in this case there is little to choose between the German and Japanese scores.

Do managers in Japanese and German firms tend to use

**Table 4.4** Satisfaction with communication (scale 1 to 5)

| Perceived by | German companies | Japanese companies |
|---|---|---|
| Top managers | 4.2 | 4.1 |
| Middle managers | 3.6 | 3.9 |

different forms of communication? Do top managers prefer the telephone or face to face communication? The results of the study show that Japanese managers do put considerably more weight on face-to-face communication than their German counterparts, whether at senior or middle management level. On aggregate, German and Japanese managers appear to use the telephone to a comparable extent, but the figures are affected by particularly high figures in Japanese production company P3 (80 per cent) and by particularly low figures in two of the German companies—top managers in one German production company scoring 10 per cent and in one transport company 15 per cent. But in an absolute sense, German managers in German companies use the telephone more. The cumulative results for all companies are shown in Table 4.5. Both groups use conferences to approximately the same extent but it may seem surprising that Japanese managers use as much written communication as they do, given their preference for face-to-face meetings.

In general, Japanese subsidiaries or branches in Germany are developing at a pace that is unusual by German standards—a pace that may be contrasted with the 'moderate expansion' aimed at by one of the German transport companies. For the Japanese

**Table 4.5** Type of communication used

| Means managers | German top managers (%) | German middle managers (%) | Japanese top managers (%) | Japanese middle managers (%) |
|---|---|---|---|---|
| Telephone | 32.8 | 31.6 | 38.7 | 38.5 |
| Written messages/notes | 15.0 | 23.0 | 9.6 | 14.0 |
| Face to face | 37.5 | 23.0 | 40.0 | 27.0 |
| Conferences | 12.0 | 18.0 | 12.0 | 16.0 |

companies, the explicit goal is the increase of market share until the position of market leader is reached. In interviews with Japanese managers it was often mentioned that price competition is only one side of the competitive struggle as a whole. The other side is the aim of offering excellent products and a high level of service, which have themselves become at least in part standards for competitors.

Because of the conspicuous successes of Japanese companies in expanding their German operations, it might be thought that the success of the firm would be more highly evaluated in Japanese than in German companies. The question was investigated by asking top and middle managers how they evaluated the company's performance in terms of profitability, growth, efficiency, quality of product or service, adaptation to the market and level of technology. The cumulative results for all companies are shown in Table 4.6.

It may seem surprising that there is virtually no difference between the perceptions of the top managers, although the Japanese middle managers' evaluations are slightly higher than their German opposite numbers. The reason may lie in the subjective factor of Japanese managers' expectations being higher, and therefore more difficult to satisfy. At the same time, there is some variation in the scores. While the success of Japanese production company P2, for instance, was rated at 3.4, that of one German production company was rated at 4.2. On the other hand, the success of Japanese production company P3 was rated at 4.4, above the other German production company at 3.4. Among the banks, the first Japanese bank scored the highest of all companies, with the maximum possible of 5; but the second Japanese bank scored 3.9. The averages for the German banks were 4.3 and 4.15, respectively. In the transport sector, the Japanese firms were perceived as outperforming their German

Table 4.6  The success of the firm (scale: 1–5)

| Japanese top managers | German top managers | Japanese middle managers | German middle managers |
|---|---|---|---|
| 4.2 | 4.1 | 4.1 | 3.7 |

competitors, while in the marketing sector the three Japanese companies received scores of 4.6, 3.4 and 4.5, respectively. The German marketing company's success scored 3.8. This is one of a number of questions that could be investigated further in a larger study.

# Conclusion

## The task orientation of Japanese management

In view of the differences between British and German management discussed in the Introduction, it might be thought that the Japanese experience in the two countries might be different, but in practice the case studies suggest that the similarities outweigh the differences from the Japanese point of view. This is not surprising when the similarities between the Japanese firms in the two countries in terms of task, size and competitive strategy are considered. Several of the same firms—particularly in the commercial, financial and marketing sectors—are found in both countries. The City of London and Düsseldorf, and the manufacturing plants in the more outlying areas, are broadly comparable.

Anglo-German similarities appear in the following areas: German managers, like their British counterparts, specialise in quite narrow areas. German firms, but not Japanese firms in Germany, make considerable use of external training courses. In both the UK and Germany the respective figures given for generalists and specialists in the firms vary widely, and there is considerable variety in the ways in which the terms are interpreted. In other words, in neither country are local managers aware of an unambiguous, unchanging and consistently promoted Japanese 'philosophy of the generalist'. Again, in spite of the attention given to the notion of 'lifetime' employment in Japan, managers in German firms appear to have a longer commitment to the same company than German managers in Japanese firms, even where the latter have been established locally for some years.

In the UK also, the remark to the personnel manager at an electronics company that '25-year men' were well known in the United States, elicited the response that 'We have plenty of 40-year men', proud of their long service and retirement celebration, award, and so on. Regarding recruitment, both Germans and British were aware of the Japanese emphasis on 'personality' or 'attitude'. No German managers had been posted to Japan or promoted within the wider organisation and nor had their British counterparts. The same information was given that Japanese managers seldom knew when and where they would be assigned. Even the Japanese criticisms of local staff were similar; 'not keen to change jobs', 'not willing to share information, because they want to make decisions on their own and are stubborn, even arrogant', 'lacking flexibility and persistence'. Finally, the importance of Japanese organisations' and managers' task orientation, to be discussed below, was similarly evaluated by the researchers in the two countries.

Differences between the sectors are significant. In the British case, for instance, the teamwork approach in the precision-manufacturing company and the emphasis on the company task contrast with the focus on the departmental task in the trading company, although the latter has fewer personnel than the former. Both contrast with the marketing company, with its entrepreneurial career and sales-orientated local staff, for whom the growth of the company as a whole, as well of their particular department, is important. All three companies are related to different sectors of the labour market.

The stereotyped views of the generalist and of the importance of the generalist concept in Japanese organisational effectiveness are only partly borne out. The cases show that Japanese managers, not to mention local staff, in the European branches of Japanese companies, do not uniformly regard either themselves or their colleagues as generalists. There are also discrepancies between the way in which Japanese managers classify themselves and the way they see their colleagues: the respective proportions of generalists and specialists do not always add up. The lack of a generally accepted definition of 'generalists' was apparent in both Britain and Germany, a lack that shows the concept was not being actively promoted by all companies as part of their corporate strategy.

Career profiles indicate a high level of specialisation among Japanese managers and that it is normal for managers to stay in the same function. Perhaps it is as normal as in Britain or Germany, although this could only be established with large-scale sample data—a research task that remains to be done. This is irrespective of whether Japanese managers who stay in the same function consider themselves specialists or not. What is different is that British or German managers would normally choose their own field and pursue it across different organisations, whereas the Japanese are assigned according to the bidding for resources between departments. Not all Japanese company entrants get their first choice of department by any means, even if they do make a request.

The larger proportion of university graduates among Japanese managers—whether engineers, marketing men or traders—in the British cases above contrasts with the generally lower educational achievement of the British managers.[1] But the latter are generally qualified by experience and, for labour market and for other reasons already discussed, are more likely to belong to a professional association and to consider themselves as professionals.

Rotation exists in Japanese firms in Europe but not in the same way as is generally mentioned in connection with the generalist training and career structure. Rotation for Japanese managers is typically an overseas assignment of five years decided by the head office. As in the case of the original job assignment in the company, this depends on the various departments who promote their own interests and make their own bids or demands. Formally, it is administered by the personnel department, where formal approval at least must be sought.

The questions of long-term, or permanent, assignment to the same department or functional area was discussed with managers in Japan. Many stated that there was 'no advanced warning' either of job assignment, posting overseas or return to Japan. One manager expressed the view that the manager either had to 'accept or leave the company'. This suggests that the rationale was the need to staff the growing number of posts in Japanese overseas operations and the effect of the different departments pushing their interests. In other words, the rotation system for assigning Japanese managers abroad has an organisational rather than an individual focus. As such, it does not match some of the accounts of the generalist career structure as being aimed at the formation of the 'well-rounded man', although this may be found at the ideological level.[2] These points do not, of course, imply that flexibility, as will be discussed below, was not important, but the frequently mentioned emphasis on flexibility is not the same thing as the full-fledged 'generalist' concept that one Japanese manager defined that is so often mentioned and which has attained something like normative status. It will be remembered that one Japanese manager defined the difference between British and Japanese specialists in terms of the flexibility of the latter.

It is not, of course, possible to arrive at a complete picture of

Table 5.1   Management training methods in Japan

| Size of firm (persons) | In-house group training (%) | OJT (%) | Job rotation (%) | Business school, external training (%) | Subsidy for self study (%) |
|---|---|---|---|---|---|
| Under 300 | 34 | 38 | 2 | 4 | 19 |
| 300–999 | 34 | 35 | 5 | 3 | 23 |
| 1,000–2,999 | 43 | 38 | 4 | 1 | 13 |
| 3,000–9,999 | 38 | 44 | 5 | 1 | 10 |
| Over 10,000 | 28 | 51 | 11 | 0 | 10 |

*Source*: Keidanren (Employers' Organisation). Quoted in Y. Funaki, 'Japanese Management and Management Training', 1981.

management development in Japan by studying the situation at its geographical extremities in branches in Europe. Discussions with managers in manufacturing, trading and financial companies in Japan confirmed the views of Japanese managers in, for example, the trading company in London. They gave similar accounts of selection, job assignments, training, overseas postings and work organisation. Their accounts present a consistent picture, but more research in Japan itself is needed in order to arrive at a more comprehensive and updated view. Tables 5.1 to 5.3 are from Japanese sources.

Table 5.1 shows the great extent to which OJT is used in Japan. The last column shows the importance of managers' own efforts to develop themselves. The table shows that OJT and self study outweigh job rotation, although the latter is the area which has so often been put in the spotlight and exaggerated. Together, the two methods of in-house training greatly outweigh the use of business schools, and so on, etc., external to the company. 'The business school can teach *universal* management skills and *theory*. However, universal management skills and theory are not of primary importance for Japanese managers. What is important is *experience in the company* and human relationships they have cultivated through the long time they have spent in the company' (Funaki, 'Japanese Management'; emphasis added).

Table 5.2 shows the differences between the composition of training for managers as they progress through their development.

Table 5.2 Aims of management training in Japan

| Aim | Would-be manager (%) | New manager (%) | Experienced manager (%) |
|---|---|---|---|
| Wider view | 4 | 2.4 | 6.4 |
| Specific job knowledge/ability | 12.6 | 7.3 | 8.8 |
| Decision-making/problem-solving | 9.6 | 9.8 | 13.6 |
| Managing change | 3 | 1.6 | 5.4 |
| Basic/advanced management knowledge | 19.2 | 30.3 | 24.1 |
| Deepen basic/advanced management knowledge | 8.1 | 2.8 | 7.1 |
| Motivating subordinates | 11.6 | 6.9 | 7.5 |
| Leadership and organisation management | 26.3 | 33.3 | 19.4 |
| Union matters | 2 | 3.7 | 3.4 |
| Others | 3.5 | 4.1 | 8.2 |

*Source*: Keidanren. Quoted in Funaki, 'Japanese Management'.

Specific job knowledge as such, largely acquired through the high proportions of OJT and self study shown in Table 5.1, is offset by the emphasis on leadership, management knowledge and decision-making or problem-solving. While assigned to specific functions, managers must develop organisational skills so that the company's task aims are met and the contrast between 'leadership' and 'management knowledge', as reflected in the table, on the one hand, and 'wider view', on the other, is interesting.

In view of some of the exaggerated accounts of training in Japan, it may seem surprising that levels of satisfaction in Japan are not higher (Table 5.3). Naturally, the reasons for dissatisfaction reflect people's expectations, and it would be unwise to assume that the reasons would be identical for managers in Japan, Britain and Germany, for example. Nevertheless, the high figure for managers dissatisfied with training because it is allegedly not systematic enough is conspicuous. This dissatisfaction, taken together with the prevalence of OJT and self study, may indicate that in practice competitive pressure dictates that expenditure on training in terms of time and money must be directed to what is considered strictly necessary. There appears to be little slack in the system.

In the European branches, job rotation according to the ideal typical generalist model did not exist. Other observers, whether in

Table 5.3  Employees dissatisfied with company training programmes

| | Managers, technical specialists (%) | Office workers (%) | Foremen and supervisors (%) | Skilled workers (%) | Ordinary workers (%) |
|---|---|---|---|---|---|
| Satisfied | 22.8 | 18.7 | 42.4 | 27.7 | 26.0 |
| Dissatisfied | 48.8 | 40.3 | 32.5 | 40.3 | 33.6 |
| Neither | 24.9 | 33.2 | 19.7 | 25.2 | 34.9 |
| No answer | 3.5 | 7.9 | 5.3 | 6.9 | 5.5 |
| *Reasons for dissatisfaction* | | | | | |
| Training only for the present job | 15.7 | 19.6 | 19.2 | 35.2 | 38.8 |
| No systematic training | 61.4 | 54.7 | 51.5 | 36.3 | 37.5 |
| To attend after working hours and on holidays | 9.0 | 4.1 | 7.1 | 10.4 | 7.9 |
| Limited no. of trainees | 7.1 | 7.4 | 10.1 | 12.6 | 11.3 |
| Limited class of trainees | 17.6 | 25.7 | 21.2 | 30.8 | 25.4 |
| Others | 16.7 | 8.8 | 13.1 | 6.0 | 13.8 |

*Source*: Japanese Ministry of Labour, 1972. Quoted in N. Sasaki, *Management and Industrial Structure in Japan*, 1981.

Britain or Germany, have also concluded that 'Few companies seem to have a clearly developed training system [for local staff]'.[3] Given the size of the firms, the tight manning policy, the recruitment of local staff for specific jobs following local labour market practice, and the need to keep costs down, this is not surprising. Given the strong task orientation and competitive strategy, it would be surprising if training costs were not kept under tight control. Visits to Japan, in terms of actual cost and the time-cost of absence from the job are expensive and, with local patterns of job changing, unlikely to be extensively used.

The clearest statement of opposition to job descriptions, as a hindrance to organisational performance, was found in the marketing company in the UK. Commenting on European job descriptions, a senior manager in Japan said that 'We don't have them. So I don't know what my job is, what I must cover. It's not clear. If I think it's my job, I will do it'. The view sums up the way the marketing company's 'basic philosophy' saw not only the advantages of flexibility but also the fostering of the attitude of initiative and of doing more.[4]

An experienced manager and Japanese consultant states that 'doing only what is ordered' is interpreted as a criticism in Japan. But an absence of job descriptions does not mean that the prevalence of 'permanent' assignment to a specific department or function and the consequent specialisation in a particular type of work that was already noted are not facts. The career profiles in the marketing and other companies show the reality.

It might have been expected that more respondents would have questioned or challenged the use of the terms 'generalist' and 'specialist', and they were given the chance to do so. In fact few did, although it was clear that how people used the terms, especially on the Japanese side, varied considerably. A senior manager at Sumitomo Rubber Company in Japan expressed the view that all managers from section chief level upwards in Japan were generalists. He saw engineers as specialists, because they tended to have technical rather than general management skills; it was therefore a company's duty to fit them into their own niche and to treat them fairly in regard to some form of promotion.[5] As well as leadership, he stresses what he termed 'followship' in Japanese organisations; in other words, the principle of teamwork, contrasting with the situation in European societies.

The definitions of the generalist used by some Japanese managers did not exclude what to most European managers would appear to be a good deal of specialisation. Equally, Japanese specialists could also see themselves as flexible; in one particular case this was singled out as the difference between a British specialist and a Japanese specialist. Other managers, both European and Japanese saw specialists as mostly lower-ranking managers than generalists, and it is true to say that most senior managers on both sides would be expected to have the broad view and overall grasp of the business of the generalist, to use the term in its most usual British sense. Clearly the semantic question and the differences between managers' subjective perceptions—both of themselves and colleagues—and, for example, their actual career profiles or 'permanent' job assignments, are all part of the problem. They suggest that the terms are often loosely used.

According to the popular view discussed in the Introduction, Japanese managers are generalists. Sometimes 'cultural' reasons are given, connected with 'loyalty' or a diffuse conception of the job or work in Japan without a job description or defined boundaries. It is suggested here that while there is a grain of truth in the image, it is in other respects a caricature.

In the public sector, the British Civil Service has both general-ists and specialists. Their qualifications, selection, job assignment and career prospects are clearly differentiated.[6] One account argues that the generalist civil servant is akin to the amateur, partly because of what seems like an exaggerated form of the ideal typical Japanese job rotation model. The opening chapter of this account discusses 'The Cult of the Generalist'.[7]

British clearing banks, like the major Japanese corporations, have been, in the words of a senior banker, 'traditionally a career employer'—what another banker refers to in a common expres-sion as a 'one-career employer'. Within this framework, banking careers have until recently been 'generalist' careers. As in Japan, the employee's recruitment to the organisation was directly after he had finished his education, in this case school, and the mutual expectation of a lifetime of work was reflected, again as in Japan, in the pay structure. The normal generalist banker's career path took him through each type of job in the branch, so that when he reached the peak of his career as a branch manager he would know all the jobs better than his subordinates who were subsequently doing them. Banks run training and assessment courses for staff at different stages of their career development, at their own residential training centres, but traditionally OJT has played a major role.

At one leading clearing bank where interviews were held, the managers in the personnel department were not personnel specialists but people who had trained as 'general bankers'. The structure resulted in the cultivation of particular house styles, as in Japan, and a number of managers interviewed claimed to be able to tell from business philosophy and general style which of the major clearing banks a random grouping of bankers in a room belonged to. In the case study of thirty-five managerial staff, thirty classified themselves as generalists or 'branch bankers'. Four classified themselves as specialists, and one 'As a generalist from the bank viewpoint, but I think I'm specialist in certain areas'—a comment that echoes those of some of the Japanese managers in the London branch of the trading company. Comments on job security and career development resembled those in a Japanese environment. Once again, no one seemed to have any difficulty in grasping the meaning. Several respondents pointed out that 'branch banker' was the term for generalist. One stated that the expression 'generalist' was not used 'but it is thought'.

This system lasted until the 1970s and 1980s, when changes in the banking business caused a major organisational change. When banking in Britain was mainly a question of lending money to individual private customers, the generalist banking structure was adequate. But when banking diversified and its product range increased, the need for specialists, in areas such as marketing, investment management, leasing, data processing, and so on, grew and the old structure, with a certain seniority element in its promotion system, was put under strain. Younger specialist managers were promoted more quickly, causing dissatisfaction among old type generalists. The training systems had to be revised. The influence of specific product areas and the consequent need for skilled expertise in them became as plain as it is in the case study of the Japanese trading company in London above.

In fact, the idea of the generalist, or the 'well-rounded manager', committed to the company ethos is not new and need not be Japanese. It was discussed many years ago in a book with a title that added a new expression to the language—'The organisation man'.[8] This was with special reference to the training and socialisation practices of the General Electric Company, USA, which with hindsight seem 'Japanese'. 'Culture' in the sense of a 'national culture' is hardly an adequate explanation. As noted above, the upper levels of organisational hierarchies, or 'general management', in different societies have a generalist orientation, and the good specialist, whether engineer or accountant, does not always make the best general manager. In the US Army, 'Officers who are to assume higher command . . . and who must function effectively in planning and in policy-making positions . . . require development as true "generalists"'.[9] There is widespread recognition of the different qualities that are required at different organisational levels.

In contrast to the stereotypical patterns of 'Japanese generalists' and 'European (or American) specialists', the reality is more complex and more changeable. 'Job security: its time has come' is an American view that 'Employees who feel secure in their jobs are more productive'.[10] In Britain, 'Matrix management at administrative levels and flexibility agreements on the shop floor have lessened the inviolability of job frontiers'.[11] In an internal labour market, job boundaries can become blurred without damaging managers' prospects as 'professionals' in the same way that they would in the external labour market. 'Lifetime employment on the Japanese model has been common in Europe for many generations', including in companies such as Krupp, Michelin, Cadbury, Fiat and ICI, even if the recession is forcing them away from the pattern.[12]

The Ataka case and its effect on Japanese trading company staff have already been referred to. In conditions of slower economic growth, it is more difficult for Japanese companies to meet the cost of long-term employment, and the structure is under strain; although it is too early to predict its end and it may be conjectured that, apart from the monetary cost, Japanese managers would not like to exchange the system's advantages of flexibility, cohesiveness and control over job assignments, for the greater degree of job changing that an external labour market of more 'specialist' job-seekers would bring. A recent Japanese Ministry of Labour survey found that 80 per cent of employees wanted the present system to continue.[13] But a Danish consultant is getting good results with his headhunting business in Tokyo and finds managers willing to discuss their job changing ambitions frankly.[14] 'The logic of the labour market process is not "culture-bound" to the West'.[15]

For Japanese firms in the USA (like those in Europe), 'Retaining highly qualified and productive workers and employees is difficult. Personnel and employee development programmes in the US must be based on periodical wage increase and promotion to be effective'.[16] The point refers back to the European system of receiving increased rewards or promotions for greater responsibility, while in large Japanese companies the order would be reversed. In commercial and financial operations in Europe the Japanese companies' solution has been to provide good rewards to suitable local staff, and as far as possible titles. In spite of these problems in some of the branches, Japanese managers with experience in the UK are aware of the levels of professional expertise available in the City and of the differences between the UK's successful financial sector and the problem-ridden manufacturing sector.[17]

There is a considerable amount of writing on other societies' experience with local branches of Japanese companies, coming from Japan, Europe and USA. How far techniques that have been so successfully used by Japanese managers can be employed elsewhere has been endlessly discussed. The 'cultural' specificity or otherwise of managerial practices in Japan has been debated,[18] though not always with illuminating or practical conclusions.

In this study the emphasis has been on empirical evidence and has shown the different situations in the different sectors. Japanese managers in production companies, particularly engineers, commonly have a training role *vis-à-vis* local staff. In banks, trading companies and marketing companies, on the other hand, young expatriates are themselves learning international business by OJT. They are not all simply 'Japanese companies'.

The meanings of the terms 'generalist' and 'specialist' and how the two orientations affect organisational performance have been discussed, and since the topic here is the Japanese management development system in two European countries, Japanese managers' opinions have been quoted extensively, both on how they see the Japanese system and how they see their European colleagues in the Japanese mirror. How far are these perceptions and how far are they real differences? If they are the latter, what implications do they have for us?

As is often the case in Japanese firms in European countries, 'American management personnel insist on having clear definition of duties and authority. They prefer to have complete authority of their job duties rather than sharing of duties as practised in Japan'. The Japanese writer's solution to this problem is that 'To make the best use of executive American talent, Japanese top management must delegate authority to American managers. Before delegating responsibility, however, Americans must go through extensive and in-depth training in Japanese management style and interpersonal relations, in addition to firm-specific practices'.[19] There is a difference between European and Japanese managers in relation to the company, career chances and the labour market. In the large Japanese company the manager practically *has* to make his career in the company, while the European manager may change his employer. The respective notions of flexibility and professionalism are correspondingly different. The problem of the job description is a real one.

From the comments of Japanese managers interviewed, especially those in the London branch of the trading company, it is clear that they are expected to be both generalists and specialists— generalists in the sense of being willing and able to deal with all aspects of a function, and of learning new skills, being retrained, reassigned, and so on; specialists in the sense of possessing and using the specific expertise required in the job. If necessary, they must learn this by themselves, through 'self study'. As one of the Japanese managers in the trading company in London put it, 'Managers need speciality and generality for promotion'. Management can therefore get the maximum of cooperation, on the one hand, and professionalism, on the other; and both serve the same end of task performance. Japanese companies have usually been very successful in getting the most out of their managers on both counts.

'Professionalism' here does not refer to a narrow or demarcated type of activity but to the ability and commitment to achieve task goals. It is task-orientated and organisation-centred. It is not centred on an individual career that can progress across different companies (see the comments above of Mr T. Ono, formerly London branch manager of the Sumitomo Bank). Nor is it orientated towards 'professional' status[20] in the sense that is normal in Britain, which fits in with the British pattern of membership in one independent professional association outside the company, membership in which is designed to help the individual career in the external labour market. It is a failing of some accounts given by or for people outside Japan that the human relations side of business organisation, which has been discussed above, is sometimes over-emphasised. While the importance of human relations, personal contacts and organisational skills are undoubtedly important, it must be asked why they should be emphasised. In most cases the reason—as can be seen from the UK case of the marketing company's basic philosophy, for example—is that they are seen to, and designed to, contribute directly to company performance. In other words, their aim is the achievement of the organisation's goals. They are task-orientated and organisation-orientated, a fact that is relevant to Lord Sieff's discussion of personnel management at Marks and Spencer, for instance (see also Lord Sieff, 'Time to alter attitudes in Industry Year', *The Sunday Times*, 27 April 1986). Whether personnel management in Britain increasingly follows the 'professional model' or whether it bridges personnel and line management functions, as advocated by Lord Sieff in a way reminiscent of normal Japanese practice, will therefore be crucial for organisational performance in Britain. How willing are people to learn from the success of Japanese managers in making their companies productive and profitable? Management is a complex activity and it would be a mistake to ascribe the successes of Japanese companies in Europe to any single aspect, or to look for a panacea in one. Competitive strategy includes such aspects as investment, engineering and design, marketing and management style, and Japanese managers in branches in Europe both act on and are acted upon by them. But a recent survey by the Japan External Trade Organisation (JETRO) of Japanese companies in Europe found that 60 per cent of the 189 firms that responded to the questionnaire were profitable.[21] Considering the relatively short period within which the branches in Europe have been established, and that it normally takes time for new business ventures to become profitable, this is a respectable figure.

Some European business competitors of the Japanese and some commentators would like to believe that Japanese business is losing its momentum; but this was not the impression gained during the study. The intensity of competition within Japan itself, which is just as fierce in overseas operations, spurs managers to greater task performance. They are continually looking to sharpen their company's competitive edge and to fight their rivals, whether Japanese or European, in the market. The recession intensifies this competition. Japanese firms are increasing in number and size in Europe and look set to continue to do so. It is their task-orientated capacity for achievement, through professionalism in the best and most effective sense of the word, that in the present study is their most valuable example for us.

## Notes

1. Seventy per cent of the managers of the main plant of the previous engineering company in Japan were university engineering graduates. The other 30 per cent had degrees in economics, humanities, and so on. Sixty per cent of the company's board are engineers. The production system in the UK is identical to that in Japan, except of course for scale.

2. NEC has instituted a system of 're-entry bosses', popularly known as 'godfathers', to oversee the foreign assignments and re-entry into the company in Japan of managers posted abroad. The aim is to improve upon the old system of 'tacit agreements between the management and the persons sent overseas without clear agreements or guarantees on how long they are going to be overseas and when they can come back to the parent company'. The system was outlined in a company memorandum of 1 November 1981 from the head office

international personnel division. NEC is a prominent investor in the UK and Ireland.

3. H. Demes et al. *Japanische Unternehmen in der Bundesrepublik Deutschland*, p. 24.

4. Honda in Japan uses the English term 'specialist' for such employees. They can 'If they choose, remain indefinitely in the same position in the factories' (S. Sanders, *Honda: The Man and His Machines*, p. 163). The manager at Sumitomo Rubber referred to also pointed to high productivity in Japanese manufacturing, in comparison with lower productivity in office work. He mentioned 'Too much telex, writing' and the problem of 'twilight zones of responsibility' creating unnecessary bureaucracy. The main successes of Japan's famous quality movement have been in manufacturing. Managers are now thinking how similar strategies can be applied throughout the office sector.

5. R. Fukuda, *Managerial Engineering*, p. xxv.

6. E. F. Ridley (ed.), *Specialists and Generalists*.

7. P. Kellner and Lord Crowther-Hunt, *The Civil Servants*.

8. W. H. Whyte, *The Organisation Man*.

9. T. J. Crockel, 'On the making of lieutenants and colonels'.

10. J. F. Bolt, 'Job security: its time has come'.

11. R. P. Dore, 'The social sources of the will to innovate'.

12. W. Kendall, 'Why Japanese workers work'.

13. 'Seniority system under pressure', *Japan*, No. 284, 26 July 1984. 'Life employment proving burdensome', *Mainichi Daily News*, 20 March 1983. It is a mistake to play down the importance of long-term employment in Japan simply because it applies to one-third of employees. It is highly relevant to the pattern of manager's careers, and the Pareto 80 : 20 principle indicates that a figure of 20 per cent frequently accounts for 80 per cent of importance. The significance of the one-third of employees is greater than the crude numbers imply.

14. G. Fabricius, 'The art of headhunting'.

15. K. Taira, *Economic Development and the Labour Market in Japan*, p. x.

16. N. Matsuura, 'Japanese management and labour relations in US subsidiaries'.

17. S. Oba, 'Japanese views of British business and industry'.

18. For example: 'Japanese-style management on trial in America', *The Oriental Economist*, September 1983; G. Bickerstaffe, 'The mixed scorecard of Japanese management abroad'; N. Matsuura op. cit.; A. Okumura, 'Management in the international age: are there universal qualities in Japanese-style management?'; 'Transferable Factors in Japan's Economic Success', *Management Review and Digest*, BIM, Vol. 9, No. 4, January 1983; A. B. Schmookler, 'An overview of Japan's economic success: its sources and its implications for the US'.

19. Matsuura. Cf. Ohmae in Bickerstaffe.
20. Of course, other types of 'status' are important in Japanese organisations, such as punctilious regard for seniority and distinctions of rank. But these primarily reflect the large number of finely graded distinctions within one organisation. Japanese organisations have standard and generally recognised ranks, such as section chief, department manager, director, and so on, but the personal and informal relations are only accessible to company 'insiders' and cannot be transferred to another organisation.
21. *Journal of Japanese Trade and Industry*, No. 3, 1985, p. 61.

# Appendix

### Research method

Britain and Germany are the principal locations of Japanese investment and Japanese manufacturing in Europe. A Japan External Trade Organisation (JETRO) survey at the end of 1984 showed thirty-four Japanese production plants in Germany, thirty-two in Britain and thirty in France, although bare numbers rather than size, number of employees, and so on, give a slightly misleading impression.[1] Japanese investment in Britain is larger than in Germany: US$2.4 billion between 1951 and 1983, compared to US$925 million in Germany. But in terms of matching cases, the Anglo-German comparison is one of the most appropriate in the Japanese context. The same types of Japanese company tend to be found in both countries, and both are keen to attract Japanese investment.

One consequence is that in both countries the Japanese companies tend to be branches of the biggest and strongest companies in Japan, even if they are numerically small by comparison with local firms. Their managers and systems therefore belong to the blue chip, or 'first class', company type in Japan, and care was taken to match the branches in Britain and Germany in the present study.

It cannot be accepted *a priori* that even all large Japanese corporations operate similarly, and samples were therefore chosen from the three main sectors of manufacturing, marketing, and commerce and finance respectively. Because major Japanese corporations operate to a considerable extent on the basis of a marketing strategy,[2] the classification 'marketing' is preferred here to 'sales and distribution', which would imply a short-term orientation. This would be inappropriate and could lead to a serious underestimation of the long-term strategic aspect of Japanese competitiveness.

The three Japanese companies in Britain in the study were among those already known from previous research and have been known over a period of years. They have therefore been treated as in-depth case studies. This has the advantage of enabling a considerable amount of qualitative data to be presented which may help to illuminate the more intangible issues, such as discrepancies in the perceptions of managers of themselves and their colleagues as 'generalists' or 'specialists', respectively. Data obtained from Japanese managers during a five-week research visit to Japan at the end of 1985 are also included.

On the German side this was the first time for most of the companies to be approached for research purposes. In general, Japanese firms in both Britain and Germany were quicker than local firms to decide when to participate in the study and were also more likely to agree: in Germany 70 per cent of local firms approached declined altogether. One firm announced that it would not participate in such studies again because of the time factor. These problems were among the reasons that made it difficult to adhere to the original timetable.

The methodology of the study consisted of semi-structured interviews. In the first two British cases the majority of the managers at the various levels in the company were interviewed. In the third case a sample of managers, particularly Japanese managers, was available for interview. In the German cases, interviews were held with one key Japanese manager, such as the managing director or personnel manager, and with one Japanese middle manager in each firm. In all cases, additional data on the organisation were obtained from personnel managers and other senior managers. These data included numbers of personnel, hierarchical levels, spans of control, absence, sickness, and so on.

The interview schedule included two open-ended questions on the nature of the firm and the reasons, or strategies, that accounted for its present position. Promising lines of inquiry were followed up during the interviews, and managers were invited to amplify comments and items that they had more to say about.

The questionnaire for all managers was designed to cover qualitative and quantitative aspects under the following main headings:

1. The firm and its present position.
2. Manager's career profile.
3. Reasons for joining the firm.
4. Manager's role and degree of flexibility.
5. Training, job rotation, promotion.
6. Communication.

7. Decision-making.
8. Job satisfaction.
9. Evaluation of the success of the firm.

Where questions of degree were asked—as regarding for example, the estimation of promotion chances or the efficiency of the firm— a standard scale of 1 to 5 was used. In accordance with normal research conventions, and in order to preserve anonymity, all companies and individuals are referred to by pseudonyms. In some cases this has made it necessary to exclude data which would have made a particular organisation too easily identifiable.

A sample survey is necessarily limited, but a study of the present type of all 450 Japanese companies in Germany, for instance, obviously poses insuperable problems in terms of resources. The subject of managers' training, job assignments and degree of flexibility, and so on, is a large one, and when it concerns Japanese practice it is desirable to carry out considerably more investigation in Japan itself than we have been able to do. Here again there is the practical question of the availability of resources. Nevertheless, we feel confident that our previous research into Japanese companies in Europe, the references from other work,[3] our own data and the reactions of managers with whom the findings have been discussed allow certain patterns to be identified that are suggestive.

In books, 'Japanese management' may appear to be something static, but in the real world of management in commerce and industry this is an illusion, because of changes in the international business environment and in Japan itself. One only has to think of the oil crisis.

While it is possible to identify patterns in organisations at a particular place and time, including certain managerial orientations towards the job that have a considerable degree of persistence, it would be an exaggeration to claim that even identifying definite patterns, as we believe the evidence has done, is something definitive. As Drucker and other management writers have repeatedly pointed out, the definitive state of organisation, the panacea and the 'quick fix' are illusions which managers may be tempted to turn to but which they must avoid. Japanese examples should stimulate European managers to look at what they are doing and to find ways of improving performance. The examples may be useful, but the actual adapting or adopting has to be done by European managers themselves. As one British manager put it, 'We have to find our solutions to our problems'.

## Notes

1. *The Economist*, 23 March 1985, p. 66.
2. P. Doyle et al., *A Comparative Investigation of Japanese Marketing Strategies in the British Market*.
3. A new study of Japanese firms in Canada, for example, draws attention to similar issues of job mobility, local wishes for job descriptions and 'individualism', and so on, with similar comments by Japanese managers in Canada on the local situation. See T. Makabe, *Japanese-Owned and Managed Businesses in Canada*.

# Bibliography

Alban-Metcalfe, B. and Nicholson, N. *The Career Development of British Managers*, British Institute of Management, London, 1984.

Amano, M. M. 'Organisational changes of a Japanese firm in America', *California Management Review*, Vol. XXI, No. 3, 1979.

Atkinson, J. 'Manpower strategies for flexible organisations', *Personnel Management*, London, August 1984.

Ballon, R. J. (ed.), *Joint Ventures and Japan*, Sophia/Tuttle, Tokyo, 1967.

Bellah, R. N. *Tokugawa Religion: The Values of Pre-Industrial Japan*, Free Press, Glencoe Ill., 1957.

Bendix, R. *Max Weber: An Intellectual Portrait*, Methuen, London, 1966.

Bickerstaffe, G. 'The mixed scorecard of Japanese management abroad', *International Management*, USA, July 1983.

Bolt, J. F. 'Job security: its time has come', *Harvard Business Review*, No. 6, November–December 1983.

Burton, F. N. and Saelens, F. *An Anatomy of Japan's Direct Investment in West Germany*, University of Manchester, 1980.

Child, J. 'Culture, Contingency and Capitalism in the Cross-National Study of Organisation', *Research in Organisational Behaviour*, Vol. 3, JAI Press, Greenwich Conn., 1981.

Child, J., Fores, M., Glover, I. and Lawrence, P. 'A price to pay? Professionalism and work organisation in Britain and West Germany', *Sociology*, Vol. 17, No. 1, London, February 1983.

Chrapary, H.-J. 'Untersuchung zur deutschen Fassung des "Performance Maintenance" Instruments nach Misumi', unpublished diploma thesis, Technical University, Berlin, 1984.

Cole, R. E. *Japanese Blue Collar: The Changing Tradition*, University of California, 1971.

Crockel, T. J., 'On the making of lieutenants and colonels', *The Public Interest*, No. 76, National Affairs Inc., Easton, Pa., Summer 1984.

Crockett, G. and Elias, P. 'British managers: a study of their education, training, mobility and earnings', *British Journal of Industrial Relations*, Vol. XXII, No. 1, London, November 1984.

Daly, A., Hitchens, D. M. W. N. and Wagner, K. 'Productivity, machinery and skills in a sample of British and German manufacturing plants', *National Institute Economic Review*, London, February 1985.

Demes, H., Merz, H.-P., Park, S.-J. and Stirn, J. *Japanische Unternehmen in der Bundesrepublik Deutschland: Ergebnisse einer Expertenbefragung zu Investionsmotiven, Managementpraktiken und Arbeitsbeziehungen*, Free University, Berlin, 1984.

De Vos, G. *Socialisation for Achievement: Essays on the Cultural Psychology of the Japanese*, University of California, 1973.

Dore, R. P. *The Social Sources of the Will to Innovate*, Technical Change Centre, London, 1983.

Doyle, P., Saunders, J. and Wong, V. *A Comparative Investigation of Japanese Marketing Strategies in the British Market*, Management Centre, University of Bradford, 1985.

Drucker, P. F. *The Practice of Management*, Pan, London, 1968.

Dumortier, J. and Hanami, T. *Japanese Multinationals and Labour Relations in Belgium*, Kluver, Amsterdam, 1979.

Eglin, R. 'Give us the tools and we'll mess up the job', *Sunday Times*, Business News, 24 February 1985.

Evans, R. 'Lifetime earnings, in Japan for the class of 1955', *Monthly Labor Review*, USA, April 1984.

Fabricius, G. 'The art of headhunting', *The Wheel Extended*, Toyota Motor Co., Japan, Vol. XIV, No. 3, 1984.

Fukuda, R. *Managerial Engineering, Techniques for Improving Quality and Productivity in the Workplace*, Productivity Inc., Stamford, Connecticut, 1983. (First published in Japanese by the Japan Standards Association.)

Funaki, Y. 'Cross culture management', *Japan in Britain*, Conference, 21 January 1982, Technology Transfer International, London, n.d.

Funaki, Y. 'Japanese management and management training', *BACIE Journal*, London, January 1981.

Gregory, G. 'Why Japan's engineers lead', *Management Today*, London, May 1984.

Harrison, R. 'Understanding your organisation's character', *Harvard Business Review*, May–June 1972.

Hu, Y. S. *National Attitudes and the Financing of Industry*, Policy Studies Institute, London, 1975.

Imai, K. and Itami, H. 'Organisation and market interpenetration', *International Journal of Industrial Organisation*, No. 2, North Holland, 1984.

Inohara, H. 'Japanese manufacturing in Western Europe', *Sophia International Review*, Vol. 4, Tokyo, 1982.

Inohara, H. 'The personnel department in Japanese companies', *Bulletin of the Socio-Economic Institute*, No. 63, Sophia University, Tokyo, 1977.

International Research Group, London. *Industrial Democracy in Europe*, Oxford University Press, 1981.

Ishida, H. 'Exportability of the Japanese employment system', *Industrial Policies, Foreign Investment and Labour in Asian Countries*, Japan Institute of Labour, Tokyo, 1977.

Ishida, T. *Japanese Society*, Random House, New York, 1971.

JUSE (Japanese Union of Scientists and Engineers). *QC Circle Koryo: General Principles of the QC Circle*, JUSE, Tokyo, 1980.

Johansson, J. K. and Nonaka, I. 'Japanese export marketing: structures, strategies, counter-strategies', *International Marketing Review*, USA, Winter, 1983.

Johnson, R. 'Adult training in Europe', *Personnel Management*, London, August 1984.

Kellner, P. and Crowther-Hunt, Lord, *The Civil Servants: An Inquiry into Britain's Ruling Class*, Macdonald, London, 1980.

Kendall, W. 'Why Japanese workers work', *Management Today*, London, January 1984.

Kidd, J. B. and Teramoto, Y. *Japanese Production Subsidiaries in the United Kingdom: A Study of Managerial Decision Making*, University of Aston, 1981.

Kono, T. 'Japanese management philosophy: can it be exported?', *Long Range Planning*, Vol. 15, No. 3, Pergamon, Oxford, 1982.

Kumar, B., Steinmann, H. and Nagamura, Y. *Japanische Führungskräfte in Deutschland: Entsendung, Einsatz und Arbeitszufriedernheit*, University of Erlangen-Nuremburg, 1984.

Kumar, K. 'Why Carlyle should be living at this hour', *Times Higher Education Supplement*, 8 May 1981.

Lane, A. 'Industrial efficiency and the West German worker', *Industrial Relations Journal*, No. 4, Nottingham University, Autumn 1984.

Legge, K. *Power, Innovation and Problem-Solving in Personnel Management*, McGraw-Hill, Maidenhead, 1978.

Lehmann, J.-P. *Japanese Management in Germany*, Institut der deutschen Wirtschaft, Cologne, 1982.

Limprecht, J. A. and Hayes, R. H. 'Germany's world-class manufacturers', *Harvard Business Review*, Vol. 60, No. 6, November–December 1982.

Lyons, N. *The Sony Vision*, Crown, New York, 1976.

McGregor, D. *The Human Side of Enterprise*, McGraw-Hill, New York, 1960.

McLoughlin, J. 'Comfort in Suntory's happy song', *Guardian*, London, 19 October 1982, p. 17.

Makabe, T. *Japanese-Owned and Managed Businesses in Canada*, University of Toronto, n.d. (1985).

Mant, A. *The Rise and Fall of the British Manager*, Pan, London, 1979.

Matsuura, N. 'Japanese management and labor relations in US subsidiaries', *Industrial Relations Journal*, USA, Vol. 15, No. 4, Winter 1984.

Mintzberg, H. *The Nature of Managerial Work*, Harper & Row, New York, 1973.

Miyajima, R. 'Managerial Values', *ESRC Newsletter*, No. 54, ESRC, London, March 1985.

Moritani, M. 'Behind the scenes of technology development in Japan', *Journal of Japanese Trade and Industry*, Tokyo, November–December 1984.

Murakami, H. and Hirschmeier, J. (eds.), *Politics and Economics in Contemporary Japan*, Kodansha International, Tokyo, 1983.

Nakagawa, Y. and Ota, N. *The Japan-Style Economic System: A New Balance between Intervention and Freedom*, Foreign Press Centre, Tokyo, 1981.

Nakane, C. *Japanese Society*, Penguin, Harmondsworth, 1973.

Nixdorf, H. in *Capital: Zeitschrift für Management*, No. 8, 1984.

Oba, S. 'Japanese views of British business and industry', *Bulletin of the Japan Society of London*, No. 99, March 1983.

Ohmae, K. 'The mixed scorecard of Japanese management abroad', *International Management*, New York, July 1983.

Okumura, A. 'Japanese and US management models compared', *Economic Eye*, Vol. 5, No. 3, Tokyo, September 1984.

Okumura, A. 'Management in the international age: are there universal qualities in Japanese-style management?' *The Wheel Extended*, Toyota Motor Co., Japan, Vol. XIII, No. 4, n.d.

Park, S. J. *Mitbestimmung in Japan*, Campus, Frankfurt, 1982.

Pollard, S. J. *The Wasting of the British Economy: British Economic Policy 1945 to the Present*, Croom Helm, London, 1982.

Reitsperger, W. *Japanese Multinationals in Europe: Management Philosophy, Personnel Policy*, International Institute of Management, Berlin, n.d.

Ridley, E. F. (ed.), *Specialists and Generalists: A Comparative Study of the Professional Civil Servant at Home and Abroad*, Allen & Unwin, London, 1968.

Rohlen, R. P. *For Harmony and Strength: Japanese White-Collar Organisation in Anthropological Perspective*, University of California, 1974.

Rohlen, R. P. 'Spiritual training in a Japanese bank', *American Anthropologist*, Vol. 75, 1973.

Sadler, P. 'Educating managers for the twenty-first century', *Journal of the Royal Society for the Encouragement of Arts, Manufactures and Commerce*, Vol. CXXXII, No. 5334, London, May 1984.

Sanders, S. *Honda: The Man and His Machines*, Tuttle, Tokyo, 1975.

Sasaki, N. *Management and Industrial Structure in Japan*, Pergamon, Oxford, 1981.

Schmookler, A. B. 'An overview of Japan's economic success: its sources and its implications for the US', *Journal of East Asian Affairs*, Research Institute for International Affairs, Seoul, Vol. III, No. 2, Fall/Winter, 1983.

Sieff, Lord. 'How I see the personnel function', *Personnel Management*, London, December 1984.

Simon, H. A. *The New Science of Management Decision*, Harper & Row, New York, 1960.

Singer, K. *Mirror, Sword and Jewel: A Study of Japanese Characteristics*, Croom Helm, London, 1973.

Smith, M. G. *Corporations and Society*, Duckworth, London, 1974.

Steslicke, W. E. *Doctors in Politics: The Political Life of the Japan Medical Association*, Praeger, New York, 1973.

Taira, K. *Economic Development and the Labour Market in Japan*, Columbia University, New York, 1970.

Taylor, D. (ed.), *Learning from Japan: Review of a Conference Held on 19 and 20 December 1983*, Work Research Unit, Department of Employment, London, n.d. (1984).

Thurley, K. E., Nangaku, M. and Uragami, K. *Employment Relations of Japanese Companies in the UK: A Report on an Exploratory Study*, Sheffield University, 1976.

Trevor, M. H. *Japanese Industrial Knowledge: Can It Help British Industry?*, Gower, Aldershot, 1985.

Trevor, M. H. *Japan's Reluctant Multinationals: Japanese Management at Home and Abroad*, Pinter, London; St Martin's Press, New York, 1983.

Trevor, M. H. 'The problem of transferability: some theoretical considerations', in Park, S.-J., Jürgens, U. and Merz, H.-P. *Transfer des japanischen Management systems*, Express, Berlin, 1985.

Trevor, M. H. 'Quality control in Japan: technology transfer and self help', *Policy Studies*, Vol. 5, Part 4, PSI, London, April 1985.

Von Mehren, A. T. (ed.), *Law in Japan: The Legal Order in a Changing Society*, Harvard University Press, 1963.

Walker, M. 'Engineering tomorrow's managers', *Management Today*, London, February 1984.

Watanabe, Y. 'The role of academic background in Japanese society', *The Wheel Extended*, Vol. XIV, No. 1, *Special Issue*, 'Behind the Japanese corporation: management and philosophy', Toyota Motor Co., Japan, 1984.

Weber, M. *The Theory of Social and Economic Organisation*, Free Press, New York, 1947.

Weiss, A. 'Simple truths of Japanese manufacturing', *Harvard Business Review*, No. 4, July–August 1984.

White M. and Trevor, M. H. *Under Japanese Management: The Experience of British Workers*, Heinemann, London, 1983.

Whitehill, A. M. and Takezawa, S. *The Other Worker*, University of Hawaii, 1968.

Whyte, W. H. *The Organisation Man*, Penguin, Harmondsworth, 1960.

Wilby, P. 'Hard work? It's just not cricket', *Sunday Times*, Business News, 19 May 1985.

Wilpert B. *Führung in deutschen Unternehmen*, de Gruyter, Berlin, 1977.

Woronoff, J. *Japan's Wasted Workers*, Lotus Press, Tokyo, 1981.

## Periodicals

*Bulletin of the Anglo-Japanese Economic Institute*, London.
*Economic Eye*, Tokyo.

*The Economist*, London.
*The Financial Times*, London.
*Harvard Business Review*.
*Japan*, Japanese Embassy, London.
*Japan Times*, Tokyo.
*Journal of Japanese Trade and Industry*, Tokyo.
*Keidanren Review*, Tokyo.
*Mainichi Daily News*, Tokyo.
*Management News*, BIM, London.
*Management Review and Digest*, BIM, London.
*Management Today*, London.
*Oriental Economist*, Tokyo.
*Personnel Management*, London.
*Speaking of Japan*, Tokyo.
*The Wheel Extended*, Toyota Motor Co.

# Index

absence from work 75, 81, 239
accessibility 26
accountancy 36, 37, 179, 205
accountants 9, 204, 207
accounts manager 133–6
achievement 6
adaptation 34
administrators 192, 201
affirm 26, 27
age distribution 160, 163–6, 222
Anglo-American professional model 10
Anglo-German comparisons 13–19
area housekeeping 26
area sales manager 123–4
arrangement 26
arrogance 5, 250
assistant (administration) to general
   manager 37–8
assistant (engineering) to general manager
   35–7
assistant manager
   accounts 203–6
   EDPS 206–9
   finance 200–3
assistant production manager 47–9
Ataka & Co. 182, 258
attitudes 171, 249
   in selection process 66
   to responsibilities 32
automation 58

banking 220–8
basic philosophy 90, 91, 100, 143, 148, 156,
   164, 226, 229, 232, 254, 256, 260
branch operations 8
British disease 30
British industry 14
British management 14
bureaucratic models 5
business schools 15, 252
business strategy 235

career advancement 146
career development 256
career profiles 144, 250
career prospects 3, 46, 53, 55, 56, 60, 90,
   113, 122, 125, 144, 151, 152, 215
career structures 3, 238
chargehand,

assembly 62–3
   inspection 60–5
   production 63–5
chartered accountant 8–9, 134, 148
Child, J. 16
combined effort 5
commercial and financial sector 167–234
committees 33, 52
communication 5, 224, 227, 230, 233,
   244–8
   banking 224, 227
   electrical 97, 107, 109, 111, 116, 118,
      123, 126, 128, 129, 131, 135, 136, 140,
      142
   electronics 86
   engineering 165
   general trading 193, 194, 198, 205, 206,
      216
   German and Japanese companese
      compared 244–8
   horizontal 5
   light engineering 77, 83
   precision engineering 38, 43, 48, 51, 55,
      58, 60, 61, 63, 158
   precision products 162
   transport 230, 233
community typification 11
companion system 170
company information 26, 50, 137, 222, 229
company performance 48
company policy 76, 82, 126
company/private life dichotomy 69, 70
company rules and procedures 36, 45, 50,
      52, 54, 57, 61, 62, 93, 123, 196, 204
competition 261
competitiveness 20
computer expert 137
controllers 201
convergence theories 198
coordination manager 180–6
cost-benefit analysis 70
courses 28, 32, 36
credit manager 183–6
Crockett, G. 14, 15
CSDP (Course of Self Development and
   Progress) 175
cultural difficulties 13, 19, 31, 57, 78, 96,
      103, 120, 130, 138, 152, 185, 202, 208,
      216, 255

Decision making 19, 253
  banking 224, 227
  electrical 97, 100, 103, 108, 109, 111,
    112, 114, 118, 120–2, 126, 129, 132,
    133, 136–8
  electronics 87
  engineering 166
  general trading 194, 202, 206
  German and Japanese companies
    compared 241, 242
  light engineering 79, 84
  precision engineering 33, 43, 45, 48, 53,
    55, 58, 60, 61, 63, 158
  precision products 162
  transport 233
delegation 259
demarcation 2, 26, 201
department manager 173–80, 186–90, 230,
  233
  engineering 101
deputy plant manager 40–3
development of new ideas and new
  business 172
disloyalty 31
dismissal 169
distribution manager 138
documentation 194
Drucker, P. F. 266

effectiveness 70
efficiency 34, 46, 70, 123–4, 203, 206, 217
egalitarianism 211
EITB (Engineering Industry Training
  Board) 13, 51
electrical marketing 88–155
electronics 85–7
Elias, P. 14, 15
employee relations 33, 79, 87, 159, 162,
  166, 244
employment legislation 168
employment systems 5
engineering 163–6
Engineering Industry Training Board
  (EITB) 13, 51
engineering liaison manager 105
engineering manager 136–7
entrepreneur 125, 178
experience 15
exportability 20

finance manager 190–1
financial director 99–101
financial system 13
four A's 26
France 17, 18

frustration 130

General Electric Company 257
general manager 32–3
general trading 167–218
generalists 4–9, 249–51, 255–7, 259
  banking 227
  electrical 93, 99, 104, 109, 111, 116, 130,
    141, 145–8
  engineering 165
  general trading 168, 174–80, 185, 187,
    188, 190, 192, 197, 207, 210–13
  German and Japanese companies
    compared 235, 239
  light engineering 84
  precision engineering 30, 36, 38, 42, 59,
    66, 159
  transport 234
German companies, compared with
  Japanese 235–48
Germany 16–19
group achievement 11
growth rate 34

hard work 89, 91, 92
harmony 10, 11, 82, 83, 86
hierarchical levels 74, 80, 85, 155, 159,
  163, 221, 226, 228, 231, 236
holidays 156, 204, 222, 229, 232, 239
human relations 8, 13, 25, 188, 213, 252,
  260
human resources 31

ideological factor 171
ideology and value 9–13
individualism 2, 4, 10, 11
industrial relations 27, 29
information flow 46
information sharing 5
Inland Revenue 214
internationalisation 198
interpersonal skills 28
interviews 32, 76, 95, 144, 161, 164, 169,
  265

Japan External Trade Organisation
  (JETRO) 261, 264
Japanese companies, compared with
  German 235–48
Japanese company model 10
job assignments 251, 255
job content 5
job definition 3
job description 8, 32, 54, 82, 86, 91, 156,
  163, 166, 222, 232, 236, 254, 255
job hopping 68

job offers 71
job rotation 6, 113, 150, 157, 193, 223, 226, 229, 232, 240, 251, 253, 256
job satisfaction,
    electrical 89, 97, 100, 103, 109, 117, 120, 122, 126, 130, 135, 140, 146
    general trading 199, 202, 206, 208, 217
    precision engineering 34, 43, 46, 48, 53, 55, 58, 60, 62, 65, 68
job security 46, 53, 126, 135, 180, 192, 194, 197, 202, 214, 217
job specifications 89, 90

Komatsu, President 182

labour market 171, 172, 183
labour mobility 11
leadership 29, 54, 188, 191, 233, 253, 255
lifetime employment 31, 86, 210, 236, 249, 258
light engineering 74–85
line management 14
line-staff organisation 8
long-term employment-generalist-flexibility model 6, 8
long-term strategies 12
loyalty 11, 70, 215

management by detail 26
management by objectives (MBO) 48, 152
management knowledge 253
management skills 252
managerial techniques 3, 27
manager's careers,
    British 40–65
    Japanese 35–40
managing director 98, 143, 148, 157
manning levels 33
manpower planning 76
Mant, A. 14
manufacturing management 17, 18
manufacturing operations 28
marketing liaison manager 102–4, 105
marketing manager 101–2, 106–9, 195–200
marketing sector 88–166
Marks and Spencer 260
Marubeni Corporation 5
MBO (Management by Objectives) 48, 152
mechanical engineer 39
mobility between firms 68
modified theory X 30
motivation 34, 42, 43, 48, 58

Nissan and Prince 183

non-bureaucracy 90–2

organisation man 6
organisation models 3
organisational structure 235–6
overseas assignments 34–5
overseas investment 25
overtime 31, 33, 69, 200

pay structures 32, 58, 82, 157, 161, 165, 258
pension schemes 30, 77, 83, 96, 157, 230, 233, 240
persistence 250
personal problems 52, 96
personal relations 215
personality 86, 193, 208, 239, 249
personnel administration 8
personnel department 8, 13, 169, 170, 197, 243, 256
personnel management 14, 27–34, 29, 76, 92–7, 167–73, 260
personnel manager 24, 28, 29, 30, 32, 33, 34, 76, 168, 169, 223
personnel officer 122, 191–5
personnel philosophy 30
personnel planning 223
personnel policy 82, 157, 161, 164, 222, 229, 232, 236–43
precision engineering 24–71, 155–9
precision products 159–63
product manager 125–32
production sector 24–87
productivity survey 16
professionalism 4, 6, 9, 15, 16, 17, 19, 130, 132, 191, 200, 258, 259, 260
profitability 34, 38, 43, 46, 97, 112, 206
promoter 127
promotion prospects 260
    banking 223
    electrical 100, 107, 111, 113, 118, 120, 122–4, 127, 131, 133, 141, 150, 151
    general trading 175, 189, 193, 197, 199, 202, 205, 208, 213, 214, 218
    German and Japanese companies compared 242
    light engineering 77
    precision engineering 45, 48, 50, 52, 54, 57, 59, 62, 64, 157
    precision products 161
    transport 229, 232–3
punctuality 18, 89, 91

qualifications 6, 15, 16, 41, 75, 81, 148, 156, 164, 222, 232, 239, 251

quality 34
quality assurance engineer 38–9
quality assurance principles 27
quality assurance systems 27
quality circles 46, 79, 86, 87, 244
quality control 3, 56
quality control manager 43–7
quality philosophy 24–7
quality standards 27
questionnaire 265

recession 26, 261
recruitment 31, 161, 170, 171, 172, 192, 200, 223, 232, 239, 249
redundancy 51
research aims 19–21
research method 264–7
responsibility 27, 45, 50, 64, 94, 204, 259
reward system *see* Pay Structure
ROI (return on investment) criterion 12, 37, 132
rotation system 77

salary prospects *see* Pay Structure
sales and marketing manager 110–15
sales manager 115–19
section leader,
   assembly 51–3
   machine shop 55–8
   planning 49–53
   production 53–5
selection criteria 157
self-development 17, 36, 43
self-development 36
self-motivation 188
self study 260
service manager 132–3
service orientation 236
setting an example 27
sick pay 62
sickness rate 75, 81, 156, 160, 222, 232, 239
Sieff, Lord 260
social relations 19
social status 9
specialists 4–9, 255, 257, 259
   banking 227
   electrical 99, 109, 131, 132, 134, 135, 138, 141, 145–8
   general trading 168, 174–80, 185, 187, 188, 190–2, 201, 207, 210–12
   light engineering 79

precision engineering 27, 30, 36, 38, 45, 46, 50, 66, 67
precision products 165
stable employment 31
staff engineer 39–40
staff problems 45
stereotypes 17, 18, 20
stock controller 140–1
success 97, 114, 117, 119, 126, 206, 209, 217, 224, 230, 234, 247
Sumitomo Rubber Company 255
survival type behaviour 10
Sweden 18

task orientation 249–61
teamwork 30, 58, 89, 91, 250
technical administration supervisor 141–2
technical advisors 75, 231, 235
technical manager 119–21
trade unions 28, 82, 160, 244
trainee section leader, inspection 58–60
training 6, 7, 249, 252–4, 256, 259
   banking 223, 226
   electrical 94, 99, 104, 130, 150
   electronics 86
   engineering 165
   general trading 170, 175, 177, 180, 181, 183, 186, 187, 190, 195, 198, 200, 204
   German and Japanese companies compared 238, 242, 243
   light engineering 77, 82
   precision engineering 32, 36–8, 40–2, 44, 46, 47, 49–51, 56, 59, 62, 65, 157
   precision products 161
   transport 229, 232
transferability 20
transport manager 139–40
transport organisations 228–34

US Army 257

vacancies 32
value systems, fundamental difference in 2

Weber, Max 19
welfare 30
work study engineer 53, 54
working climate 33, 48, 51, 53, 61, 64, 224, 230, 240
working conditions 60, 203, 218
working environment 25
working hours 48, 49, 51, 69, 89, 149, 213
working methods 25
works councils 244